# Candidates, Consultants, and Campaigns

To my mother and father, from
whom no sacrifice was too
great, to whom all credit is due,
this book is lovingly dedicated

# Candidates, Consultants, and Campaigns

## The Style and Substance of American Electioneering

FRANK I. LUNTZ

*Foreword by*
*Richard B. Wirthlin*

Basil Blackwell

First published 1988

Basil Blackwell Ltd
108 Cowley Road, Oxford, OX4 1JF, UK

Basil Blackwell Inc.
432 Park Avenue South, Suite 1503
New York, NY 10016, USA

*British Library Cataloguing in Publication Data*

Luntz, Frank I. (Frank Ian)
  Candidates, consultants and campaigns:
  the style and substance of American
  Electioneering.
  1. United States. Elections. Campaigns
  I. Title
  324.7'0973

  ISBN 0–631–16262–3

*Library of Congress Cataloging in Publication Data*

Luntz, Frank I.
  Candidates, consultants, and campaigns.

  Bibliography: p.
  Includes index.
  1. Campaign management—United States.
  2. Electioneering—United States.    I. Title.
  JK2281.L85    1988        324.7'0973        88-6358
  ISBN 0–631–16262–3

Typeset 10 on 11½ point Sabon by Columns, Reading
Printed in the USA

# Contents

# Foreword

In less than two decades, the way the American people elects its representatives and presidents has been dramatically and permanently changed. Frank Luntz chronicles the source, nature and implications of that change accurately and with a keen analytical eye.

At the turn of the century, the Austrian economist Joseph A. Schumpeter described the unsettling but dynamic impact of innovation on the capitalist economic system. Innovation, he believed, involved the emergence of new combinations of technologies, markets, and organizations that either generated new methods of production, or new goods and services, or a reorganized or a newly-created industry. The birth and evolution of what Luntz names the "campaign consulting industry" followed precisely Schumpeter's lines, inducing revolutionary impact not on our economy, but on the way Americans select candidates and the way those candiates run for election.

The "new methods of production" most paramount in revolutionizing campaign techniques were television and the computer. These two new tools completely altered both the way candidates communicate with the electorate – directly and personally through words and pictures crafted by the political media consultants – and the way candidates conceive and implement their campaigns through the guiding hand of the pollster and the strategist armed with the analytical and statistical tools of the computer. In turn, the conjuncture of television, the computer, and campaign consultants spawned a whole range of new campaign services never before used. A new industry emerged through these innovations – the campaign consulting industry.

Despite its importance and impact, no major systematic review of the political consulting industry's evolution, its present nature and possible future influence has been undertaken until now. The author assumes that task and performs it well.

Using both in-depth, unstructured, personal interviews along with a structured questionnaire, Luntz gathered information and insight from thirty-seven of the major campaign practitioners. This group represents an impressive cross-section of the major campaign consultants in the United States and provides the author with both a frame of reference for his analysis as well as a new vehicle to gather information about this industry in a systematic fashion. Clearly, the responses that were gathered were candid and, in my view, reliable. It is quite unexpected that any one person could encourage those in this new industry to describe the pressures, pleasures, and pains of political consultants as faithfully as is reflected in this book.

To understand American politics as we move into the twenty-first century, it is imperative to recognize three major forces exogenous to the candidate that strongly impinge upon his running a successful campaign. These are the emergence of campaign consultants; the changing role of the national parties; and the way the Federal Election Laws and its Commission have restructured the political rules of the game, giving rise to the uniquely American phenomena of the Political Action Committee and the Independent Committee.

Twenty years ago few campaigns employed consultants. In 1986, 94 per cent of all senate and gubernatorial campaigns had at least one consultant and most had two or more. Luntz chronicles the variety of roles assumed by the campaign consultants, the contributions they make, and the conflicts they can generate.

Just ten years ago many astute political observers noted that television and direct mail cut the candidates loose from the apron strings of their parties. No longer were candidates beholden to the party for nomination, or to the boards of volunteers needed to carry the message into the precincts. Direct mail and sophisticated fundraising provided the candidates of the 1970s with financial independence. Some of those pundits concluded, prematurely, that political parties in the United States would wither and die.

The role assumed by the Republican National Committee (RNC) under the direction of Richard Richards and Frank Fahrenkopf in providing strategic attitudinal data for the White House and the party captures just one dimension of the new and powerful influence of modern American political parties.

Beginning in January of 1981, before Ronald Reagan was inaugurated the 40th President of the Union, I initiated through the resources of the RNC both a series of monthly national cross-sectional studies and, between 1981 and 1988, during times of crisis, daily tracking studies to provide timely measures of the public mood. Space permits referencing just two strategic uses the generation of such a large and uniform attitudinal data bank allowed.

In 1981 and 1982 the RNC surveys picked up a growing concern, especially among older voters, that the Republicans were going to cut social security benefits. Further research defined precisely the specific dimensions of the issue and provided input into the development of a series of television ads which were produced under the aegis of the Republican National Committee. The Wirthlin Group then measured, using a pre–post design in a key television market, the change in perceptions toward the Republican party the ads induced – before they were run on a national scale. (A major media campaign was then launched.) The social security issue, which might have impinged unfavorably on the 1984 re-election of President Reagan, was to a large extent neutralized.

The way the RNC dealt with the "gender gap" provides a second example of the development and implementation of political strategies made possible solely because of the continuity of the party and its commitment to keep an open and listening ear to the voice of the American electorate.

In late September of 1980 I noticed with growing concern that female voters were much less supportive of our presidential candidate, Ronald Reagan, than male voters. Hence, right after the elections, working in conjunction with the RNC I developed several hypotheses about which types of women were more or less supportive of the President and why. By the Spring of 1982 we had developed, on the basis of our access to the RNC survey research data bank of 21,000 interviews, eight female prototypes which brought into clear perspective which female voter groups needed to be targeted and with what messages. Between late 1982 and the re-election of President Reagan in 1984 the "gender-gap" was cut in half.

The present scope and viability of political parties is best captured in just one number cited by Luntz. In 1985–6 the political parties spent $316 million dollars. How that money is generated, what it is used for, and how parties now influence American politics are questions that the author answers in one of the best chapters of this book.

If money is the mother's milk of politics then two different cows were added to the American herd with the legislative creation of Political Action Committees (PACs) and Independent Committees. One of the most clear-cut consequences of PACs has been to provide incumbents with almost a guaranteed resource advantage over all challengers. Luntz provides an excellent analysis of this phenomenon, and goes beyond it to outline where the trend of PAC financed campaigns may lead. Luntz says that it is the rise of Political Action Committees and Independent Committees, spawned by congressional legislation, that impinges unfavorably on the way we select and elect our candidates because these committees distort campaigns' access to resources.

In sum, many of these campaign innovations could, *ceteris paribus*, depersonalize the political process and unhinge the candidate from his campaign. But "other things" are *not* equal. Luntz points out that the net impact of these electoral innovations have fostered the democratic process, they have not diminished it. For example, direct mail clearly has broadened campaign involvement and financial participation. No longer can a few millionaires drive the political system.

Campaign consultants, rather than blurring the contact between candidates and voters may have enhanced it, because survey research enables the candidate and his associates to determine more precisely what drives the vote. Specifically, the voter was found in the late 1970s and early 1980s in many campaigns to build perceptions about the candidates more rapidly through issues than through imagery alone. And never before has the voter's voice been so carefully listened to as it is today. The pollster provides an accurate and timely feedback mechanism between candidates and constituents. But many of these same tools and techniques can of course be misapplied and misdirected to the detriment of all. In part, the net positive or negative impact of the political consulting industry may turn on the ethical and professional commitments of its practitioners.

In a broad sense, then, the ultimate consequence of the rise of the campaign consulting industry is not found in the power of the consultant, nor even in the power of the candidate, but rather in the power of the voter. Through the medium of television a candidate now has more direct and personal access to the voters' living room than ever before, and because of modern survey research the candidate and his campaign know more precisely what the hopes, fears and aspirations of the voters are. Thus candidates who succeed are generally those who use that access to convince the voter, on the voter's terms, that the candidate can lead and govern well.

Perhaps the most basic challenge now facing both consultants and candidates, given their enhanced power and potential to persuade and motivate the voter, was best summed up at the dawn of this political era by a Democratic contender for the presidency, Adlai Stevenson: "I am not an old, experienced hand at politics. But I am seasoned enough to have learned that the hardest thing about any political campaign is how to win, without proving that you are unworthy of winning." Students and scholars of US politics, practitioners like myself, and interested observers of the US political scene should find this book to be of indispensable value.

Richard B. Wirthlin
White House pollster,
Reagan administration

# Acknowledgements

The existence of this book owes much to the generous and thoughtful assistance of friends, scholars, and individuals in the world of politics with whom I have had the pleasure of working. I thank them all.

I am most grateful to John and Jane Thouron, who placed their confidence in me well before it was due. The Thouron Award enabled me to study at Oxford and complete my doctorate thesis in politics. Without the award, this book would never have been written. Similarly, I am deeply indepted to Gillian R. Peele for her assistance and supervision at Oxford. A true scholar of American politics, her patience, encouragement, and advice are greatly appreciated. I shall forever be in her debt.

I also wish to thank specifically those consultants who went above and beyond my selfish requests for time and information. First and foremost are media consultant Raymond Strother, and pollsters Richard Wirthlin and Harrison Hickman. Despite an impossible workload and other endless demands on their time, they managed to provide many hours of wisdom and insight. The political consulting profession needs more individuals like them. In addition, among media consultants, Roger Ailes, Ed Blakely, John Deardourff, Robert Goodman, Frank Greer, Bob Squier and Ken Swope were particularly kind. Also generous with their time were pollster Bob Teeter; fundraisers Roger Craver, Bruce Eberle, Peter Kelly, Bob Odell and Brad O'Leary; and campaign strategists Dave Keene, Bill Lacy, Ed Rollins and Stuart Spencer. I am also grateful to Bill McInturff from the Republican National Committee, and Ed Brookover and Paul Curcio from the National Republican Senatorial Committee. In addition, Senator Gordon Humphrey and former Senators George McGovern and Jim Abdnor provided particularly thoughtful insights on the life of a candidate. Finally, a special heartfelt

*Acknowledgements*

thanks to Arthur Finkelstein and James Buckley for that first campaign opportunity so long ago.

I am deeply indebted to Bernard Sosnick, who most thoughtfully, patiently, and intelligently improved a draft of this book. An expression of thanks is also due to Victor Wolski, Gary Christopher, Robert Snyder, Andre LeTendre, Craig Shirley, Robert Barber, Katherine Watson, David Welch and Cheryl Altmire in Washington, Jon Case, Ben Sharav, David Donabedian, and Steve Sosnick in New York, and John Vlahoplus and Mark Montgomery in Oxford, all of whom contributed in some way to the completion of this work. Also, my gratitude is extended to Fiona Sewell for her editorial services, and a particular thanks to Sean Magee at Basil Blackwell for pursuing this project.

Finally, I would like to express my gratitude to Jim and Sue Calhoun, who have taken almost as much interest in my activities as my own parents; Michael Francis, who I hope one day will be governor of New Jersey; James Cappellano and Robert Derosier for their learned advice all those years ago; Professor Melvyn Hammarberg at the University of Pennsylvania, where the idea of this study first began to take shape; the staff at *Campaigns and Elections*, the finest election journal in America today, my relatives, and the "bridge club," who have endured stories of my trials and tribulations for too many years, and especially to my friends at the University of Pennsylvania and Oxford University.

I had no research assistants, secretaries, typists, or stenographers. All errors in the pages that follow are therefore my own. I hope that they can be forgiven.

Frank Luntz

# Introduction

The only way I'll lose is if I got caught in bed with either a dead girl or a live boy.

Edwin Edwards, Louisiana Governor (prior<br>to his re-election defeat in 1987)[1]

It is often said in politics that victories have many fathers but defeats are all orphans.

Bob Teeter, pollster

There is a regrettable shortage of academic material for those seeking a factual account of present-day electioneering, modern campaign technology, and the candidate's role in the campaign process. While numerous scholarly works have been published about voter attitudes and behavior, there is comparatively little literature in the area of campaign decision making. Moreover, of the small number of publications that have explored the substance and style of a modern American political campaign, most have already become outdated because of the rapid, continual change in the electioneering process.

Fundamental to every campaign are the voters and the candidate. Yet studies of the former do not automatically shed light on the latter. What is rational for the voter is not necessarily rational for the candidate, whose major goal is to win the election. Voters want unbiased, undistorted facts about the candidate and his views.[2] Candidates, however, want to censor the information about themselves, highlighting those factors positive to the image they seek to create, while suppressing the negative. In effect, they seek "limited enlightenment" of their constituents, providing only that which will help their own candidacy or detract from their opponent's. Clearly, the aims and actions of candidate and voter are not necessarily compatible.

An examination of voter behavior represents only one side of the political process. To complete the picture it is necessary to provide a comprehensive study of the other side of the equation – the role played by candidates and consultants in an election. This book proposes to present a factual account of the process and problems of actually conducting a modern campaign, from the complexities involved in the selection of advisors to the determination and eventual implementation of campaign strategy. It seeks to explore the particular roles played by candidates and consultants, and specific methods used by those seeking public office to influence their electorate. It is thus an intimate study of candidates, consultants, and today's modern technological campaign. For the purpose of clarification, modern campaign technology is here defined as the strategy, techniques, and hardware currently used in campaigns to influence voter behavior. Much of the technology was developed in conjunction with the introduction of television as a political tool, and with the rapid expansion of computer capabilities. More specifically, modern campaign technology embraces the recent electronic innovations in campaigning, as evidenced in new and sophisticated methods of polling, advertising, and direct mail fundraising. Modern campaign technology has changed – completely and forever – the traditional styles of campaigning once common in American politics.

Basic to electioneering, yet relatively neglected by social scientists, is the marketing of the candidates. This book will examine, in detail, how candidates are marketed in a modern American campaign, who is doing the marketing, and the relationship of the consultants to the candidates they are marketing. The survey of political consultants found in appendix I is entirely original and was systematically administered by the author in conjunction with personal interviews, thereby allowing the immediate opportunity for further direct questioning and clarification.[3] The resultant data collected was then methodically compiled and cross-tabulated. I believe this to be the most current systematic study of the private viewpoints and conceptions of America's leading political consultants regarding both the electoral process today and their clients – candidates actively seeking federal office.

The reader may ask: "Why have consultants been surveyed and not candidates?" The answer is two-fold. First, active candidates are often so caught up in their own campaigns that they may be unable to offer an impartial and dispassionate view of their role in the political process. Almost all politicians use marketing techniques and ideas, but few wish to admit it openly. Incumbents are frequently unwilling, both for personal and political reasons, to discuss the process of decision making that went on in their campaign, while unsuccessful challengers often fade away from the political scene and therefore can be difficult to trace, as well as uninterested in participating in research studies.

Second, candidates generally have only limited electoral experience. House members participate in a single campaign every two years, senators every six years. Political consultants have ten, fifteen or even twenty clients in each election cycle, and can be involved in more campaigns in a two-year period than will be experienced by the most senior members of the US Senate in their entire lifetime. The consultants interviewed here are dominant in the American election system and have had more clients than their clients have had consultants. Because they operate in a much larger and more diverse universe, they are in an excellent position to discuss their roles, their clients, and the campaign process in general. In actuality, they are more attuned to the practical aspects of electioneering than are the candidates themselves.

Interviews with thirty-seven consultants, selected because they are widely acknowledged as outstanding in the consulting field, provide the basis for the aforementioned survey. These consultants comprise a senior partner in each of the eight largest media and the eight largest polling companies (determined by the number of statewide candidates for senator and governor that they have advised), partners in prestigious general consulting and direct mail firms, and several acknowledged pioneers in the political consulting field. (See appendix II.) Almost all have handled presidential races, and all are experts in their particular area.

Interestingly, certain of the survey findings may be antithetical to the conventional wisdom. For instance: technological innovations in electioneering do not begin at the presidential level and filter down, as numerous pundits have suggested; consultants are more concerned about a potential client's ideology than about his personal wealth or ease of electability; and a majority of those surveyed candidly admitted that unethical practices and misrepresentation of qualifications do occur in their profession, but usually blame the media gurus and general consultants, not the fundraisers or pollsters. Moreover, although the independent political consultants have been accused of having helped destroy the national party organizations, the author's survey strongly suggests that the national parties have since regained their importance in the election of their candidates, and furthermore, that the significance of parties in the campaigns of their candidates is growing – not diminishing.

The material in the chapters to follow has been directly obtained not only from political consultants but also from a cadre of national party leaders, and from candidates themselves. Often it is presented in their own words, particularly where it seemed that the flavor might be lost in paraphrasing. It should be pointed out that many of the facts, observations, and incidents contained herein are appearing in print for the first time. And since several of the consultants cited in these pages seldom grant interviews, their unexpectedly extensive and candid responses may well constitute a special contribution to this particular study.

Now a word of explanation about the organization of this book. The first chapter provides an overview of American electoral politics and examines the common qualities generally found in state and congressional political campaigns of the late 1980s. In particular, it details the changes in federal election laws and their impact on electioneering, the limited role of the candidates in their own campaigns, the phenomenon of the personality-based campaign, and the increasing role of money in politics; and, finally, it offers a look at incumbent advantage in recent elections. Chapter 2 examines, in detail, the candidate–consultant relationship and the current use of modern campaign technology, as well as the process of hiring consultants, consultant influence over the candidates and their campaigns, disputes between consultants and candidates, and accusations of unethical behavior among consultants. Chapter 3 covers media consultants and political advertising, and presents a precise, original catalog system to aid in the understanding and analysis necessary for the proper study of television commercials. The expanding role of the national party organizations is the subject of chapter 4, which includes interviews with the leading administrators from both national party organizations. Chapter 5 explores the candidate's quest for money and votes through direct mail, and his relationship with the practitioners in this specific area. Chapter 6 covers the role of political action committees (PACs), and the means by which candidates solicit PAC funding, concluding with an in-depth look at independent expenditure campaigns. Anticipating the future look of political campaigns in the 1990s constitutes chapter 7, which describes some of the latest in campaign innovations. Chapter 8 concludes the book with a discussion of modern campaign technology and its decided impact on American electoral democracy.

Although there seems to be a general awareness of major changes in the American electoral process, it struck this author that no updated, systematized study of modern campaigning had as yet been produced and made readily available. This book hopes to fill that void. It presents new and original material on the use of current political campaign technology (from the early 1980s up to and including the 1988 presidential election), accompanied by revelatory and remarkably frank interviews with the political consultants directly responsible for the drastic innovations in modern campaigning. It is hoped that this work will provide an interesting and useful addition to what has already been written.

# 1

# So you want to run for office? An overview of electoral politics in America

When I first ran, you didn't have to worry about having your hair all fluffed up and you didn't have to worry about what color necktie you wore, just so you had one on, or what shirt; you didn't even care much about the language you used, just so you got the message across. But today . . . you are told what to say, when to say it, how to say it.

Former US Senator Barry Goldwater[1]

All of us want to use or have access to every new discovery or technique. . . . This desire to take advantage of the newest developments becomes a very personal thing in a political campaign, and I am no different from anyone else in this regard.

US Senator Wendell Ford[2]

We've now run races where the only thing being done was polling and television. We have seen the demise of political bosses and the demise of campaign organizations. Campaigns are now very personal, very man-made, require a lot of television, polling, good information, and tons of paid media.

Robert Goodman, media consultant

Vital to the ultimate success of a modern campaign is the early commitment of the candidate to what has become a complex and highly technical election process, costing an enormous amount of money and requiring long, arduous advance planning. No longer can candidates announce for Congress only a few months before election day and then rely on political machines and party bosses to secure their victory. The political machine has been replaced by the comprehensive use of modern campaign technology, which has revolutionized electioneering in America. Under the new setup, which is technologically based, the once separate and independent campaign functions of polling, fundraising, and political advertising have been merged by the modern-day political bosses – the campaign consultants – into a system of coordinated, interrelated, and interdependent procedures that operate until election day or until the money runs out – whichever occurs first.

The significant changes in electioneering tactics and the integration of modern campaign technologies that have taken place in the 1980s can be directly traced to specific congressional legislation: the Federal Election Campaign Act of 1971, the 1974 Campaign Law (also known as the FECA amendments), and the amendments of 1976 and 1979. These legislative acts placed strict limits on individual campaign contributions, required public disclosure of major contributors and expenditures, regulated the financial involvement of the political parties in the campaigns of their candidates, legalized the formation of political organizations representing organized labor and large corporations, and created a federal organization, the Federal Election Commission (FEC), with the legal power to enforce the new rules. The American political system and structure has been transformed by the new laws, and nowhere is the transformation more evident than in the new style of political campaigning that they induced.

When leading political consultants of the 1970s and 1980s were asked to name the single greatest change in electioneering in the past decade, the change in election laws was second only to the use of television. (See appendix I.) According to veteran Republican advisor Eddie Mahe, "The dramatic changes in electioneering have been caused by one thing – the federal election laws. That more than anything else has dramatically changed the nature of my business." Although the new regulations were designed to limit the power of money in the election process, they only altered its dynamics, not its influence. Instead of opening up the electoral process, as was intended, the laws have served to inhibit political activity. Congressman Daniel Lungren concluded, "If you seek to be a candidate for membership [in Congress], the very first thing you should do is hire yourself a lawyer and hire yourself an accountant so that you will not run afoul of the law."[3] The election laws directly resulted in the rising utilization of expensive modern campaign technology, along with virtually total candidate dependence on professional political advisors who, unlike most candidates, understood the new environment.

Before 1971, the amount of money any individual could legally donate directly to a candidate or a political committee was limited to no more than $5,000, a restriction first instituted in 1940 as a major provision of the Hatch Act. However, it was perfectly legal for an individual to contribute unlimited funds to state, county, and local political committees, even if they were all supporting the same candidate. The money was then passed on to the candidate in the name of the particular political committee – and the donation was thus within the law. Moreover, since it was also legal to subsidize gifts given in the names of one's relatives, it was not uncommon to find wealthy individuals subsidizing family donations of $25,000 or more to a particular candidate.

Corporations, prevented by the 1907 Tillman Act from making direct contributions to political candidates, also were able to circumvent such restrictions.[4] The corporations did this by providing executives with bonuses or salary increases which were then expected to be turned over to candidates favored by the corporation. In addition, some non-financial assistance to a campaign was legal, such as the lending of billboards, mailing lists, and office furniture and equipment, and providing for a candidate's transport. It was even possible for a corporation to rent items to a candidate and then write off the rental fee as uncollectable. However, the use of corporate funds to establish and administer political action committees (PACs) had been prohibited by the Federal Corrupt Practices Act of 1925.

Restrictions on labor unions were not as extensive as those on corporations, although the Smith–Connally Act of 1943 prohibited unions from making direct campaign contributions to candidates, and the 1947 Taft–Hartley Act reimposed laws on union leaders that prevented them from contributing money taken from union dues. However, money collected from members that was apart from union dues could be donated legally. Moreover, money could be taken directly from union treasuries and used for voter registration drives, get-out-the-vote efforts, and other technically nonpartisan, informational services that are, in actuality, directed to aid specific candidates. Despite all the restrictions, federal and state limitations on the total amount of money a candidate could receive or spend were easily evaded, as long as the money was raised and spent without the candidate's knowledge and consent.

The Federal Election Campaign Act (FECA), signed into law in 1971, was the first in a series of significant recent pieces of electoral legislation designed to limit illegal campaign finance activity and institute specific disclosure procedures. FECA required full and timely disclosure of campaign contributions and expenditures, thus strengthening previous disclosure regulations which had been almost ignored for many years. Under FECA, federal candidates and political committees had to file quarterly spending and receipt reports, listing contributions of $100 or more, along with the contributor's name, address, occupation and place of business. During election years, additional reports were required that had to be filed fifteen days and five days before an election, and any contribution of $5,000 or more had to be reported within forty-eight hours of receipt. A candidate and his immediate family were limited to spending $50,000 on his campaign for president or vice-president, $35,000 for senator and $25,000 for representative. However, all previous spending and contribution limits were repealed except for restrictions barring contributions directly from corporate funds and union dues money.

Several of the FECA regulations had an immediate effect on the candidates and their campaigns. Many Senate and House campaigns were forced to hire an extra staff member whose sole job was to oversee compliance with the new disclosure regulations. With spending limits now placed on paid political advertising, a flood of candidates sought professional advice for the first time, anxious to make the greatest impact with the least amount of expenditure. Most importantly, wealthy candidates were suddenly (but only temporarily – thanks to a 1976 Supreme Court ruling) faced with the necessity of seeking new contributors to help fund campaigns previously paid for by the candidate himself. This was the first in a series of reforms that developed candidate dependence on direct mail solicitations.

Congressional leaders had hoped FECA would remove financial corruption from the electoral process without overly hampering the candidates seeking election. However, the effect of the legislation was quite different. The 1972 elections were marred by flagrant abuse of the intent, if not the letter, of the new FECA laws. A single individual, W. Clement Stone, alone donated more than $2 million to the re-election campaign of Richard Nixon before FECA disclosure rules took effect, on 7 April. Yet, to the General Accounting Office, he reported giving less than 5 percent of that amount. The Finance Committee for the Reelection of the President refused to publish its list of major contributors who had given prior to 7 April, provoking considerable resentment among electoral reformers. The list, released after a successful Common Cause lawsuit, revealed frequent breaches of electoral ethics as well as a number of illegal corporate donations.

Having observed both the successes and failures of the 1971 FECA, and influenced by the anti-Washington mood of the Watergate period, Congress decided to make another attempt at electoral reform. The FECA amendments of 1974 were considerably more extensive than the original legislation, and doubtlessly would have changed the shape and style of elections for many years to come if the Supreme Court had not stepped in two years later to declare several sections unconstitutional.

Highlights of the 1974 amendments for congressional candidates were the limits of $1,000 for individual contributions to each primary, runoff, and general election, and $5,000 to each political action committee and state party organization; strict spending limits placed on House and Senate candidates in both the primaries and the general election; the repeal of the media spending limitations in the 1971 FECA; and the establishment of a Federal Election Commission to enforce all electoral legislation. For presidential candidates, the new law provided for public (that is, the federal government) funding of their pre-nomination campaigns and the general election, and mandated a $10 million spending limit for each candidate in the primary cycle, and a $20 million limit, fully financed by the government, for each candidate in the general election – both limits to increase with inflation.

Opponents of this electoral reform wasted no time showing their disapproval, and filed suit just hours after the new laws went into effect. It was their contention that the law's new restrictions on campaign contributions and expenditures curbed the freedom of contributors and candidates to express themselves in the political marketplace, and provided unfair advantage to well-endowed major party candidates at the expense of the minor parties with limited fundraising capabilities. Former United States Senator James L. Buckley particularly opposed the clause preventing a candidate from spending unlimited funds on his own campaign. It was "quite clearly a flagrant unconstitutional abuse of the right to unlimited free expression," he said reflectively years later.

The Supreme Court eventually agreed to hear the case, and handed down its ruling on 30 January 1976. In the landmark *Buckley* v. *Valeo* case, the Court upheld the limits on individual and PAC contributions, and on the public financing of presidential campaigns, as well as the public disclosure requirements. However, other facets of the law were overturned, the most important being the removal of limits on campaign spending, as an unconstitutional violation of the First Amendment guarantee of free expression. According to the majority ruling:

A restriction on the amount of money a person or group can spend on political communication during a campaign necessarily reduces the quantity of expression by restricting the number of issues discussed, the depth of their exploration and the size of the audience reached. This is because virtually every means of communicating ideas in today's mass society requires the expenditure of money.[5]

The Court also threw out limits on independent expenditures, thereby freeing candidates to spend as much as they wished on their own campaigns, and struck down the validity of the Federal Election Commission (although Congress was given thirty days to "reconstitute the commission by law or adopt other valid enforcement mechanisms").

Congressional reformers then went back into committee early in 1976 and came out later that year with a new set of amendments to FECA. A reconstituted Federal Election Commission, with altered responsibilities, was the major provision of the new legislation. Other amendments set new limits on the amount individuals could donate to PACs and the national committee of a political party, strengthened disclosure regulations, and placed further requirements on presidential candidates accepting federal matching funds. Finally, all independent expenditure campaigns by PACs or individuals were required to state that the expenditures were not being made in collusion with the candidate.

Further changes in election laws occurred in 1979, with the passage of several additional FECA amendments, spurred on by the general complaint from academic and political circles that the new federal election laws had seriously weakened the national party organizations and removed any remaining role they may have had in the election of their candidates for the House and Senate. The 1979 amendments permitted state and local parties to purchase, without limit, campaign materials for volunteer activities promoting any federal candidate. These items included political buttons, bumper stickers, posters, and yard signs. State and local party organizations were also allowed to conduct, without financial limit, certain kinds of voter registration and get-out-the-vote drives, done under the guise of "party building" activities.

The national party organizations, particularly on the Republican side, immediately exploited a loophole in the new election amendments and obtained rights, similar to those previously granted the state and local parties, to conduct "party building" and volunteer activities. Of enormous benefit to the national parties was the Federal Election Commission ruling that the 1979 amendments removed all financial limits covering national party registration drives and get-out-the-vote efforts. In addition, the FEC allowed the national parties, on behalf of their candidates, to use direct mail in the name of a specific candidate as long as volunteers had a major role in the process. Despite several challenges brought before the Federal Election Commission by Common Cause and the Democratic National Committee, the FEC has continued to uphold the Republican National Committee activities as being within the scope of the federal campaign law and its amendments, even though several national Republican officials admitted off-the-record that their organizations stretch their interpretation of the federal election laws to the "maximum limit." The national Republican organizations, and to a lesser extent their Democratic counterparts, have used the 1979 amendments, the related loopholes, and the FEC rulings to assert themselves actively in the campaigns of their candidates once again, by providing both cash and services. The 1979 amendments thus enhanced the potential usefulness of the national parties, helping them regain a meaningful role in the campaigns of candidates running for office.

Faced with strict limits on the size of contributions but blessed with unlimited expenditures, many candidates abandoned the old campaign methods of the 1960s and 1970s and entered the 1980s with a different approach to electioneering. Many were forced to turn to professional political advisors for ideas on squeezing the most out of tight budgets.

The most controversial new ingredient in the electoral process, however, was the political action committee. As author Burton Sheppard observed, "The FECA itself created a whole new structure of entities – the PACs – ready to work for their self-perpetuation and self-enhancement."[6] PACs, with their legality affirmed by the Supreme Court, now found themselves sought after by financially hungry campaigners, rather than being the seekers themselves of suitable candidates to support. According to journalist Elizabeth Drew, candidates were now forced to add an additional responsibility to their electioneering activities: "A candidate entering politics now must systematically make the round of the interest groups [PACs] and win their approval, and their money . . ."[7]

Independent expenditure campaigns, an electioneering vehicle used almost exclusively by the political action committees, allows organizations to spend unlimited amounts for – or against – candidates, as long as these expenditures are entirely independent of (that is, neither at the direct request of nor in direct cooperation with) the candidate they wish to help. Since they face no financial restrictions, independent expenditure campaigns have become the new wild card in electoral politics, and they too can be traced directly to the FECA. According to former Republican National Committee Chairman Richard Richards: "Some of the election law reform prompted, if not specifically caused, the creation of independent expenditure groups that have injected a great amount of irresponsibility in political campaigns."[8] An important example was the one million dollars spent in the 1984 Illinois Senate race by a millionaire in his successful independent expenditure effort to defeat a single incumbent – Senator Charles Percy.

Challenges to the constitutionality of several current laws have made their way to the Supreme Court, and thereby altered the electoral landscape. One of the most important decisions affecting political action committees came on 18 March 1985, when the Supreme Court ruled that limiting independent spending by PACs on behalf of publicly funded presidential candidates was an infringement on freedom of speech and association, and therefore unconstitutional. The vote, by a seven to two margin, following an earlier four to four vote in 1982, finally ended the legal controversy surrounding independent expenditures in presidential and other federal races. These expenditures have undergone dramatic increases in PAC allocations – from $1.6 million in the 1976 presidential election to $16.7 in 1984.[9] The Supreme Court decision can only lead to further independent expenditure efforts in future presidential races.

The Federal Election Commission has also had an impact on those running for office, though more often by default than by action. Since 1979, only in rare circumstances has the Commission obtained the necessary four votes from the six-member panel to take action on a regulatory issue. It has not recommended a criminal prosecution in years, and settles most of its cases through "conciliation," a civil plea-bargaining process that rarely ends in any substantial penalties.

First in 1979 and again in 1986, the FEC refused to ban an electioneering practice known as the "bundling" of campaign contributions. Bundling is a practice by which PACs and other political committees gather together the contributions to a candidate from their membership and then turn them over to the candidate without having to account for the contributions under the statutory limits restricting what a political committee can give to a federal candidate. Before the 1974 campaign laws, the Council for a Livable World, an antimilitary organization, would solicit members for cheques made out to specific candidates selected by the organization. These cheques were then "bundled" and handed over to the specified candidates by the Council, which took credit for the total amount contributed by its members. The 1974 laws apparently made this procedure illegal, but the Council went to court in 1979 and received a ruling that allowed them to resume bundling as long as they could show that the contributors, not the organization, had made the final determination of who was to receive the money.

After the National Conservative Political Action Committee (NCPAC) received the same ruling, other PACs also adopted the procedure. In a typical example of the financial power of PAC bundling, Alignpac, a political action committee composed of insurance agents, gave Senate Finance Committee Chairman Bob Packwood a $1,000 contribution in preparation for his 1986 re-election campaign. But in addition, Alignpac collected $215,000 from its members and turned over the entire sum to the Packwood campaign – without breaking any law.[10] Thus, political action committees, with many contributors, are now legally able to exceed previously imposed contribution limits when aiding preferred candidates.

The bundling loophole is exploited by the national party organizations as well. The National Republican Senatorial Committee channeled about four million dollars to Senate candidates in 1986 in contributions collected from party donors.[11] In a September fundraising letter signed by George Bush, contributors were urged to donate to candidates in specific states, thus complying with the law. But the names of the Republican candidates were never mentioned, and the contributors were instructed to send their checks not directly to the specific candidate of their choice but to the Senatorial Committee. The national Republican organizations were thus able to flood close races with additional funding in the latter stages of the campaign, demonstrating how current election laws have returned influence to the national parties.

The national Democratic organizations also bent election laws to their advantage when they adopted a fundraising practice similar to the illegal system of "laundering" campaign contributions. Wealthy contributors were sent a direct mail package on behalf of 1986 North Carolina Senate candidate Terry Sanford by the Democratic Senatorial Campaign Committee that asked the recipient to write three separate checks, one for $2,000 directly to the Sanford campaign, one for $5,000 to a state party organization called "North Carolina Victory Fund," and the third for $15,000 to the Democratic Senatorial Campaign Committee. The $2,000 check, double what federal law allows, was legal because half the money went to pay leftover bills from the primary. But the $5,000 and $15,000 contributions were dubious. The direct mail piece instructed potential donors to send both checks to the Sanford headquarters for fowarding to the state and national committees. There, the letter said, "Funds equivalent will be directed [that is, returned] to pay Sanford campaign expenses."[12] This process of laundering money through "earmarking" donations was declared illegal by the FEC in the mid 1970s, but the Democratic Senatorial Campaign Committee skirted the rule by avoiding a guarantee, at least publicly, that every dollar raised to help Sanford would eventually find its way into his campaign coffers. Further attempts by the two national party organizations to bend the existing rules are likely.

Bundling and laundering campaign contributions are not the only attempts by PACs and the national parties to circumvent the spirit of current federal election laws. In an important 1986 "non-ruling," the FEC refused to investigate or further regulate the use of political "soft money" in the electoral process. Although candidates and national political parties are prohibited by federal election law from accepting direct contributions from corporations and unions, many corporations and unions evade the legal restrictions by donating instead to state parties, where regulation is almost nonexistent. According to the *Washington Post*, the Democratic National Committee, the Democratic Congressional Campaign Committee, and the Democratic Senatorial Campaign Committee manage to raise over 20 percent of their budgets from these "soft money" contributions, asserting that the cash is not used directly to further the efforts of candidates for public office.[13] However, this extra money does, in turn, enable the national Democratic party, and to a lesser extent the Republican party, to utilize other funds for candidate activities.

The most recent regulatory change, enacted by the Federal Communications Commission (FCC) in time for the 1988 elections, was the abolition of the "fairness doctrine," a rule which generally required broadcasters who aired controversial shows or commercials to give opponents the opportunity to respond. There are a number of Senate and House candidates who have used the FCC rule to force broadcasters to provide them with an opportunity to respond to particularly harsh and unfounded criticism. It is doubtful, however, that the elimination of the fairness doctrine will have any significant impact on the election process; since 1980, the FCC has received about 50,000 complaints, but found only one violation.[14] Nevertheless, a battle looms between congressional supporters of the regulation, led by Senator Ernest Hollings, and the FCC that may last into the next decade before the issue is finally resolved.

Clearly the 1971 FECA and the amendments of 1974, 1976, and 1979 have profoundly affected the style and substance of modern electioneering, and in many ways altered the role of candidates in their campaigns. Contrary to what was intended, the new laws have made the never ending search for campaign funds the primary focus for many candidates. With strict contribution limits in effect for federal races, the task of raising private funding has become more difficult and time consuming than ever. "One of the sad things about the process created by the federal law is that it forces candidates to spend too much time fundraising," commented former National Republican Senatorial Committee (NRSC) finance director Rodney Smith.[15] Lyn Nofziger, formerly President Reagan's political advisor, concurred: "Candidates are forced to spend far more – and far too much – time on fundraising because of the federal election laws."

Candidates, unless independently wealthy, had no choice but to turn to direct mail consultants and other fundraising specialists for the then primitive – but nevertheless proven – technology needed to raise the significant sums required to replace the now illegal large donations. Political fundraising eventually evolved into what Smith calls "a technician's game."[16] Said fundraising consultant and former Democratic National Committee treasurer Peter Kelly, "The Federal Election Campaign Act has replaced the major donor with the major fundraiser. I have replaced the moneymen of politics."

At the same time that the federal election laws contributed to and hastened the evolution of modern campaign technology, they also contributed to the demise of volunteer-centered campaigning. Besides direct mail, candidates have also become dependent on paid media to reach their constituency, and on pollsters and media experts to research and produce an effective message that will prevail on election day. Each election cycle seems to bring an added level of technical sophistication, often going beyond the understanding and interest of the candidate. Dependent on professional consultants, candidates have become less involved in decision making in their own campaigns, sometimes appearing more like spectators than participants in the electoral process. Gone are patronage and the old-time political bosses, replaced in the 1980s by political consultants, PACs, and direct mail.

Much of this new technical sophistication has been greatly facilitated by advances in computer technology. Prior to 1976, the costs of computerizing a campaign were too high for most statewide campaigns. But with the development of minicomputers, and more recently microcomputers, data processing capabilities have quickly permeated the political world. Traditional internal campaign chores, such as scheduling, opposition research, and the financial reports required by the Federal Election Commission are routinely computerized in most statewide campaigns. But it is in the areas of polling, direct mail, media placement and assessment, voter analysis, demographic analysis, and voter identification, that the computer has truly revolutionized politics. The integration of these specialized techniques, through computerization, has allowed campaign consultants to develop highly defined campaign messages, determine the manner of communication, target precisely the intended audience, and then measure the campaign's success or failure.

Polling has become an indispensable ingredient in the modern political campaign. Even the safest congressional incumbents and most naive (or underfunded) challengers will expend campaign dollars for at least one professional public opinion survey. "It used to be, if you couldn't use a poll for strategy, you could always use it for a paperweight – those things weighed about 18 pounds," joked pollster Vince Breglio.[17] Today, speed is of the essence, and political pollsters can now monitor the public mood on a day-by-day basis through tracking polls that use an abbreviated questionnaire and a limited number of interviews as compared with the usual political survey. Although political survey research is not new, prior to this decade tracking polls were almost unheard of as a means to test last-minute changes in voter opinion. Today, however, a typical statewide campaign will poll 100 to 200 voters a night, every night, sometimes weeks before election day, in an effort to detect any shift in public sentiment. The campaign thus has a constant finger on the pulse of the electorate. With advances in demographic research, pollsters can also divide the electorate into small, refined subgroups for precise analysis and strategy planning. Under the guidance of pollster Richard Wirthlin, the 1980 and 1984 Reagan presidential campaigns made great use of these technical advances in determining which voting blocks to target, and which to ignore, during crucial periods in both election cycles. Thus, the political image merchants are better able to fine tune their client's words in accordance with intricate polling data, sharpening the quality and speedily adjusting the content of the candidate's message.

Candidates are guided by what the polls tell them concerns or worries voters – or what issues could concern or worry voters if the proper stimuli were introduced. TV spots declaring the candidate tough on the issues and the opponent soft, or depicting the candidate as honest and hardworking and the opponent corrupt and irresponsible, are intended to boost the candidate's poll ratings, which are then used (in his name) to raise more money for additional TV spots that reflect the information gleaned from the polling data. Money and polling are thus supremely important elements in the modern election because, in the final analysis, the major campaigns of the 1980s have been won and lost on television. Wrote the *New York Times* in 1986: "The most striking change [in elections] is the way in which television, an important but not dominant element in American politics ten years ago, is at the center of the electoral process."[18]

The impact of television in recent years cannot be overstated. The extensive literature on the role of the media in politics is evidence of this, as is the fact that nearly one-half of the leading political professionals interviewed by this author consider the importance and use of television to be the single greatest change in electioneering over the past decade. (See survey 1.1.)

**Survey 1.1**  *What has been the single greatest change in electioneering in the past decade?*

|                                                           | %  |
|-----------------------------------------------------------|----|
| Importance/impact/use of television                       | 43 |
| Federal election laws                                     | 14 |
| Money in politics                                         | 11 |
| Use/integration of modern technology and consultants      | 9  |
| Role of the computer                                      | 6  |
| Reduced role of the parties                               | 3  |
| Negative campaigning                                      | 3  |
| Other responses                                           | 11 |

Although newspaper coverage of politics continues to have some influence on the way voters perceive a campaign, it is really through television that images are created or destroyed. It was at a competition of woodsmen in New Hampshire that 1984 dark horse presidential candidate Gary Hart, dressed in blue jeans, checkered shirt, and red suspenders, created an image through television that was to take him all the way to the Democratic national convention. Hart was filmed throwing a large, long-handled axe at a target on a tree stump some distance away. When the axe hit the target dead center, a proud Gary Hart spread his arms wide and took a showy bow, as the image of a youthful, active, and confident presidential candidate was instantly beamed across America – to be shown day after day in reports about the Hart candidacy. But what viewers did not see – and therefore did not know – was that this was Hart's second throw. The first one had missed. No other current medium of communication has equal power.

Media consultant Bob Goodman cites 1988 Republican presidential candidate Al Haig as an illustration of a candidate destroyed by television: "Haig just has the most unfortunate television personality I've ever seen. If you listen to [or read] what he says, a lot of it makes a lot of sense. But the delivery, and the mood of the delivery, is kind of frightening."[19]

In the past, candidates had to demonstrate previous success in local campaigns before attempting a federal race. In presidential contests, only the acknowledged front runners received significant coverage. Back in 1975, recalled Jimmy Carter's press secretary Jody Powell, the only way he could have gotten Carter on television would have been to have the former Georgia governor "set his hair on fire in public – with ample advance notice."[20] Television advertising has changed all that. "Candidates can come from nowhere, thanks to television advertising, and run for Congress or the Senate," claimed Edward Rollins, former White House political director and 1984 Reagan–Bush campaign director. Added campaign strategist Charles Black, "Television advertising can overpower print coverage of campaign events."

Many consultants even go so far as to advise their candidates to ignore unfavorable newspaper coverage and concentrate their efforts solely on achieving a winning TV image. Sometimes this can backfire; Pat Robertson attempted to use his old Brooklyn neighborhood as a backdrop when he announced his candidacy for the 1988 Republican presidential nomination, but the protesters and hecklers who shouted him down received more attention than the announcement itself. Yet for many candidates, particularly dark horses, television can be everything. Bruce Babbitt, 1988 Democratic presidential hopeful, quickly accepted an invitation to appear on the popular *Saturday Night Live* comedy show because he was lagging far behind his rivals in all public opinion polls. "If I had Babbitt's numbers in the polls, I'd do *Saturday Night Live*, too. I'd do the Thanksgiving Day Parade as one of the balloons if they wanted me to," commented leading Republican media consultant Roger Ailes.[21] "Unless you have a television campaign," argued 1986 New York gubernatorial candidate Andrew O'Rourke, "nobody thinks you exist."[22]

In fact, newspaper coverage becomes an important factor in electioneering only when coupled with television. Said Robert Squier, a veteran media consultant: "Even if people don't read the articles, if they are devastatingly one-sided, we can use them in television commercials and then they become part of the dialogue." The *Los Angeles Times* summarized the 1986 campaign effort by incumbent Senator Alan Cranston: "A dozen 30-second Cranston commercials have aired in the general election so far, and perhaps three more are still to come. It adds up to a story $7\frac{1}{2}$ minutes long, painstakingly crafted in video-editing laboratories. . . . This is the backbone of the Cranston campaign."[23]

That campaigns have come to recognize the importance of television is clearly demonstrated in the quantity and quality of the paid political advertising. No longer do a candidate's television commercials look like someone's home movies. With the development of portable professional video cameras, improved editing equipment, satellite technology, and express mail, it is possible for a campaign to respond to an opponent's actions or accusations far more quickly than in the past. "It used to take two or three weeks for information to reach the voters. But now it's film at 11:00," concluded pollster Harrison Hickman.[24] Elections have taken on all the aspects of a video war.

These great strides in mass communication could be expected to aid candidate–voter rapport, yet many observers have noted that elections, which are increasingly costly, and highly proficient technically, are severely lacking in content. Along with (or perhaps because of) the technological advances, American politics have become personality-based and candidate-based, rather than issue-based. (See survey 1.2.) The *perception* of a candidate's character and judgment have become more important than the reality of his issue positions, and to the extent that issues remain important, they are used by media consultants and pollsters to build a desired image for their client. The consensus among leading consultants (particularly in the polling and media professions) is summarized by Republican media advisor Robert Goodman: "Now and then you may have an issue, like abortion or nuclear power, which can dominate. But today it's all basically personality." Added Bill Lacy, a leading strategist in the 1988 presidential campaign of Senator Bob Dole, "There are not many issues out there that by themselves will elect or defeat candidates."

Issues of themselves are becoming less important than the way in which they are being packaged and marketed to the voters. "People are even willing to vote for someone they disagree with," said Ed Rollins, 1984 Reagan–Bush campaign manager, "as long as they think the person is honest." The early months of the 1988 presidential campaign

**Survey 1.2**   *Overall, which is more important in recent congressional and senatorial campaigns: issues, or the candidate's image and personality?*

| | Total % | Pollsters % | Media consultants % | General consultants % | Fundraisers % |
|---|---|---|---|---|---|
| Image/personality | 73 | 100 | 71 | 67 | 33 |
| Issues | 15 | 0 | 0 | 33 | 67 |
| Not separable/ of equal importance (response volunteered) | 12 | 0 | 29 | 0 | 0 |

were dominated not by economic, foreign or social issues but instead by the issues of personal integrity and morality. A majority of candidates had to face, at least once during the campaign, charges of flawed judgment or character weakness. For several, the accusations could not be overcome. "We live in an age without secrets," observed media consultant Bob Goodman. "We come to know each other too well."[25] For candidates Gary Hart and Joseph Biden, the public came to know them too well.

A campaign's message, like the candidates themselves, varies from one campaign to another, since it is primarily designed to highlight the unique qualities of the candidate rather than his ideology or partisan affiliation. Many candidates openly resent any attempt to label their politics, if only because it restricts their ability to define themselves. Following an endorsement from the liberal publication *Village Voice*, a spokesman for South Dakota Senate candidate Thomas Daschle said, "We don't pay much attention . . . [and] don't call Tom liberal."[26] At one time, issue-laden slogans were a campaign's rallying call, but they have little place in the modern political campaign. Florida Senator Paula Hawkins ran her 1986 re-election campaign on the issueless slogan "The senator for people who don't have a senator." Opponent Bob Graham responded by referring to Hawkins as "A cheerleader for causes no one can oppose." That same year, "Governor not guru," said the political buttons distributed on behalf of Pennsylvania gubernatorial candidate Robert Casey. The reference was to the college days of opponent William Scranton, who admitted having smoked marijuana and having been a disciple of the Maharajah.

This noticeable shift in campaigning style can be traced back to the 1980 election, when voters went to the polls and surprisingly supported candidates who had waged patently negative campaigns. According to pollster Harrison Hickman, it was the candidates themselves that were at least partially responsible for the shift in emphasis: "Candidates normally have trouble distinguishing themselves from their opponents by simply making a positive argument. The relative quality of any two people running for office today is more or less equal. It is easier to make a distinction by finding some little episode in someone's past or a bad vote to make a clear distinction between people."

Apparently, voters also found it easier to distinguish between candidates when negative campaigning was used. Post-election studies conducted in 1980, 1982, and 1984 by professional advisors showed a far greater public tolerance for negative advertisements than they had expected; it was this that laid the groundwork for the increase in anti-candidate campaigns in the 1986 and 1988 election cycles.[27] The rise of negative advertising has placed heavy emphasis on personality traits as well as on the misrepresentation of the opponent, at the expense of issues and almost everything else.

In some instances, the campaign itself has become the biggest issue. Candidates are appealing for support by criticizing an opponent's campaign tactics, which by implication means his character. In the 1986 Colorado Senate race, one of the major issues in the campaign was whether Democratic candidate Tim Wirth acted improperly in paying professional actresses to star in his television commercials. Republican opponent Ken Kramer maintained that voters really needed to know "not what he [Kramer] is, but what the women in the [Wirth] commercial are," and began airing commercials to that effect.[28] Headlines similar to "Campaign tactics stir up old animosities in Louisiana" and "Senate candidates' commercials cause outrage in Maryland race" were common across the country.[29] Concluded Senator John Danforth, sponsor of the Clean Campaign Act of 1985: "Negative political campaigns have drawn such general expressions of revulsion — that some ask why they are used. The answer is that they are used because they work. They wear down and tear down opponents, and they win elections."[30]

Modern American politics have two alternative re-election campaign strategies. In what is commonly referred to as the "high road" approach, the candidate points to accomplishments he has already achieved and promises even more if re-elected. Over the past decade, however, a different strategy has become popular. A candidate adopting the "low road" strategy does not trumpet recent achievements but seeks, instead, to focus voter attention upon intellectual, moral, and other personal defects of the opponent. In 1986, nearly every campaign featured the lower road strategy.

Although negative campaigns have been conducted in politics since the earliest elections, the extent to which some candidates and campaigns are now employing odious methods to attain victory at the voting booths stretches morality to the limit. Candidates are digging deep into the past of their opponents in search of any potentially embarrassing episode that would fit conveniently into a 30-second TV spot. Some do not have to dig much at all. The 1988 presidential campaign of Massachusetts Governor Michael Dukakis temporarily came unglued after his campaign finally admitted producing and distributing a videotape showing that a Dukakis rival, Senator Joseph Biden, had plagiarized lines from a speech delivered earlier in the year by British Labour Party leader Neil Kinnock. At first claiming to have had no involvement or knowledge of the video, Dukakis was slow to accept the resignations of the two top aides involved. "Anything for the sake of winning" appears to be the current motto of many politicians.

The hiring of private detective agencies became an issue in several 1986 statewide campaigns. In North Dakota, a close friend of Republican Senator Mark Andrews hired a detective to investigate the private lives of two possible Democratic contenders, Congressman Byron Dorgan and Andrews' eventual Democratic opponent, Congressman Kent Conrad. Copies of documents and press clippings relating to their divorces and to the Washington lobbying activities of Dorgan's wife were sent anonymously to newspapers and wire service bureaus. In the 1986 Texas gubernatorial campaign, a surveillance sweep for the campaign of Republican gubernatorial candidate William Clements unearthed an eavesdropping bug in the private office of his campaign consultant. In the 1988 Republican presidential sweepstakes, it was reported that Craig Shirley, a part-time consultant to the presidential campaign of George Bush, resigned his two thousand dollar a month position in protest after refusing to take part in a dirty tricks effort by some members of the Bush campaign staff. Several months later, the campaigns of Senator Bob Dole and Congressman Jack Kemp also accused the Bush staff of improper electioneering tactics.

Negative campaigns and improper tactics have infiltrated gubernatorial and House elections as well. A Democratic candidate for Congress from Long Island paid female investigators to meet his Republican opponent, Representative Raymond McGrath, in a Washington restaurant and, secretly, tape record their conversations with him. The Democratic candidate, Michael Sullivan, thereby obtained fourteen hours of recordings at a cost of $18,000 – nearly a third of his campaign war chest. But on his FEC campaign expense record, it was reported as payment for "research."[31] In one campaign, a House incumbent urged voters to "break the back of Satan" by returning him to Congress. In the 1987 Kentucky race for governor, Republican candidate John Harper suggested on various occasions that Democratic opponent Wallace Wilkinson was "sleazy," "seedy," "tacky," and even "a little weasel." For his part, Wilkinson conceded that his campaign tipped the news media onto stories about Harper's son, who was shot to death attempting a burglary.[32] Although few current races have provoked such strong measures, many political consultants see a marked increase in negative campaigning in elections that are considered marginal.

Even among practitioners of the negative style, a growing number of candidates have begun to express dismay that the attacks and counterattacks between themselves and their opponents have become unnecessarily vicious and are occurring too early in the election cycle. "I have never been so angry with the political process," said South Dakota Congressman Thomas Daschle in response to attacks by Senator James Abdnor in August 1986, two and a half months before election day.[33] "What Tom Daschle did to me and my record is disgraceful," Abdnor responded later. Said a state Democratic leader: "It's a little early for an exchange this tough in South Dakota. The question is whether it's too early."[34] The success of those candidates who adopted negative strategies may very well result in still earlier negative attacks in upcoming election cycles.

Paradoxically, at the same time that candidate personalities have become the primary focus in American elections, personal campaigning by candidates has been sharply reduced, if not virtually eliminated. As the *Wall Street Journal* reported in 1986, "If you want to look at what the future of politics is like, look at this election. The campaign points to a brand of politics that is personality-oriented but impersonal."[35] Rarely are elections won any more by shaking enough hands or giving speeches to live audiences. Said four-term Senator Alan Cranston during the 1986 campaign, "Door-to-door work is harder to do when you are interrupting people watching their favorite television show. Rallies take a lot of staff work, a lot of time. It's hard to get people away from their TV sets to come out to rallies."[36]

True, some politicians still go through the motions of personal campaigning, but usually it is only to impress a visiting reporter or for filming, under the direction of the campaign's media advisor and film crew. California Lt. Governor Leo McCarthy, 1988 Senate candidate, recently embarked on a highway caravan tour designed more for media opportunities than to meet the public. Florida Senator Lawton Chiles walked the entire length of Florida in his first run for the Senate in 1970, but his hiking activities were sharply curtailed in his two subsequent re-election campaigns. Except for a few lightly populated localities where voters still expect to meet and talk with their senators, governors, and congressmen, personal campaigning is almost nonexistent. "A campaign rally today is three people around a TV set," said media consultant Robert Shrum.[37] Added author and political columnist Michael Barone, "Personal campaigning seems to be going the way of the torchlight parade, the whistle-stop campaign and the deadlocked convention."

The phenomenon of the absent candidate also extends to other areas of the campaign. Changes in the method of winning elections have come so rapidly that some pundits have suggested the candidate has been left behind. Only a small number of leading professional consultants appear to agree, however. (See survey 1.3.) Concluded Richard Viguerie, "There is some truth to the old cliché that you can't teach an old dog new tricks. It is the younger candidates who are interested in trying the new techniques and ideas." Candidates often do not understand the intricate details of survey research or the software packages that automate their computer operation or the equipment used in editing their campaign commercials. Furthermore, no candidate interviewed for this book expressed any interest in learning polling techniques, designing campaign software, or being taught how to use film editing equipment. Nevertheless, they are usually well versed in the

**Survey 1.3** *What is the single most important factor in a political campaign today?*

|  | % |
| --- | --- |
| Candidate | 66 |
| Money | 11 |
| Issues | 8 |
| Television | 6 |
| Strategy | 6 |
| Other | 3 |

general functions and operation of a modern campaign. (See survey 1.4.)

Although the professionals feel that candidates are now relatively familiar with the new technology, many consultants still prefer that the candidate take a limited role in his campaign. More than half of the leading consultants interviewed did not want their candidates "very involved" in the inner workings of the campaign, particularly in the execution of campaign strategy and tactics. (See chapter 2.) Even important campaign activities such as direct mail and television advertising are often made without the direct participation of the candidate. But since enormous sums are required to pay for professional services and for the costly television commercials that currently dominate most campaigns, few consultants will take on a campaign if there is any doubt about the candidate's fundraising ability. Thus the "candidate-centered campaign" might be considered a misnomer if it were not for a vital factor in modern electoral politics – money. The need for huge amounts of money to be raised by the candidate has reaffirmed the importance of the candidate in his campaign, at a time when the growing power of consultants and the intricacy of the new technology seemed to be threatening to eliminate him from the election process.

The oft-quoted California politician Jesse Unruh once said that money is the mother's milk of politics. Added former Missouri Senator Thomas Eagleton, "Fundraising has gone from a campaign ingredient to an all-pervasive campaign obsession."[38] Both observations are even

**Survey 1.4** *Are candidates better versed in the various aspects of the new campaign technologies than they were five years ago?*

|  | % |
| --- | --- |
| Yes | 75 |
| No | 25 |

**Table 1.1**  *Money spent in Senate/House campaigns*

| Cycle | No. of candidates[1] | Expenditures Total ($ million) | % increase |
|---|---|---|---|
| 73–4 | * | 73.9 | – |
| 75–6 | * | 125.5 | 70 |
| 77–8 | 2,163 | 194.8 | 55 |
| 79–80 | 2,288 | 239.0 | 23 |
| 81–2 | 2,240 | 342.4 | 43 |
| 83–4 | 2,036 | 374.1 | 9 |
| 85–6 | 1,868 | 450.0 | 20 |

% increase in House and Senate expenditures 1976–86    259%
% increase in House and Senate expenditures 1980–6    88%

| Cycle | Senate No. of candidates | Senate Expenditures ($ million) | House No. of candidates | House Expenditures ($ million) |
|---|---|---|---|---|
| 73–4 | * | 28.9 | * | 45.0 |
| 75–6 | * | 46.3 | * | 79.2 |
| 77–8 | 254 | 85.2 | 1,909 | 109.6 |
| 79–80 | 344 | 103.0 | 1,944 | 136.0 |
| 81–2 | 283 | 138.4 | 1,957 | 204.0 |
| 83–4 | 254 | 170.5 | 1,782 | 238.9 |
| 85–6 | 262 | 211.1 | 1,606 | 238.9 |

% increase in Senate expenditures 1976–86    356%
% increase in Senate expenditures 1980–6    105%

% increase in House expenditures 1976–86    202%
% increase in House expenditures 1980–4    76%

[1] Including unsuccessful primary candidates.
* Not available.

*Source*: Compiled from FEC Press Releases of 29 June 1979; 7 March 1982; 2 December 1983; 8 December 1985; 10 May 1987; and FECA Rules Hearing 1986, p. 326

more appropriate today than ever before. Campaign spending has been driven relentlessly upward by nervous candidates who feel compelled to make maximum use of the new techniques for reaching voters. (See table 1.1.) Candidates need substantial resources to be able to hire the best campaign consultants, who bring with them expert knowledge of the latest campaign techniques. Poorly funded campaigns, with limited access to technological innovations, have to settle for a lower standard in campaign functions, such as less sophisticated polling, inferior quality of paid political advertising, less computerization, etc. Financially strained challengers, in particular, are at a severe disadvantage when competing against well-funded incumbents. With minimal funds, challengers are often forced to depend almost entirely on free media sources and grassroots campaigning, while money-laden incumbents can utilize many of the latest, expensive campaign techniques.

There is no question that money has become a key requirement, on which paid advertising, polling, and all other campaign techniques depend, a fact that has not been lost on candidates, consultants, or party leaders. "As I began my candidacy," said 1986 New York Senate candidate Mark Green, "many leaders of my party said to me not who are you, not what you stand for, not what you have done, but where is your $5 million up front?"[39] Green's opponent in the primary, John Dyson, even made money an important campaign issue during a public debate: "[I am] the only Democrat . . . who has the resources and ability to raise funds to make a real contest," he said, a reference to Green's failure to attract sufficient funding to wage a credible campaign against Republican incumbent Alfonse D'Amato.[40] In his official concession announcement, former Arizona gubernatorial candidate David Moss informed his audience that lack of funds had forced him to quit. If there had been more money, "it could have been a darned good race. All I would have had to do is get on the tube and be nice."[41] Senator Rudy Boschwitz in a letter to GOP Senate incumbents in 1986 advised: "Raise $1 million or more in advance to buy television time a la Budweiser . . . and waste little time on speeches and debates."[42] Florida Governor Robert Graham had seven professional fundraisers on his 1986 Senate campaign payroll, including six who were full time. One even worked entirely out of his Washington office. The day after his election, the victorious candidate told reporters: "The most important decision we made was to do the things necessary to be competitive financially. We spent the better part of a year raising the money to spend in the last fifteen to thirty days of the campaign."[43] Media consultant Frank Greer, who won three of his four statewide races in 1986, concurred: "If there are two lessons of this campaign, it's that money has become a determining factor, and second, I am absolutely convinced that the issues and the agenda get set by the people who have the money." Concluded veteran political advisor

Stuart Spencer, "While starving artists have produced great paintings, starving campaigns produce few winners."[44]

The number of candidates spending vast sums of money seeking election continues to grow, even though the rate of increase in campaign expenditures for House and Senate candidates has slowed somewhat in recent elections. (See table 1.2.)

Since extensive personal campaigning by candidates is no longer required, and most consultants do not want their clients loitering around the headquarters, fundraising has become the candidate's main function in his campaign. With the rapid escalation of campaign spending, experts like Keith Abbott, finance director of the Democratic Senatorial Campaign Committee, recommend that candidates devote at least 50 percent of their campaign hours to raising money, and that they start years, not months, before election day.[45] Most candidates do not appreciate such advice. Democratic presidential hopeful Bruce Babbitt muttered about "the absurdity of all this" after being forced to devote as much as two full days a week exclusively to fundraising, a degrading process he once compared to "root-canal therapy."[46] Senate candidates are no less pressed for funds. On election day 1986, more than $10 million in campaign contributions had already been been raised by the 1988 Senate candidates, including six candidates who each already had accumulated more than half a million dollars in the bank.[47] California Governor George Deukmejian had already collected almost two million dollars for his re-election bid – three years before election day. Even after their elections are over, candidates often continue allocating a significant portion of their time to raising money. "We are still working to retire debt on a daily basis," said Massachusetts Senator John Kerry a full year after his election victory. "On some days 50 percent of our time is just trying to get out of debt."[48]

**Table 1.2**  *Top Senate and House Fundraisers*

| | Senate | | House | |
|---|---|---|---|---|
| Cycle | No. of candidates raising over $3.0m | No. of candidates raising over $5.0m | No. of candidates raising over $0.85m | No. of candidates raising over $1.0m |
| 79–80 | 1 | 0 | 3 | 2 |
| 81–2 | 10 | 4 | 10 | 6 |
| 83–4 | 15 | 7 | 16 | 4 |
| 85–6 | 24 | 12 | 37 | 19 |

*Source*: FEC Press Releases of 7 March 1982; 2 December 1983; 8 December 1985; and 10 May 1987

It is therefore not surprising that the average amount of campaign expenditure by successful candidates has increased dramatically in the past five election cycles, usually setting a new record every two years. (See table 1.3.) Although the average for expenditures by all congressional candidates did not increase from 1982 to 1984, the average cost of winning a seriously contested House seat, where the winner had 55 percent of the vote or less, reached $484,949 in 1984, up one-third from 1982.[49] Expenditures also continued to rise on a per vote basis. In 1984, the total expenditure by the two candidates for US Senate in West Virginia came to $18.37 per vote cast, a new spending record.[50] The 1984 North Carolina Senate race, the most expensive statewide contest in American history, ranked second, with a per vote expenditure of $11.66.[51] As Senator David Boren concluded, "When we are in the midst of a campaign we are worried about winning; if an additional million dollars is made available to us, we are probably going to spend that million dollars."[52] Added media advisor Greg Stevens, "It's a vicious circle. If people don't see us spending money on television, they'll think we're losing and stop contributing. Then we get a shortage of money which forces us to cut back on television, which only makes the shortage worse. Pretty soon there's no money left at all."

Fundraising is one aspect of modern electioneering that the candidate cannot personally avoid. According to Abbott, "It is the candidate who has to make the final sale. Donors want to hear from the candidate, to rub shoulders with the candidate, to develop a special relation with him or her."[53] Every year the demand for personal contact escalates, and candidates accommodate the demand to compete. Florida Senate candidates Robert Graham and Paula Hawkins between them attended close to 260 fundraising events from late August 1985 to October 1986, an average of approximately four "fundraisers" a week for over a year.[54] Not surprisingly, of all the political rituals, fundraising appears to be the least popular among candidates. Although recognized as a necessary evil, it is usually regarded with aversion. "The price for running for the Senate today," said 1986 Missouri Senate candidate Harriet Woods, "is spending more time than you'd like to spend asking people for more money than they'd like to give."[55] Senator Charles Mathias retired in 1986 rather than face another cycle of perpetual fundraising. "I certainly won't miss raising the maybe $4 million it would have cost to get reelected. That's the worst thing that's happened in politics in my time."[56] Added Senator Barry Goldwater, "If there was one thing that made up my mind not to run more than anything else, it was the fact that I could no longer go to my friends and say, 'Can you give me some money to run for office?'"[57]

It has become almost impossible, even for statewide candidates in wealthy states or districts, to raise sufficient money from their own

**Table 1.3** *Campaign expenditures of successful candidates*

| | Senate ($ million) | | |
|---|---|---|---|
| Cycle | Raised | Spent | Average spent per candidate |
| 75–6 | 21.0 | 20.1 | 0.61 |
| 77–8 | 43.0 | 42.3 | 1.28 |
| 79–80 | 41.7 | 40.0 | 1.18 |
| 81–2 | 70.7 | 68.2 | 2.07 |
| 83–4 | 100.9 | 104.0 | 3.14 |
| 85–6 | 106.8 | 104.0 | 3.14 |

% increase in average spent per candidate 1980–6   166%

| | House ($ thousand) | | |
|---|---|---|---|
| 75–6 | 42.5 | 38.0 | 87 |
| 77–8 | 60.0 | 55.6 | 127 |
| 79–80 | 86.0 | 78.0 | 179 |
| 81–2 | 123.1 | 114.7 | 264 |
| 83–4 | 144.8 | 127.0 | 292 |
| 85–6 | 173.3 | 155.4 | 357 |

% increase in average spent per candidate 1980–6   99%

*Source*: Compiled from FEC Press Release "FEC Releases Final Report on 1984 Congressional Race", 8 December 1985; and 10 May 1987

constituents. Candidates are now seeking new sources of capital, in big (even if distant) cities like Los Angeles, Dallas, Houston, Chicago, Miami, New York, and, above all, Washington. "The feeling is that campaigns are won or lost in the Washington, DC money centers rather than in the district [or state] sought to be represented," said House Task Force on Elections Chairman Al Swift.[58] The $1,000-a-ticket Wall Street fundraiser has become a mandatory event for most presidential candidates, and few thought it improper when 1986 Maryland Senate candidate Barbara Mikulski conducted elaborate fundraisers 3,000 miles from her state that brought in $1,000 contributions from several Hollywood celebrities.

Plainly, candidates are being stretched to their creative limits to raise the necessary funds. For $5,000 per couple, 500 persons had the opportunity to attend Barbara Streisand's first public concert in six years, laugh at a comedy routine by popular funnyman Robin Williams, and rub shoulders with the rich and famous of Hollywood, as they contributed to the 1986 Senate campaign of Alan Cranston. A 1986 Kentucky lieutenant governor candidate sold look-alike Halloween costumes of himself at $30 each. Recent Georgia Senate candidate Wyche Fowler appeared in a $250 per couple fundraising concert with folk singers Peter Yarrow and Mary Travers that raised $50,000 for his campaign. In Oregon, 1986 GOP gubernatorial candidate Norma Paulus arranged for supporters to fly with Air Force hero Chuck Yeager to a fundraising barbecue that cost $500 per ticket. For a $1,000 donation to a 1986 Republican Senate candidate, GOP suppporters could have their picture taken with President Reagan while he was on the campaign trail.

There is strong evidence to suggest that "cash on hand," a factor which is often overlooked by political observers and the news media, has become nearly as important as the total amount raised and spent during the campaign. Of the fifteen most contested Senate races in 1986, as determined by the *Washington Post*, two-thirds of the eventual winners had more cash on hand than their opponents on 30 June four months before election day – the "decisive period" of the campaign because voter perception of the candidates is then most fluid and open to suggestion.[59] Examined another way, none of the eight incumbents, and only one of the three challengers, who had at least $1 million in the bank on 30 June, was defeated in November.[60] However, by 15 October, the FEC's final date for required financial disclosures, fewer than half of the eventual winners maintained cash-on-hand balances above their opponents.[61] In fact, six of the top twelve Senate fundraisers lost their election bids.[62] For many of these losers, even the late influx of money was too late to undo the damage of earlier months. In the elections of the 1980s, money has always been a crucial factor, but its overall importance has depended almost as much on timing (that is, on when it was available to be used) as on the total amount raised and spent. Early funding helps build political credibility which is necessary before a candidate can successfully appeal for support. Noted political finance expert Herbert Alexander concluded, following the 1986 elections: "This election shows that there are absolute limitations on what money can do."[63] Added Fred Wertheimer from Common Cause, "Money never guarantees winning, but having money makes a big difference."

Somewhat less crucial to recent campaigns is the origin of this political money. An increasing number of wealthy candidates successfully seeking elective office are personally financing their own campaign. Personal fortunes have turned more than a few unknown and politically inexperienced millionaires into senators, governors, and congressmen. In 1974, the last election cycle before new federal election laws took effect, candidate contributions to their own campaigns, as a percentage of total campaign receipts, averaged about 4 percent. Since 1974, the average has been just under 11 percent, although in 1982 it reached a high of 20 percent for Senate candidates. (See table 1.4.) With fundraising setting new records in each election cycle, the amount of money the average candidate needs to contribute to his own campaign is also growing, at a rate equivalent to that for funds from other sources.

**Table 1.4** *Congressional candidates' own contributions as a percentage of total campaign receipts, 1974–1984*[1]

|         | 1974 | 1976 | 1978 | 1980 | 1982 | 1984 |
|---------|------|------|------|------|------|------|
| House   | 6    | 11   | 9    | 10   | 12   | 6    |
| Senate  | 1    | 12   | 8    | 10   | 20   | 11   |

[1] General election candidates only.

*Source*: 1986 Rules Hearings, p. 332

The phenomenon of candidates routinely spending hundreds of thousands, or even millions, of dollars on their own campaigns can be traced directly to the current federal election laws. When there were no legislative contribution limits, it was not difficult for wealthy individuals to attract sufficient funding from other wealthy persons, and therefore it was usually unnecessary for candidates to spend great sums on their own behalf. However, the 1974 Federal Election Campaign Act placed a strict ceiling on contributions, both by candidates and their supporters. But in early 1976, the Supreme Court, in *Buckley* v. *Valeo*, overruled limits on candidate spending while upholding other individual contribution restrictions, and thus made the self-financed campaign almost a necessity for candidates with low name recognition or a limited political base. Many millionaire incumbents found themselves forced to dip into their personal resources to replace the large contributions that had now become illegal. "That is a constant in politics today," remarked New Hampshire Senator Gordon Humphrey. "What scared me most about running was that I had to financially dip into my life savings. If I had lost, it never would have been repaid." Timing is crucial in politics, and the existing law has thus served to enhance the prospects of wealthy candidates who can afford to use their own resources to augment their campaigns continuously, while others must devote valuable campaign time (and often postpone major expenditures) to concentrate on fundraising efforts in order to stay competitive. "The wealthy candidate knows all through the campaign that they have the resources to conduct the campaign," offered leading media consultant Robert Squier. "The poor candidate has to just wonder whether they will. And that in itself means that you cannot plan a campaign in a way that is most efficient," he concluded.[64]

Despite the advantage of wealth, there have been a few candidates with huge, personally funded campaigns who were still unsuccessful. In 1982, when Lew Lehrman spent $8.5 million of his own money, which was twice the amount of his opponent's entire war chest, he still lost the New York governor's race. In Minnesota, department store heir Mark Dayton spent $7 million of his own money in an unsuccessful attempt to unseat the US Senate incumbent in the 1982 race. Adam Levin and Andrew Stein, respectively the biggest personal spenders in the 1982 and 1984 House campaigns, were both defeated. Nashville millionaire businessman Phil Bredesen actually refused to solicit donations from the public in a 1987 special House election, choosing instead to finance his campaign with an interest-free $1.1 million loan.

For John Dyson (who had made money a campaign issue), a $6 million personal contribution to his campaign war chest (a financial advantage of about ten to one over his opponent), an extensive media advertising campaign, and the endorsements of New York's two most popular Democrats, Governor Maurio Cuomo and Mayor Ed Koch, were still not enough to defeat an opponent who spent no more than $600,000 in the 1986 primary for US Senate in New York. Dyson received only 46 percent of the vote. Mark Green, his opponent, was entirely dependent on free media coverage, yet received 54 percent. A *Washington Post* editorial suggested that "Mark Green's victory shows there may just be an anti-Goliath vote out there."[65] The Post editorial might also have pointed out that when a candidate is defined by the money he spends, it fosters the image of a candidate without a cause, whose rationale is his electability as suggested only by his cash. According to Green, "Money matters, but money without message is an echo chamber."[66] Dyson notwithstanding, the financial Goliaths of politics are usually successful.

Money has become so important to political success that it is no longer uncommon for campaign expenditures to exceed campaign receipts, sometimes by a large margin. These debts are the responsibility of the campaign committee and are not transferable to the candidate. In practical terms, this means that the candidate is not personally liable for any campaign debts, except personal loans, and is therefore less inhibited about going into the red. The 1988 presidential campaign of Republican Jack Kemp ran up debts of roughly $1.3 million in an effort to finance a costly direct mail program that his staff regarded as crucial to the campaign's long term financial health. Among the dozens of creditors still owed money by John Connally's 1980 presidential campaign is Connally himself, who loaned his campaign more than $500,000. Gary Hart's 1984 presidential campaign had debts in excess of four million dollars when it came to an end, though he had whittled down the debt to one million by the start of 1988. Ohio Senator John Glenn currently holds the largest outstanding debt, owing more than $2.1 million to creditors across the country. Said one of those creditors, "I was really hoping he would run again so I could sue his campaign when it came to Iowa. . . . Glenn may be a quality senator, but he has people on his staff who belong in a penitentiary."[67]

The weighty combination of television and money have led to the disappearance of other once important campaign features. According to Stuart Spencer, "Because of the new technology, few campaigns are 'people campaigns' any more. You don't need a bunch of little old ladies stamping envelopes to send out a direct mail piece." Most conspicuous by their absence are the campaign volunteers. The 1986 Pennsylvania Senate campaign of underdog Congressman Robert Edgar was the exception, bustling with volunteers and activists. This was nothing new, for Edgar had always run labor-intensive campaigns, depending on volunteers to help him to victory in his congressional races. Edgar had ten field offices across the state that coordinated literally millions of hand delivered campaign literature drops – this in addition to the 400 volunteer-staffed telephones. However, while other less volunteer-intensive underdog Senate campaigns were closing the gap, Edgar's campaign merely remained constant, because his campaign was so pinched for money that he did not air any television ads. He was one of the few strong Democratic challengers in 1986 that failed to unseat a vulnerable Republican incumbent.

Along with the reduced emphasis on volunteer activities has come the reduction in, or elimination of, political buttons, bumper stickers, and lawn signs, once the most visible evidence of an approaching election. The number of televised debates, a major part of the 1988 presidential contest, has actually decreased among US Senate candidates. According to the National Association of Broadcasters, 56 percent of the nation's TV stations offered free time for political debates in 1986, but nearly half of them were unable to air even one of the debates offered, because one or more of the major party candidates refused to participate.[68] Successful statewide campaigns of the mid 1980s consisted basically of fundraising and paid media, and little else.

Even the press has changed its focus. Gone are the page-long comparisons of the various candidates and their positions on numerous questions of the day. Reports on campaign rallies, motorcades, and press-the-flesh events are also rapidly becoming a thing of the past. Reporters are cutting back on coverage of what happens on the campaign trail and, instead, are increasingly watching what goes out over the tube. Today's news stories tend to report on internal campaign strife, production of the latest campaign commercial, the results of a recent public opinion poll, and who is spending more money and what those expenditures are buying. The print media and radio, which lacks the visual, pay close attention to the latest polling data, now often their own. Even in television, it has been found that live footage of the candidates themselves can be replaced by substituting a montage of ad clips and anecdotes about their professionally produced campaign commercials. Said Michael Barone, "We have begun to realize that it matters almost not at all what a candidate says to some audience out in Squeedunk, while what is said in those 60-, 30- and 15-second spots matters a great deal." At a cocktail party following one of the presidential debates, the crowd of journalists surrounding candidates Jesse Jackson and Bruce Babbitt was dwarfed by the journalists and politicians around media consultant Bob Squier. His opinions of the campaign were more important than the candidates' opinions on the issues. In fact, interviews and news conferences with the candidates will often center on rebuttals of their opponents' commercials. The mechanics of campaigning have become a better story than the campaign itself.

Moreover, all across America news organizations have jumped into the polling business, in an effort to gauge the direction in which the electorate will turn. "Political polls from coast to coast far apart in predicting favorites," read a *Washington Times* headline in October 1986.[69] The story detailed several examples, among them the polling results of three Pennsylvania television stations, one of which put Republican gubernatorial candidate Bill Scranton ahead by thirty points, while the other two had him leading by only two points. Under the headline "Pollsters in a state of confusion," the *Washington Post* ran a front page story in 1986 detailing the weekly results of six different Florida news organizations that showed Senator Paula Hawkins trailing Governor Robert Graham by anywhere from two to eighteen points, a difference well beyond any acceptable margin of error.[70] As the article noted, "Poll results are of vital concern to candidates in most campaigns today. Political money follows winners, or those perceived as winners. And poll results create a perception of winners and losers."[71]

The changes that are currently occurring in electioneering because of press interest in public opinions polls should not be underestimated. Campaigns manipulate perceptions of strength by releasing (or leaking) favorable findings, withholding unfavorable ones, and promoting those public polls that will put their candidates in a good light. The sharp increase in public opinion polling has been an advantage for some candidates and a detriment to others. Often, campaigns will invest thousands of dollars on ads for no other reason than they believe it likely that the major media organizations will soon be polling. The proliferation of independent surveys allows campaigns to pick and choose from a greater number of poll results (one favorable result can be sufficient) in an effort to enhance their credibility as they search for dollars. Thus, it is not surprising to find an increasing number of races where candidates spend a great deal of time battling over whose poll results are correct. But as Bob Teeter noted, "There used to be a few media polls, and most of them were pretty good. Now you have a great many . . . some that are pretty good, some that are mediocre, and some that are frankly quite bad." Mervin Field, California's leading independent pollster for the last forty years, endorses this judgment: "There is a new wave of [media] pollsters who are short on methodology. Some of them look at polling as something very easy. They don't go through all the steps."[72] In a similar vein, the *Washington Post*, under the heading "Sun cancels publication of gubernatorial poll," revealed that the highly regarded *Baltimore Sun* had to cancel plans to publish its poll on the Maryland gubernatorial race after one of the candidates publicly alluded to flaws in its methodology.[73] The disputes over methodology and the frequent disparity of results have already begun to reduce the credibility of media sponsored independent polling.

Although the incumbency factor in politics has been extensively examined by numerous political and social scientists, it is important to note that the activities and opinions of incumbents regarding their own re-election efforts have undergone significant change in the past decade. Few now regard their re-election as assured, and incumbents are therefore raising and spending more money in each election cycle. Yet over the past two decades, incumbency has become the greatest single determining factor in the election of Senate and House candidates. Reelection rates for incumbents in both Houses of Congress are impressive. (See table 1.5.)

**Table 1.5**  *Incumbent re-election rates*

| Year | House % | Senate % |
|------|---------|----------|
| 1974 | 87.7 | 85.2 |
| 1976 | 95.8 | 64.0 |
| 1978 | 93.7 | 60.0 |
| 1980 | 90.7 | 55.2 |
| 1982 | 90.6 | 93.3 |
| 1984 | 95.1 | 89.7 |
| 1986 | 98.0 | 75.0 |

*Source*: USA Today, 25 November 1986

In every election since 1976, House incumbents have been re-elected at a rate of over 90 percent. In the 1986 elections, 385 out of the 393 congressmen seeking re-election were successful. In fact, the 1986 re-election rate of 98 percent was the highest in history, and included 77 House seats (18 percent) that went uncontested.[74] On the Senate side, the re-election figures are somewhat less impressive. Only once since 1976 has the re-election level for incumbents reached more than 90 percent, though it has never fallen below 55 percent. In 1986, a relatively good year for challengers, 75 percent – 21 of the 28 incumbent senators – were re-elected. In campaigns of the 1980s, the incumbent's advantage has become nearly insurmountable.

One reason for the electoral success of incumbents, particularly House members, is the wide range of privileges and benefits they have voted themselves, including ever-increasing congressional staff and office allowances, free trips home, and free use of the Congressional radio and television studios for the production of news clips that are then made available to the media outlets in their states and districts. (See table 1.6.)

Allowances for such things as computers, automobiles, telephones and travel have more than doubled since 1979. Forty years ago, the typical House member had only three personal staff employees; today the average is seventeen.[75] The number of House staff members working in district offices has more than doubled since 1972, and Washington staff assistants are often responsible for assisting constituents at home in the Congressman's state or district rather than drafting legislation in the Capitol.[76] House members have long since learned that although nearly every vote they cast alienates someone, providing favors for a member's constituents has no downside risk. Congressman Tom Daschle, before he became the newly elected Senator from South Dakota, spent a great deal of time writing to constituents by hand. Indiana Representative Philip Sharp operates a toll-free line to his office, holds scores of town meetings, and is a regular visitor to local

**Table 1.6** *Estimated financial value of House incumbency*

| Item | Value ($) |
|---|---|
| Constituent-service staff | 400,000 |
| District office expenses, travel, phones, computers, etc. | 400,000 |
| Unsolicited mailings to constituents | 250,000 |
| Total | 1,050,000 |

*Source: Wall Street Journal,* 24 September 1986

shopping malls. Many members of Congress have vans that cruise their districts in search of voters who need, and would be grateful for, assistance. Said veteran advisor Eddie Mahe: "All this money and effort is devoted to persuading the electorate to believe about the incumbent what they want the voters to believe, that they are some great gift to mankind."

One of the major advantages available to House and Senate incumbents is the congressional "frank," the free mailing privilege that has saved some candidates hundreds of thousands of dollars. Appropriations to pay for franked mail have soared from $32 million in 1972 to $144.5 million in the 1986 fiscal year.[77] In a three-day period, Florida Senator Paula Hawkins, in her bid for re-election in 1986, sent 1.9 million pieces of mail to constituents at public expense, at a cost of about $247,000.[78] When Patrick Leahy faced a tough challenge in 1986, he flooded the state with free newsletters whose positive content was in sharp contrast to his opponent's paid negative advertising. Leahy was the fourth largest user of the franking privilege during the election cycle, despite Vermont having one of the smallest state populations in the nation.[79]

But the major advantage of incumbency is the ability to raise money. (See table 1.7.) From his desk in Washington, Senator Alan Cranston can "do $50,000 in five hours of phone work," claimed an assistant, a feat only the wealthiest challenger can hope to match.[80] "The whole strategy," said Senator Gary Hart, "is to get several hundred thousand dollars in the bank, intimidate your opponent so that you do not get a

**Table 1.7** *Incumbent advantage in fundraising (in $ million and percent)*

| | | Senate | | | | | |
|---|---|---|---|---|---|---|---|
| | Total | Incumbent | | Challenger | | Open Seat[1] | |
| Cycle | Receipts | $ | % | $ | % | $ | % |
| 81–2 | 115.7 | 55.1 | 48 | 35.4 | 30 | 25.2 | 22 |
| 83–4 | 147.3 | 74.8 | 51 | 31.7 | 21 | 40.8 | 28 |
| 85–6 | 185.5 | 90.3 | 49 | 47.7 | 26 | 47.5 | 25 |
| | | House | | | | | |
| 81–2 | 183.7 | 108.7 | 59 | 44.4 | 24 | 30.5 | 17 |
| 83–4 | 195.9 | 131.5 | 67 | 45.8 | 23 | 18.6 | 10 |
| 85–6 | 228.8 | 149.3 | 65 | 41.4 | 18 | 38.1 | 17 |

[1] Republican and Democratic general election candidates only.

*Source*: Compiled from FEC Press Releases of 2 December 1983; 8 December 1985; and 10 May 1987

strong opponent."[81] Said newly elected Arizona Congressman John Rhodes III, just one day after his election victory, "I'm going to start right away raising more money to run again."[82] As former House Speaker Thomas P. "Tip" O'Neill observed in 1986, "Too many [incumbents] have big money and no opponent."[83]

Along with the demonstrated relationship between incumbency and fundraising, there is also a clear relationship between challenger spending and electoral success, particularly among House candidates. (See table 1.8.) This was particularly evident in 1980, the most successful year for House challengers in the past decade.

The average expenditure by a House challenger has risen considerably since 1980, though average amounts spent by House incumbents have increased by an even greater margin. Thus, as the total number of successful challengers has dropped, the total amount spent by a challenger relative to that of the incumbent has actually grown more important in predicting the eventual outcome of closely contested races. (See table 1.9.)

Although other factors beside campaign spending do figure in successful campaigns, there is no statistical evidence that even the most formidable challengers can expect to do well without spending a great deal of money. The benefits of incumbency are so numerous that only by significant expenditures can a challenger hope to defeat the incumbent. According to former Republican National Chairman Richard Richards, an incumbent "has an advantage that is so great that we would never defeat [him] unless we had a reasonable amount of money to go after him."[84] Former National Conservative Political

**Table 1.8** *Financial pattern for the 1980 House elections*

| Challenger spent ($ thousands) | Average vote of challenger (%) | % of victories | No. of cases |
|---|---|---|---|
| Less than 50 | 28 | 0 | 201 |
| 50–99 | 38 | 7* | 42 |
| 100–149 | 42 | 5* | 19 |
| 150–199 | 44 | 17 | 18 |
| 200–249 | 45 | 21 | 14 |
| 250–299 | 46 | 27 | 15 |
| 300 or more | 49 | 59 | 27 |

* Of the four challengers who won in 1980 while spending less than $150,000, two defeated incumbents under criminal investigation and two defeated incumbents who had just been elected in spring by-elections and did not have full opportunity to use incumbent perks.

*Source*: 1983 House Hearings, p. 644

Table 1.9  *Average disbursements of House general election candidates*

| | 1979–80 | | 1981–82 | | 1983–84 | | 1985–86 | |
|---|---|---|---|---|---|---|---|---|
| | No. of can. | Amount ($) | No. of can. | Amount ($) | No. of can. | Amount ($) | No. of can. | Amount ($) |
| **Won – 60% or more** | | | | | | | | |
| Incumbent | 279 | 124,818 | 268 | 202,192 | 315 | 228,432 | 333 | 274,766 |
| Challenger | 5 | 277,781 | 5 | 208,639 | 2 | 385,482 | 1 | 382,663 |
| Open Seat | 13 | 184,350 | 22 | 398,145 | 7 | 401,213 | 15 | 586,276 |
| **Won – 55%–59%** | | | | | | | | |
| Incumbent | 52 | 214,298 | 52 | 382,177 | 48 | 390,531 | 33 | 599,474 |
| Challenger | 8 | 316,298 | 5 | 189,177 | 2 | 527,876 | 1 | 854,616 |
| Open Seat | 8 | 317,557 | 13 | 321,145 | 6 | 427,146 | 8 | 613,592 |
| **Won – less than 55%** | | | | | | | | |
| Incumbent | 33 | 300,996 | 38 | 382,998 | 32 | 495,993 | 23 | 592,649 |
| Challenger | 27 | 322,386 | 21 | 310,526 | 17 | 448,447 | 5 | 457,046 |
| Open Seat | 15 | 302,155 | 15 | 392,739 | 11 | 508,907 | 20 | 467,371 |
| **Lost – 45% or more** | | | | | | | | |
| Incumbent | 25 | 269,563 | 23 | 466,393 | 15 | 425,449 | 5 | 541,410 |
| Challenger | 35 | 234,577 | 41 | 234,588 | 30 | 344,375 | 22 | 360,714 |
| Open Seat | 11 | 173,480 | 13 | 320,577 | 9 | 380,370 | 13 | 509,572 |
| **Lost – 40%–44%** | | | | | | | | |
| Incumbent | 5 | 269,840 | 4 | 439,399 | 2 | 553,759 | 1 | 665,782 |
| Challenger | 46 | 168,854 | 45 | 257,087 | 48 | 250,318 | 32 | 313,271 |
| Open Seat | 10 | 251,181 | 11 | 154,273 | 7 | 377,473 | 11 | 329,659 |
| **Lost – less than 40%** | | | | | | | | |
| Incumbent | 4 | 332,397 | 2 | 424,769 | – | – | – | – |
| Challenger | 171 | 48,413 | 172 | 84,038 | 187 | 171,430 | 205 | 91,965 |
| Open Seat | 18 | 81,187 | 28 | 195,305 | 11 | 116,669 | 17 | 176,289 |

*Source:* Federal Election Commission Report

Action Committee director Terry Dolan concluded, "Any time you defeat an incumbent, you're bucking the odds." It is an opinion universally held by consultants and pundits alike. Moreover, as a challenger demonstrates fundraising ability, and thus begins to present a serious challenge to the incumbent, the incumbent himself is likely to raise and spend additional sums. Wrote author Burton Sheppard in 1985: "While most practicing politicians do not keep up with the political science literature, incumbent congressmen intuitively grasp the point that the level of challengers' funding is a crucial factor in their likelihood of success. The deterrence approach to fundraising is the incumbents' answer to the prospective challenger."[85] It is, therefore, no surprise that Congressman David Obey, in testimony to the House Task Force on Elections, defended the fundraising practices of his fellow incumbents and insisted even relatively safe incumbents, in the 1980s, are still forced to go out and raise significant sums to insure their re-election:

They don't know, even on the basis of polling, whether they are going to have to spend money. . . . You can have 2 weeks left to go and all of a sudden, whammo, you have $100,000 poured into your district, and if you haven't spent money ahead of time, in order to try to solidify your position in the polls, you run the risk of being blind-sided, and I have seen that happen in a number of cases.[86]

Congressman Matt Rinaldo added, "We are talking about an incumbent with all the advantages of incumbency, and two times the amount [spent by the opponent] is not enough, three times the amount is not enough, four times the amount is not enough."[87] Political scientist Richard Joslyn summarized thus: "The more convincing an electoral victory, the less likely it is that a serious challenge will appear in the next election . . . [and] the easier it is to raise campaign contributions the next time around."[88]

Yet some candidates are finding incumbency a mixed blessing. While challengers are free to raise money and mingle with the voters, the incumbent is often locked up in Washington for as much as five days a week. A barrage of negative advertising against incumbents with poor voting records in the 1984 election forced many anxious senators to remain in Washington in 1986 for fear they might be caught in the state when an important vote was being taken at the Capitol. Yet many of those who maintained a diligent vigil of answering all roll call votes were later criticized for not spending sufficient time back home with the voters. Since Congress often continues to meet until late September or early October, incumbents are deprived of valuable campaign time in their states or districts, and the lack of presence back home can come back to haunt incumbents on election day. Moreover, with the rise of negative advertising, every legislative vote has the potential to become the focus of an opponent's campaign commercial. "Senator McIntyre was a very personable guy, but his philosophy and voting record were quite inconsistent with New Hampshire," claimed Gordon Humphrey, McIntyre's successful 1978 opponent. Humphrey won only because he was able to use the new technology to bring McIntyre's political history into the homes of New Hampshire voters. "When you become an incumbent,the issues really swing differently," commented Indiana Congressman John Hiler on his narrow 1982 re-election victory. "We really didn't understand the difference between being an incumbent and being a challenger. I was suddenly held accountable for every issue, every problem unsolved by my office." Added freshman Congressman Dean Gallo prior to his 1986 re-election campaign, "As a challenger, you can say almost anything and get away with it. Now I'll be more on the defensive since I'm the one with a record." Exclaimed former Republican Congressman Joel Pritchard about the hazards facing Senate incumbents in the 1986 elections: "They've got to get the damn guys out of Washington. Just close the Senate down. Every day they're there now, they cast another vote that makes someone mad."[89]

There are several distinct differences between House and Senate candidates, even though the campaign technology used is somewhat similar (House campaigns operate on a smaller scale). Because House candidates have to stand for re-election every two years, many start running as soon as they take the oath of office. They are virtually forced to stay in continuous touch with the voters in a way that senators, with re-election campaigns every six years, are not. House members are identified primarily with local rather than national issues, and with providing services to constituents.[90] In addition, since House members generally represent smaller areas and fewer people than their Senate colleagues, their constituents are more cohesive and therefore easier to represent. Electorally, House challengers are in a particularly difficult position because they are seldom seen on television. According to 1980 election surveys conducted by the University of Michigan, only 24 percent of those surveyed claimed to have seen a House challenger on television.[91] "House challengers are invisible," said William Schneider of the American Enterprise Institute. "They can't afford TV advertising, and most don't get covered by local stations. As a result, voters don't know who they are. If you're not on TV, you don't exist."[92]

Senators, in contrast, are more easily identified with national issues and problems. Because of this linkage with major national concerns, senators can be caught up in tidal waves of feeling that periodically sweep across the country, as in 1980 when voters were angry with the high inflation rates and tired of weak national leadership. Moreover, senators, particularly from the larger and more politically and geographically diverse states, are often forced to vote on issues that benefit some constituents at the expense of others. Senators occasionally have to take stands that ingratiate them with voters in one part of the state while alienating those in another part. Unlike House challengers, Senate hopefuls receive substantial press coverage, which will generally enable them to achieve a basic level of recognition with voters. According to the University of Michigan study, 70 percent had seen the Senate challenger on television, three times the number of those that had seen a House challenger.[93] As media coverage of Senate campaigns continues to intensify, challengers may find themselves as well known as their opponents on election day. It is through this recognition that Senate challengers then can establish credibility, and perhaps even gain equal footing with the incumbent.

In the campaigns of an era now past, candidates would rely on the door-to-door canvassing by party workers and volunteers to keep abreast with voter attitudes. Now they commission private pollsters to inform them about public opinion. Formerly, candidates depended on political bosses for advice, and political machines for turning out the voters. Now they have expensive consultants, with their intricate strategies for maximizing public support. Television and radio were once a luxury and a rarity in a campaign. Now they are commonplace. "The business was more exciting and a lot more fun in the early days when we didn't have as many rules," remarked veteran political consultant Stuart Spencer, "but we have them now and we have to live with them." The reform legislation of the 1970s, designed to open up the political process and free candidates from the pressure of wealthy contributors and special interest groups, has, in actuality, indentured them to the political consultants and consigned them to modern campaign technology. "What we have now is the survival of the most enthusiastic and the most extreme," said Montana Republican Congressman Bill Frenzel.[94] Competitive election strategy in the late 1980s is aptly described by a White House aide who advised, "Be the first in the field with a machine gun when everyone else is using arrows."[95] This strategy is what modern day victories are made of.

# 2

# The wizards of American politics

The old [party] bosses are long gone and with them the old parties. In their place has grown a new breed of young professionals whose working skills in the new politics would make the old boys look like stumblebums.

Theodore White, author[1]

It is a very precarious decision for a candidate to choose his consultant. Too many candidates do not shop around enough, and too frequently they are uninformed buyers. Not all the consultants are worth the prices they charge.

Richard Wirthlin, pollster

I recently spoke with a prospective candidate who told me he had talked with the people at the top of our profession and that we all made the same claims and used the same techniques. I told him that if he thought that was bad, wait until he interviewed the next five guys and found the same claims and the same techniques and *virtually no experience.*

Raymond Strother, media consultant
(in a campaign memo to Gary Hart)

The burgeoning growth of campaign technology and the accompanying complexities have contributed to the increasing recognition and influence of the professional campaign consultant. The fact is, modern campaign technology has so complicated the process of running for public office that it has passed the stage where a statewide candidate can independently and competently manage his own campaign. Most candidates recognize the need for expert advice, not just at the beginning of the campaign for the initial planning, or near the end, when tactics become all important, but throughout the duration of the campaign. Candidates now view electioneering as a legitimate pro-

42

fessional activity, and the political consultancy profession has arisen to meet their needs.

The minimum tools required to compete in politics today – the benchmark survey, computerized fundraising, television advertising – each requires consultation with an expert in the field. Computerized fundraising and television advertising, which are to some extent self-explanatory, will be examined elsewhere in these pages. The benchmark survey differs from other campaign polls in that the questionnaire is longer and more detailed, and more individuals are polled than in other surveys taken during the election cycle. Moreover, the benchmark survey is usually the first major poll undertaken by the candidate, and is therefore crucial in determining campaign strategy. Likewise, external factors – political action committees (PACs), the national party organizations, and independent expenditure efforts – also benefit from handling by a professional. Successful campaigns are usually those that can best exploit the external factors in their favor, and best manipulate the tools of contemporary American politics. It is the acknowledgement of these realities that has given rise to professional campaign consultants, and altered, probably forever, the candidate's role in his own campaign.

The primary elements of modern campaign technology are no longer new to the political process or its participants. Prospective candidates have viewed political TV commercials, received direct mail fundraising appeals, scanned the results of voter attitude surveys, and are familiar with PACs. Yet even with a relatively extensive knowledge of electioneering, statewide candidates and many congressional hopefuls still have the need for professional advisors; and over the past decade the use of campaign consultants has grown dramatically. "In today's politics," concluded fundraiser and former Democratic National Committee official Peter Kelly, "a candidate either has to understand the new technology or have faith and follow the advice of someone who does."

Advising candidates, political parties, and political action committees has become a new growth industry in America. Candidates have learned that the right campaign strategy can survive a mediocre campaign, but even a brilliant campaign is likely to fail if the strategy is incorrect. As both an observer and a participant, veteran advisor Eddie Mahe reflected on the consultants' meteoric rise to power: "Ten years ago, consultants were largely a rarity in the business. There were survey research consultants, but they were the exception in congressional races, not the rule. There was perhaps one poll, or at most two. Media consultants did exist, but again there was only one or two in the business and . . . general strategists were almost unheard of." Today, the number of political consultants has reached an all-time high in American politics, and the widespread involvement of consultants in campaigns is still growing. (See table 2.1.) In 1986, 85 percent of the total 138 candidates for the US Senate or for governor hired professional pollsters, 94 percent had professional media consultants, and only 4 percent hired no consultant at all.[2]

Challengers, in particular, are vulnerable to those twists and turns of events that, unexpectedly, may complicate a seemingly easy race. A reputable political consultant can provide a challenger with the expertise and guidance necessary to survive the intricacies of the electoral process and, possibly, defeat a more experienced and credible opponent. All thirteen newly elected senators in 1986, both challengers and open seat competitors, had both a media consultant and a pollster on their campaign payroll.[3] Author and political scientist Stephen Salmore concluded: "To run effectively against an incumbent who has typically been planning the race for a year or more, a challenger must be able to compress time, creating an instant organization by hiring experienced consultants."[4] According to fundraiser Robert Odell, "Consultants are in the game twenty-four hours a day, seven days a week, so we obviously keep a certain knowledge base far and above what the average candidate can have."

Candidates seeking office without any political consultant are a vanishing breed. Only the least competitive Senate and House challengers failed to hire at least one consultant in 1986, which may help explain why they were unsuccessful. In fact, in that election year

**Table 2.1**  *Candidate's use of consultants in statewide campaigns*[1]

| | Total | | |
|---|---|---|---|
| *Year* | *No. of candidates* | *Media consultant* (%) | *Private pollster* (%) |
| 1984 | 88 | 87 | 80 |
| 1986 | 138 | 94 | 85 |

| | Senate | | | Governor | | |
|---|---|---|---|---|---|---|
| *Year* | *No. of candidates* | *Media consultant* (%) | *Private pollster* (%) | *No. of candidates* | *Media consultant* (%) | *Private pollster* (%) |
| 1984 | 64 | 84 | 75 | 24 | 96 | 91 |
| 1986 | 68 | 97 | 85 | 70 | 91 | 84 |

[1] General election major party candidates only.

*Source*: Compiled from *National Journal*, 20 October 1984, pp. 1976–83; *National Journal*, 11 October 1986, pp. 2432–41; *Campaigns and Elections*, November/December 1986, Vol. 7, No. 4, pp. 33–40

not a single challenger for the US Senate or for state governor managed to unseat an incumbent without having at least one professional consultant.[5] The outcome was much the same in 1984. According to Mahe, "No serious candidate for statewide office would not have a political consultant because, if for no other reason, if they don't have one, they are not seen as a serious contender by the press, the PACs, and the national party organizations." Said New York gubernatorial candidate Andrew O'Rourke, when he hired several media consultants from President Reagan's 1984 "Tuesday Team" organization to bring credibility to his 1986 campaign: "I think that when people see the panache of the Tuesday Team, they will say, 'Maybe O'Rourke has a fighting chance and we should help him.'"[6] Fred Rainey, chairman of the American Medical Association political action committee, speaking before the Senate Committee on Rules and Administration, acknowledged that the candidate's professional advisors become an important consideration in his PAC's decision on whether to contribute to a campaign.[7]

The number of congressional incumbents forgoing the use of consultants in the face of a serious challenge are also few in number, after several suffered upsets at the hands of skillfully guided opponents in so-called "safe" races that the incumbent should have won. Explained media consultant Raymond Strother: "As soon as you learn the lessons, you lose – because the lessons always change." Apparently in agreement, every Senate incumbent in the 1986 elections had at least one consultant.

Former Oklahoma Congressman Jim Jones, a high-profile member of the Democratic House leadership until his Senate campaign defeat in 1986, typified the increasing reliance on professional advice. When Jones first ran for Congress in the early 1970s, he relied on a few close friends and his wife for campaign strategy, and adamantly refused to hire any professional consultants. But in 1984, with the National Republican Congressional Committee targeting him for defeat, the Oklahoma Congressman turned to three out-of-state consulting firms for help. Defending his decision to use professional advisors, Jones said, "I want the best advice, the best talent that money can buy."[8] Jones paid more than $500,000 to the three firms, and survived a tough re-election battle.

Of course, there still remains a small number of incumbent congressmen and senators who are in safe districts and actually have no need for consultants or any of the modern technological trappings. Pennsylvania Congressman William Goodling was first elected in 1974 following the death of the veteran incumbent, who was his father. Goodling has never hired a consultant and probably never will. Since 1961, a member of his family has represented the district for all but two years, and Goodling has rarely received less than 70 percent support in seven elections. Senator William Proxmire holds to the same opinion. He has spent less than $1,000 on each of his last three elections, and received at least 60 percent of the vote in all three. As political consultant Paul Manafort observed, "Some incumbents don't feel they need us any more because they are incumbents and their seat is safe. Others don't see the value."

The few candidates that are, for whatever reason, unable or unwilling to pay for independent professional advice need no longer depend only on their own resources. Dean Gallo, in his successful 1984 bid for Congress from New Jersey, was such a candidate: "We checked with consultants because we were initially planning to use them, but we couldn't find any. They were already committed, the good ones, and could only give us a day. We decided it wasn't worth it and instead received our help from the NRCC [National Republican Congressional Committee]." As a last resort for such candidates, the national Republican and Democratic organizations currently offer, at no cost, able in-house consultants who can assist candidates in the technical aspects of electioneering. Although increasingly competent and effective, and with a record of success on both sides of the aisle, national party consulting is often criticized by the independent professionals. According to consultant Jay Smith: "The party committees can be very helpful. They can also be a pain in the neck. . . . Other than giving us the money, access to contributor lists, getting national speakers to do fundraising events – other than that, I don't look for them to do a damn thing."[9] Admittedly, political assistance from the national parties is usually the last resort for the desperate candidate. Although the quality of advice and consistency of performance may not be up to the standards of the best professionals, nevertheless, every candidate and consultant interviewed agreed that utilizing party personnel was still a better alternative than having no outside help at all; and most agreed that the national party organizations can be a helpful resource for financially strapped candidates.

But for the most part, reputable, independent consultants are preferable. According to political scientist Dan Nimmo, a critical quality found in the best consultants, and largely absent in candidates, is "the capacity to look at political reality without reading one's own biases, dreams, or wishes into it."[10] Candidates have come to realize the importance of internal campaign objectivity, external media relations, and the necessity of obtaining competent advisors who can provide both. As Senator Edward Kennedy concluded, "Events matter less than what is now widely referred to as spin control – who in which campaign can explain why something doesn't mean what it seems."[11]

The selection of a campaign consultant (or firm), whether it be an overall strategist or a particular technique specialist, is crucial, since the proper match of consultant and client can be of utmost importance to the success of the campaign. There are a number of factors that influence the match-up, and by examining them from both the candidate's perspective and the consultant's, one can gain an understanding of the dynamics of a modern campaign. It is usually the candidate that seeks the consultant. (Of the consultants interviewed, not one said that a major part of his business came from his own solicitation, though most admitted to seeking specific clients or races from time to time.) The process of acquiring professional advisors often begins with the candidate visiting Washington and meeting with the campaign committee of the political party with which he is affiliated. Although the committees do not tell the candidates whom to hire, they do maintain lists containing vendors of campaign services. Party officials have also found it necessary to advise unsuspecting candidates to be selective and cautious in obligating themselves to any consultant, and to warn them against the financial dangers of signing expensive contracts with too many professional advisors. Aided by the advice received from the committee, which often favors the large, well-established firms as well as those consultants friendly with the party's administrators, most candidates will begin to interview potential advisors from eighteen months to two years prior to the election.

Assessing campaign consultants can be difficult, since some professionals want to assume credit for their clients' victories and pass the blame onto someone else for the failures. Advises general consultant David Keene:

Candidates have to realize that when they put their team together, that team, just by their past experiences, will shape the final strategy even before that strategy is written. As the candidate considers his race, he ought to ask himself what it is he wants to do, what kind of race he wants to run, and whether the background of his consultants is appropriate for that purpose.

Although requirements and priorities can vary with each candidate, a consultant's track record, reputation, fees, accessibility, ideology, and party affiliation were suggested by all the major campaign consultants as important considerations when a candidate seeks professional assistance. According to pollster R. Harrison Hickman, candidates interviewing potential consultants should also ask "why they are better or worse than their competitors and what are their strong points and weak points compared to other consultants." Media consultant Roger Ailes advises candidates to choose advisors that "are fighters who absolutely hate to lose." Except for minor differences in emphasis, the criteria that consultants advise candidates to consider seldom vary.

Notwithstanding the fact that the ceremonial search for professional talent has become a recognized ritual of modern campaigning, there remains strong evidence that some candidates still know comparatively little about the process of securing a consultant, and even less about the qualifications of the practitioners they are considering. "Of the hundreds of candidates I have dealt with in the last several years," claimed Jeffrey Browne, associate publisher of *Campaigns and Elections* magazine, "fewer than 5 percent have been able to ask the right questions to obtain answers crucial to their campaigns."[12] The evidence from interviews suggests that few consultants resent being questioned by a potential client, and many actually prefer it. Lee Atwater, chief consultant to the 1988 presidential campaign of Vice President George Bush, is the notable exception. "Candidates should know enough about me that when I meet with them, they won't have to ask me much." Said media advisor David Doak, "Most candidates are not well informed consumers. They ought to ask us about our losers, [to] show them tapes of their commercials, and then arrange to contact them. Most candidates don't do this." Media consultant Robert Squier agreed:

There is a widening gap in understanding how the technologies can be used by candidates, and the candidates' actual understanding of the technology. I am often appalled when I hear candidates tell me about the process they went through to hire us, the reassessing they used and what they thought the criteria should be. It was really quite appalling.

Pollsters have had similar experiences. White House pollster Richard Wirthlin established a system whereby potential clients who do not wish to view the actual polling operation can instead dial directly into the Wirthlin Group phone banks in Provo, Utah, and listen to the interviewing process. Commented veteran Democratic pollster Peter Hart, "Most candidates never visit my shop so they have no idea what goes on. All they ever see is me, and a set of numbers on a piece of paper. It is absolutely important that clients see where the polling is done, but most don't understand the technical part."

Even the (nonspecialist) general consulting firms are often hired by misguided, naive, and uninformed candidates, who know nothing about the strengths and weaknesses of the various firms or of the individual consultants within the firm. The consulting company hired by Richard Snelling for his 1986 Vermont Senate race was highly regarded, but primarily for its tough, aggressive campaign style. Thus, according to media consultant Ken Swope, they were entirely unsuited for Vermont politics. "Snelling was badly advised. The firm he hired wasn't able to do that kind of work, accentuating his positive qualities. Their stuff was flat. They're only good at attack media." Former South Dakota Senator Jim Abdnor had similar feelings about one of his 1986 consultants: "I liked my consultant very much, but he didn't know his front end from the back about farming. He had to learn everything from me, and I didn't have enough time to spend with him."

Despite the onrush of new practitioners into the political consulting field, there are more candidates in search of "name" consulting firms than the major consulting firms can handle. Said media advisor Greg Stevens,

The political consulting community is very small and tightly connected. It's a high burnout business. Campaigns are incredibly tough physically, mentally, and psychologically. Banging around in airplanes is not a great way to live. There are a lot of so-called consultants around, but in the long term, only a few firms remain successful.

Because the demand for well-known consultants exceeds the supply, even an extensive search can prove disappointing, and it is not uncommon for candidates to be forced to settle for their second or third choice of consulting firm or, temporarily, none at all.

According to several consultants, the situation can induce a firm to take on more clients than it can manage. Some firms, in an effort to increase profits, knowingly refuse to hire the staff necessary to manage their client list properly. "I've seen too many cases where consultants overpromise their clients," claimed Wirthlin. "They just can't be in four places at one time." But occasionally an over-burdened operation occurs by accident. Media consultant Charles Guggenheim candidly recalled a period when his firm found itself trapped in such a situation:

One year we did twelve or thirteen candidates at one time. There were times when I would come home late at night and say, 'What am I doing?' Eventually we began to choose candidates more indiscriminately. The press was calling us every day and I found my name in the paper a lot. That becomes very attractive, and the money was good. It was hard to put the brakes on.

But most consultants are careful not to overreach their limits. Richard Viguerie once claimed he turned away 98 percent of those seeking to hire his direct mail outfit.[13] Media consultant David Garth was approached by statewide candidates from thirty-nine different states in one election cycle, but he took on only five races.[14] "I do less campaigns than most media consultants," admitted Kenneth Swope, "but I put more time into research, writing, thinking, and interviewing. My commercials are much more custom made than most of the bigger firms." Other media consultants, by necessity, are less selective. Said Raymond Strother, "There is an art to consulting. You can't just afford to do only one campaign. You have to do seven or eight. The consultant must be able to balance that business, keeping a lot of people happy at one time." In a private memo to Senator Gary Hart in preparation for his 1988 campaign, Strother noted: "The problem with media consulting is that it is not a one-man show. . . . An organization the size of mine or [Robert] Goodman's or [Robert] Squier's costs between $60 thousand and $80 thousand per month. . . . It takes six to eight people to back up the work of one consultant, if he or she is performing at maximum capacity for the client."

Since the amount of time a consultant will devote to his clients is a fundamental consideration, a candidate who hires an overloaded firm will quickly find himself short-changed and dissatisfied. Roger Ailes blamed the unreasonable expectations of the candidates for their discontent:

Most candidates are totally unrealistic about the consultant's time. They think that if the guy spends two days on an airplane to fly out for a one-hour meeting, it's helpful. What he's doing is draining the consultant, making him exhausted, reducing his creativity, and making him hate their guts. They'd be better off with a 20-minute conference call."

Other leading professionals felt candidates often would be better served with a lesser known but more attentive firm. Fundraiser Robert Odell suggested: "If I were a candidate, I'd get one or two trusted consulting-type friends and wouldn't let them get too far from the campaign. You shouldn't have to share them with twenty other candidates as well. They can't be attentive if they are not involved enough." Former White House Deputy Political Director William Lacy agreed: "Rather than having a junior partner in one of those larger firms handling your race, candidates would do better hiring someone less well known and less expensive but who could spend a lot more time advising them."

It seems clear, from this author's extensive interviews, that consultants have their own personal criteria for accepting clients. According to former American Association of Political Consultants president Sanford Weiner, "As professionals . . . we have a duty and a responsibility to screen would-be candidates more carefully than ever."[15] Today, party affiliation is by far the most important factor considered by consultants in selecting their clients, outweighing a candidate's electability, ideology, or financial standing. In 1976, author Robert Agranoff quoted the president of the American Association of Political Consultants as saying, "The fact that no one in California cares that my firm represents both Democrats and Republicans . . . is symbolic of politics around the nation as well. Strict partisanship just isn't important any more."[16] Yet only a decade later, none of the ten largest polling firms or media production agencies had clients from both parties in the 1986 races. Currently, Richard Morris (polling) and David Garth (media) are among the very few well-known political consultants that still accept clients from either party. Said former bipartisan media advisor Robert Goodman, "For business reasons, I only do Republican races because when I did Democrats, we were given a lot of hell."

There still exists, however, the misconception that consultants are mercenaries, that they are unconcerned with and inclined to disregard the ideas and beliefs of their clients. Larry Sabato, whose book *The Rise of Political Consultants* still serves as the unofficial guide to modern campaign technology, claimed in a 1983 Senate Rules Committee hearing, in concurrence with many leading political scientists, that most consultants are not overly concerned with their prospective client's ideology.[17] According to a 1984 *National Journal* article on political consultants, "ideology seems to be a minor factor in their [consultant] decisions about which candidates to work for."[18] However, those opinions are quite contrary to the survey and interviews of consultants recently conducted by this author, which reveal, perhaps for the first time, that one-half of the nation's leading consultants strongly prefer candidates with a particular ideological background, and only 21 percent consider ideology to be unimportant. (See survey 2.1.) "There's a great deal more zing in the victory if you not only put a good man in office but also removed a bad one," said Democrat Bob Squier. Charlie Black, a partner in one of the fastest growing political firms in the country, concurred: "In addition to being in politics as a business, we are in politics to make a difference." Added media consultant Frank Greer, former advisor to Walter Mondale:

We have been very fortunate to always be able to work for people I believe in. If I don't really believe in that person and the message he stands for, I can't do a good job for him. In the [1986] Georgia [US Senate] race, for example, I can't go out and choose Hamilton Jordan, because of his positions. I could never produce his spots.

The campaign specialists most concerned with the ideology of their clients are the direct mail consultants. "The old saying that a professional could write successful direct mail appeals for anyone is just not true," said conservative fundraiser Bruce Eberle. "You have to believe in your client." Added liberal fundraiser Roger Craver, "The only requirement we have is that the candidate has a sufficiently polarized stand on the issues which we can raise money around. Candidate electability is of no consequence to us. Our job as fundraisers is to create public awareness of issues." In direct mail, the practitioners

**Survey 2.1**　*The following factors are sometimes considered by consultants in their decision whether to take on a prospective client. Which factors are highly important, somewhat important, or of little importance in your decision? (responses rotated)*

|  | Highly important (%) | Somewhat important (%) | Not important (%) |
|---|---|---|---|
| Ideology | 50 | 29 | 21 |
| Electability | 41 | 24 | 35 |
| Candidate's personal wealth | 6 | 21 | 73 |

(as well as the clients) tend to place more emphasis on ideology than do other campaign technologists.

On occasion, the philosophical beliefs of a candidate and his consultant may come into conflict, but as veteran advisor William Roberts pointed out, "Most consultants realize that they will not always agree with the candidate, and that they are supposed to subvert their own philosophical beliefs to the interests of the candidate and campaign." Ideology is rarely the source of major campaign disputes, mainly because few candidates and consultants want to work with someone who is philosophically incompatible. Media consultant John Deardourff advised, "You make sure you understand your candidate before you go to work for them, before the process begins."

Not all candidate–consultant relationships are initiated by the candidate. In some elections it is the consultant, not the candidate, who actively seeks a client to work for. Consulting firms have often been accused of taking on numerous "no-hopers" primarily for the financial gain, although on occasion such a no-hoper may actually finish quite well. But money alone cannot always buy the desired services. Pollster Peter Hart turned down a lucrative offer from 1982 Minnesota Senate candidate Mark Dayton, even though it would have brought in nearly $500,000 to his firm, because he had no interest in the candidate or the race.

Some firms seek out candidates in highly visible races in order to improve their own standing and reputation. Presidential campaigns, in particular, offer the rewards of instant credibility and fame for those firms fortunate enough to be on the winning side. Pollster Pat Caddell, anxious to remain active following the defeat of Jimmy Carter in 1980, was widely ridiculed for candidate-shopping in the 1984 presidential elections. Caddell was turned down by four candidates before finally settling with Gary Hart.[19] It is also not uncommon for consultants to approach candidates in statewide races in California and New York, for the reason that those states attract much media attention. Most of the largest Republican polling firms and media outfits had candidates in the profitable 1986 California Republican Senate primary, as did dozens of other consulting firms. Consultants also enjoy David and Goliath scenarios, and occasionally will search for candidates they believe can defeat well-known but potentially vulnerable incumbents.

On a cruder level, a current leading Republican consultant is known to have offered his services at a sharply reduced rate to any candidate willing to challenge his (the consultant's) major political adversary. Similarly, in an effort to defeat an ex-client – a 1988 presidential contender who had fired his firm in a previous statewide campaign – a top media consultant on the Democratic side gladly advised *several* of that candidate's opponents. There have even been occasions when consultants who have had disputes with their clients have then gone to work, officially, for the opposition.

There are some consultants who prefer working for incumbents. For the most part, incumbents have a clearer idea than challengers of the message they wish to convey, better general knowledge of the important issues in the campaign, far greater fundraising ability, and an understanding of what it takes to win an election. "An incumbent, typically, has been before a television camera and knows how television works," said media advisor Greg Stevens. "Many challengers know nothing about television advertising." For these reasons, media professionals, in particular, tend to compete more for the business of candidates seeking re-election than do other campaign specialists. (See table 2.2.)

**Table 2.2**  *Percentage of incumbent clients among primary media and polling firms*[1]

|          | Incumbent | Challenger |
|----------|-----------|------------|
| Media    | 54        | 46         |
| Polling  | 32        | 68         |

[1]  Firms with at least five statewide candidates in 1986. An equal number of Democratic and Republican firms are represented in media and polling categories.

*Source*: Compiled from *National Journal*, 10 October 1986, pp. 2432–3

"That is not to say we don't take difficult races," emphasized Squier. "We took [New Jersey Senator] Frank Lautenberg when he was 32 points behind his opponent. When Bob Graham first came in 1976 and said he wanted to be governor of Florida, he had no support and no recognition." Media experts, more than other consulting specialists, depend on their "won–lost" record and high profile for future business. Unlike pollsters, fundraisers, and general consultants, established media firms do not have the capability to work with more than eight to ten statewide candidates in an election cycle. Every loss, therefore, will clearly affect their won–lost ratio. Some general consultants, many pollsters, and nearly all media advisors prefer a significant percentage of their clients to be incumbent candidates who, by the nature of their position, have a high likelihood of success. (See survey 2.2.)

Consequently, pollsters and media consultants will often reject challengers who they feel cannot be marketed effectively. "If you buy insurance, you probably would prefer working for an incumbent," suggested Reagan pollster Richard Wirthlin. "But if you are a risk taker, you probably like working for challengers." Some, like pollster Peter Hart, make these decisions for purely personal reasons: "If I think a race is hopeless, if I think I can't make a difference for the candidate, I

**Survey 2.2**   *Is your won-lost record very important to you and your firm?*

| Total | Yes (%) | No (%) |
|---|---|---|
| Total | 59 | 41 |
| Media consultants | 78 | 22 |
| Pollsters | 62 | 38 |
| General consultants | 50 | 50 |
| Fundraisers | 0 | 100 |

will probably turn him down. I only have so many hours in the day. If I spend x number for a candidate I don't see winning, I don't see that being helpful." But for other consultants, choosing clients is more of a financial decision. While media advisors will usually acknowledge that they occasionally receive undeserved credit for certain "wins," along with the unfair blame for "losses" that were not their fault, nevertheless it is the overall record that attracts most candidates. "If a political advertising or consulting firm is not able to win, consistently, more races than it loses," explained Deardourff, "it is simply not an attractive firm." Added David Doak, a partner in one of the most successful new media firms in 1986: "A good won–lost record is the only way we'll stay in business." As author Richard Joslyn wrote: "Professional campaigners not only want their client-candidate to win, but they also have the goals of future business and the enhancement of their profession in mind. Their involvement and conduct in a campaign is also often motivated by such long-term considerations."[20] Concluded Democratic pollster Harrison Hickman: "We tilt at windmills occasionally, but ultimately we are a business. Our business is to be right in terms of polling, but it is better to be right and win."

A consultant's decision that a potential client has poor marketing characteristics may be due to the candidate's unimpressive personal appearance, a speech impediment, or other physical detraction, but not always. Author Stephen Salmore pointed out that such a decision may actually be made solely on the strength of the prospective client's opponent:

Because in most races challengers are assumed to be the underdogs, and consultants' reputations depend on their "win and loss" records, they find it more difficult to persuade the leading consultants to work for them. . . . The challengers' need for hired guns, and the difficulties in retaining the well-known ones, who are most likely to be both competent and credible, becomes a vicious circle.[21]

Mario Cuomo ran into this difficulty when he was an underdog candidate for the New York gubernatorial nomination in 1982. David

Garth was his first choice of consultant, but Garth decided to go with Cuomo's opponent, New York City Mayor and election favorite Ed Koch. Cuomo's next choice already had a statewide New York race and was uninterested in adding a second. The embattled candidate, a veteran campaigner, was fully aware of his electoral difficulties. He wrote in his diary: "The value of a Garth is clear from the way our campaign is shaping up – or rather, isn't. It has no form. It is not being driven by anyone along any particular path."[22]

Senator Bill Bradley's entry into electoral politics was similar. Bradley first sought the services of David Garth in his 1978 bid for the US Senate from New Jersey, but Garth refused. "I didn't like Bradley. I interviewed him. It was awful. . . . He didn't know anything."[23] Bradley was forced to turn elsewhere for professional advice.

Not all consultants like incumbents, however. In fact, most find challengers easier to work with. (See survey 2.3.) "Incumbents often do what they want, irrespective of the advice given them," said pollster Lance Tarrance. "There are six layers of bureaucracy working with incumbents," complained pollster Hart. He, like certain of his colleagues, enjoys the less defined and more exciting environment of a challenger race – even if the chances of success are considerably reduced. Said Hart, "With challengers, it's a very easy one-on-one relationship. You don't have the various factions." According to Robert Goodman, "Challengers are easier to work for because they are dying to get there." Especially among longstanding consultants, the opportunity of doing something different can be more important than the chance of victory. "They [challengers] have nothing to lose so they are often more courageous and likely to say what they really think," said media consultant Ken Swope, notable among his colleagues for taking on difficult challenger races. Veteran Democratic advisor Walter DeVries agreed:

If you want to do some experimenting, trying new things in campaign techniques, you are better off working with challengers. It's more fun and

**Survey 2.3** *In general, which candidates are easier to work with, incumbents or challengers?*

| | Total (%) | Fundraisers (%) | Pollsters (%) | Media consultants (%) | General consultants (%) |
|---|---|---|---|---|---|
| Challengers | 65 | 100 | 86 | 56 | 55 |
| Incumbents | 22 | 0 | 14 | 33 | 17 |
| Equal (response volunteered) | 13 | 0 | 0 | 11 | 28 |

challenging. They're not yet wedded to a particular technology. I was working for a black Catholic Republican candidate for governor [Bill Lucas] in Michigan in 1986. That is a set of combinations and circumstances that we've never seen before. That kind of race interests me.

The degree of rapport and trust between the candidate and his professional advisors significantly influences the structure and style of the campaign. According to Bob Squier, who has been involved in more successful Democratic Senate campaigns than any other media consultant: "When you have a long-term relationship with a candidate, you develop a trust. If you're in a situation where the candidate is going to have to make tough or unpleasant decisions, that trust will carry you over the rough spots." Moreover, the increasing responsibilities and power being absorbed by political consultants have themselves forced a change in the complex candidate–consultant relationship. In the past, consultants were of the belief that, in the words of one media consultant, they didn't have to "love [their] candidates, only respect them." Today, many of America's most sought after professionals won't enter a race unless they truly *like* the candidate. Advisors Lee Atwater, Roger Ailes, Bob Goodman, Harrison Hickman, and Ray Strother, among others, volunteered in interviews with this author (before the question was asked) that they must "like" the candidate if they are to accept him as a client.

Admittedly, the personal chemistry between candidate and consultant is particularly important to professionals with more potential business than they can accept. Consultants with a wealth of possible clients can afford to be highly selective in their choice of clients. Those just starting out in the profession undoubtedly take whomever they can get. But a majority of the consultants interviewed agreed with Hickman that personal ties often develop between candidates and their advisors. Said Hickman: "We like establishing a personal relationship with all our clients. With just a couple of exceptions, I would count almost all our clients as close friends. You give too much time and energy to the process not to get something back in return on a personal level." Added Ailes: "If I develop a friendship with the candidate, it can make me more effective. You hate to let a friend down. If you care deeply about the candidate as a person, it is easier at 3:00 a.m. in an editing room to push your self the extra mile and come up with that extra idea."

Although the rapidly increasing use of consultants has brought an aura of professionalism to political campaigning, it has correspondingly lessened the involvement of candidates in their own campaigns. Said Congressman Dean Gallo, "It is important for the candidate to be involved in the campaign strategy, but too often they are not. They leave it to the high priced consultants." However, there is a noticeable trend among many of the largest consulting firms to encourage, or even insist upon, a limited role for the candidate in setting the campaign's strategy and tactics. (See survey 2.4.) "On a scale of one to one hundred, zero is the level a candidate should be involved in setting his own strategy. Candidates should know very little about the day-to-day affairs of the campaign," claimed Andre LeTendre, perhaps the only person in American politics to have been a congressional candidate (unsuccessful Wisconsin hopeful in 1970), campaign manager (1980 Wisconsin Senate candidate), and political consultant. He added, "The less they know, the better candidates they are." Said Bob Goodman, "The candidate really must understand that he is the candidate – the star – but not the stage manager." Bob Squier concurred: "It is very possible to go through an entire campaign with a candidate, and when it is all over, they have no idea what went on. It is not to our advantage to explain it to them. It is to our advantage to get them to do what we want – what's best for them – with the least amount of fuss."

Survey 2.4  *How involved should the average candidate be in setting and executing the strategy and tactics of his campaign: very involved, somewhat involved, or little or no involvement?*

|  | % |
| --- | --- |
| Very involved | 39 |
| Somewhat involved | 46 |
| Little or no involvement | 15 |

Peter Kelly, a major Democratic fundraiser, also wants his candidates as far away from the strategy as possible:

I was asked to do a campaign program for an incumbent congressman elected to the Senate in 1984. He asked that I meet with his staff for a four hour meeting. At the end of this meeting, I said, "Look, there's one guy in your state who absolutely will screw up everything in this campaign if you let him near it. He has no judgment, he is totally ego driven." Finally, somebody said who was I talking about. I said, "The man you are sitting next to, your Senate candidate. He is the worst person to say anything about his campaign. Keep him out of it."

Campaign consultant Matt Reece believes campaign control is not only preferable but usually essential to the eventual victory of his clients: "The races I was happiest with were those where I had complete control of the campaign. Most of the time when I do that I win. Most of the times that I lose I had less than complete control." One final reason for the consultants' lack of enthusiasm for candidate involvement may be the frequent problems with the candidate's family. Complained pollster Lance Tarrance, "There is always a mother-in-law or wife near the candidate, telling him things in a very unsystematic-like fashion."

Despite the extensive influence of consultants over the campaigns and candidates that they advise, there is little evidence to suggest that candidates become clones of their advisors. The ideal candidate–consultant relationship was typified by the 1986 Florida Senate campaign of Robert Graham. Said the candidate: "I've got to do the things that only the candidate can do. There are other people deciding what the schedules should be, when commercials go on the air, that sort of thing. . . . But I make the final decisions."[24] Responded Squier: "Bob Graham is one of my best friends. He knows I'm not going to let him down. It would have been very embarrassing if I had to explain how I allowed one of my best friends to lose."

Not a single one of the more than forty-five consultants interviewed by this author wishes to remove the ultimate power of the candidate to approve or veto those major decisions that need to be made during the course of a campaign. Offered Frank Greer: "In the end, it is the candidate's decision. It has to be this way in a democracy. When we walk away from a campaign after the election, it is the candidate that has to represent the people. We owe it to our candidates to let them be the final arbiter in how their campaign is run." Candidates themselves are generally unwilling to allow all their power to be usurped by outside professionals. "In 1984 we hired one consultant," said Indiana Congressman John Hiler. "Sometimes I took his advice. Sometimes I didn't. It was important just to get an outside view, and our consultant was comfortable in that role." The main advisor to Maryland congressional candidate Helen Bentley realized there was little he could do to keep his candidate away from the management process, so he had to pick his battles carefully. "A couple thousand brochures didn't make much difference . . . but when it came to cancelling a television buy, that was a totally different story."[25] According to journalist Michael Barone, "You sometimes see candidates change their emphasis, based on advice taken from a consultant, but you seldom see a candidate changing a position on an issue because a consultant told him it was unpopular."

Although consultants want to control the campaign, no consultant surveyed here indicated he had ever asked a client to switch his position on an issue just to help himself in the election. Reagan pollster Richard Wirthlin echoed the comments of many consultants when he said,

Some people mistakenly believe that consultants tell the candidate how he should look, what he should say, and what issues he should feel strongly about. That is grossly mistaken. The single most important selling proposition for a candidate is trust and believability. If you stretch a candidate to take a position he really doesn't believe in, you endanger his most important asset, the ability to communicate that he cares.

Added Roger Ailes: "Candidates have to be aware of their campaign.

They have to have ideas. If a candidate called me up and said,'Do whatever you want and call me on election day,' I'd think he was a fool. But if he told me, 'I don't like that cutaway shot,' if he tried to do my job for me, I'd tell him to go to hell."

The matter of candidates and consultants prematurely severing their relationship has seldom been examined, probably because it is not a common occurrence. According to Paul Manafort, "It is rare that an issue between the candidate and the consultant is so dramatic that it cannot be worked out. A good consultant can find a way to massage the candidate's concerns and still get the objective accomplished." Said Roger Craver, "Virtually every candidate is problematic at some point, in terms of my being able to tell them something with the bark off and still make them listen." Sometimes, however, if the chemistry between candidate and consultant is poorly matched, the traumas of electioneering can exacerbate an already difficult situation. Manafort and his partners – Charlie Black, Roger Stone, and Lee Atwater – have joined a growing number of firms that now have an escape clause in all their contracts, giving both the client and the firm the opportunity to opt out if their relationship has soured. The reasons for the failure of a candidate–consultant relationship vary: consultants will often blame the candidates' ego, or their indecisiveness, campaign staff, friends and advisors, or even their spouses, for the continued differences of opinion. Candidates, on the other hand, often cite the consultants' aloofness, lack of availability, failure to understand the constituency, or their desire for total control. Remarked David Keene: "When the campaign begins to fall apart . . . you can't replace the candidate, so the candidate replaces the consultant." When the consultant is replaced, rarely is the consultant or the candidate willing to discuss the true circumstances behind the split.

The most publicized break-up of a candidate and consultant in the 1986 election cycle occurred in the Missouri Senate campaign of Harriet Woods, and included the firing of media consultant Bob Squier and the resignation of the polling firm Hickman–Maslin. According to Squier, the Woods campaign staff believed the key to their success in 1986 rested solely on avoiding the mistakes of their failed 1982 Senate attempt: "What they wanted to do was rerun the 1982 campaign, clean up the problems, and then they would win. They were stuck in the mire of that old campaign. I take some blame since we really never understood that. We didn't read them correctly." Squier's firm, the Communications Company, had produced a set of three political ads that struck hard against Kit Bond, Woods's Republican opponent. Woods, who had consistently trailed Bond throughout the campaign and had been searching for an issue that would cut deeply into Bond's support, nevertheless panicked when the Squier commercials, which tied Bond to the farm foreclosures in Missouri, drew heated protests from some voters. She responded to the criticism by hastily firing her media consultant. Said Squier:

We were really stunned, and so were the pollsters, at what happened. The Woods campaign met for two days by themselves, excluded us, excluded the pollsters, came out of the room, and fired us. We didn't even get a chance to explain. Woods got blown over by her friends who just didn't like the ads. Her campaign just climbed into a bunker. It's sad because I'm absolutely sure we could have elected her to the US Senate.

The ads that caused Squier's dissmissal had been viewed and approved by the candidate before airing, yet the intense pressures of the campaign trail can sometimes lead to highly emotional and even irrational behavior. The Woods campaign proved that a candidate's inherent distrust of modern campaign technology (or of modern campaign consultants) can sometimes prove electorally fatal. In this case, it was the candidate's total rejection of professional advice that caused her campaign to rupture at a crucial stage in the election process. By firing Bob Squier, Harriet Woods not only lost her highly respected media consultant, but also her pollsters – who quit out of frustration with the candidate and her campaign. According to Harrison Hickman:

They wanted us to do polls, mail in the advice, and let them make all the decisions. If they were people of impeccable political judgment, we might have been able to work with them. But they weren't. We weren't willing to be held responsible for the campaign without having any authority. There would have been as big a fight within the Woods campaign as there was between Woods and Bond. . . . A different candidate could have prevented the problem.

The ousting or resignation of well-known consultants often receives press coverage, and this instance was no exception. Wrote political journalists Jack Germond and Jules Witcover of the July 1986 Woods shake-up: "The departure not only of Squier but also of the Washington polling firm of Hickman–Maslin Research has created an impression, justly or not, of disarray in the Woods camp."[26] Woods was never able to shake this impression, and it irreparably damaged her fundraising efforts and also the campaign.

Candidates often have a predetermined, though possibly incorrect, idea about the message they should be sending to the public, and may resent continued interference by the consultant, particularly when the candidate and the consultant clearly do not agree. In such circumstances, consultants often attack the candidate's judgment and voluntarily offer to leave. Said Joseph Napolitan, the dean of political consultants:

In a situation like this, I usually tell the candidate and/or his campaign manager, "Look, you are telling people I am the media director in this campaign, but I really am not, because you are not accepting my recommendations. You are paying me money for advice you are not using, and I am spending my time working in a campaign where my advice is not needed or wanted. Why don't we part company . . . ?"[27]

Concluded Peter Kelly: "It always comes down to who controls what. Some consultants consult. Other consultants command." Former presidential candidate Joseph Biden came to this realization about pollster Pat Caddell too late to save his 1988 campaign, but nevertheless found this issue important enough for him to release a statement following his withdrawal: "The Senator wants it to be known that he has no animosity toward Pat Caddell, but that he has ended his relationship with him."[28] Republican media advisor Edward Blakely blamed poor diplomacy for many of the problems between media consultants and their clients:

Very few media consultants are really good at this. In one situation, they'll present an ad to the candidate, and say, "That's it." There will be heated words, and somebody ends up leaving the campaign. Or, you'll have the other extreme where the consultant will roll over and play dead. They'll do anything the candidate wants without any argument.

Even after a successful election, candidates and their consultants are not necessarily members of a mutual admiration society. It is not uncommon for a recently elected official to change consultants soon after the last votes are counted – provided, of course, that money owed the consultant has been paid. Since candidates tend to minimize the role of their consultants, particularly following election day, changing advisors between campaigns is not as noteworthy as might initially appear. Keene explained why:

If the candidate wins, he knows deep down in the darkest recesses of his mind that he won because he is a genius and the best politician to ever come along. The fact that he had all these consultants is almost an embarrassment to him, because he knows that he won it, they didn't, and when they present him with the bills, he doesn't want to pay them.

But if he loses, he knows that the consultant messed it up, and that he would have won if he did it *his* way.

Usually, the worst disputes between candidate and consultant are financial in nature, although both the candidate and the consultant are extremely reluctant to admit it publicly. One well-known example was the direct mail efforts of conservative fundraiser Richard Viguerie on behalf of 1980 Republican presidential candidate Phil Crane, a conservative, grassroots activist. Though unknown to over 99 percent of the electorate at the time of his announcement of candidacy, Congressman Crane used his early-bird status (as the first announced presidential candidate) to build up a sizeable war chest. By the spring of 1979, Viguerie had amassed almost $3 million for his obscure candidate, much of it qualifying for federal matching funds. The trouble arose when Crane became aware that about two-thirds of the money raised was being pocketed by Viguerie (lawfully) in fees and expenses. After a series of heated arguments, the congressman dropped Viguerie's firm. In retaliation, Viguerie quickly signed up with one of Crane's opponents, at the same time filing a major lawsuit against his former client. Even today, both men still refuse to discuss their differences or the details of what actually happened.

More recently, consultants have begun to "front-load" their contracts, requiring clients to pay most or all fees before any work is undertaken, but even this has not completely prevented significant financial disputes from occurring. The inability of Bob Odell to collect money due his direct mail firm from Colorado Congressman Kenneth Kramer's campaign for the US Senate led to a particularly bitter break-up. Privately, Odell blamed the disagreement on the candidate: "Almost always these things break down when the candidate decides not to be involved, which is the disaster of campaigns." Odell may be correct, since Kramer went through three different media consultants during his Senate campaign. On the other hand, when unsuccessful 1986 Maryland Senate candidate Michael Barnes ran out of money, he (uncharacteristically for a candidate) informed his general consultant, pollster, and media advisor that he could no longer afford to pay them. In spite of the information, the professionals continued to give advice on an "ability-to-pay basis" (that is, free of charge) because of the candidate's truthfulness about his finances.

Another factor in the candidate–consultant relationship is the role and authority of the campaign manager. "Campaigns are enormously taxing, don't allow enough time to do the job right, and don't have good managerial talent," claimed fundraiser Roger Craver. "My vision of hell would be to die and go down there and run only campaigns."[29] There are a growing number of specialists in politics who prefer the lead role in a single campaign rather than serve as one of many advisors to multiple candidates. Unfortunately, it is not uncommon for a surging electoral effort to be derailed by internal conflicts over strategy and its execution, with the candidate trapped between the consultant and the campaign manager. "The job of a campaign manager today is to set the strategy, pick the staff, and then serve as marriage counselor," offered David Keene. But to some consultants, the new generation of campaign managers all too often make the wrong choices. In a private memo to Senator Gary Hart before the 1988 campaign, media consultant Ray Strother warned Hart about the dangers of the new breed of campaign manager: "The next generation of . . . young campaign managers judge media producers by the cuteness of their product, and the Squiers, Strothers, and Sawyers are forced to produce reels of crap. We are diminished, but crap is easier to produce than tight communications, so we shrug our shoulders." Along with the rapidly growing importance and utilization of political technology, the incidents of rivalry between consultant and manager – as each courts favor with the often befuddled candidate – have increased in number and intensity. The end result may be more resignations and firings in the future than occurred in the past.

Judging from this author's interviews with candidates, consultants, and campaign managers, there appears to be a correlation between the power of the consultant and internal staff strife, particularly in re-election campaigns. With incumbents, a high degree of tension and rivalry often exists between the outside consultant, who only comes into the office around election time, and the regular staff people, who labor there daily. When an inordinately high level of discontent or dissension from the challenger's "headquarters" personnel falls on the consultant, it is generally due to what they perceive as the consultant's control over their employment during, and after, the election. Because of this, suspicion, resentment, and jealousy are frequently directed at the political consultant, who is paid thousands of dollars for one-day-a-week appearances. Specifically, it is the ability of the consultants to step into a campaign, provide an unbiased assessment, and then have their recommendations immediately accepted and implemented, that generally causes the most problems between the consultant and the campaign staff. In many races, according to one consultant, "You're always fighting the guy who's the candidate's best friend or next-door neighbor, the guy who always has his ear."[30] John Deardourff faced such a situation in 1986, in his successful effort to have William Clements elected governor.

All during the race in Texas, there were people inside the Clements campaign that were complaining that our advertising was not as good as our opponent's. There was one woman in particular, an old-time party war horse, who was a very dedicated person. But I had to keep reminding myself that her motivations were honorable, even though I found myself disliking her intensely. She kept saying, "I got seventy calls this week about how bad our ads were."

Some candidates have even gone so far as to conceal their consultants in an effort to avoid charges by their staff of pandering to outsiders. Florida Senate candidate Robert Graham restricted the interviews given by his paid professional fundraisers after an article written about them upset several of his volunteers. Usually, the best way to end discord is for the candidate to settle any dispute promptly and directly, though initially he may be inclined to side-step the issue for a while. Said Deardourff about his candidate in Texas: "Clements was terrific. He would almost always say at the end of the meetings, 'John, I hired you because I have confidence in your judgment. These people are important to me for other reasons, but understand that I am with you.'"

The most common dispute between consultants and campaign managers concerns the issue of control. "Amid the generally bitter factional strife of a campaign," reads one volume on electioneering, "consultants adore control; the more established demand it before accepting a campaign."[31] It is not unusual for the campaign manager to have a close but volatile relationship with the candidate, which consultants will often exploit. For example, according to a rival pollster, Patrick Caddell has acquired a legendary reputation "for being someone who jumps up and down on the table and says it has to be done his way," intimidating both the candidate and the campaign manager. "Losing wasn't as bad a memory as having had to work with Pat Caddell," said Oliver "Pudge" Henckel, Gary Hart's 1984 campaign manager.[32]

A few candid consultants will admit to their internal power struggles with the campaign manager and staff. "I would argue and fight with my candidates and their staffs, pounding the desk, screaming and sulking," acknowledged Joe Napolitan, the dean of political consultants, who added that, with age, he had become more patient and tolerant of his clients.[33] Media consultant Edward Blakely, commenting on the tension between candidate, consultant, and campaign manager that can arise from the consultant's inordinate desire to control the campaign, was strongly critical of campaign managers: "Most campaign managers are insecure people," he emphasized, adding that a powerful consultant is thus allowed to destabilize a campaign. In fact, Roger Ailes blames the managers more than the candidates for the difficulties that can arise in a campaign. Some months ago, Ailes told this author that he quit a US Senate race for a candidate he liked, rather than work with a campaign manager he detested.

To avoid or at least contain these problems may rest with the ability of the consultant to ensure a "friendly" campaign manager. Blakely described how he minimizes disputes in the campaigns he is involved in: "What I do when working with the campaign is first, to determine the key people, and second, make them part of the process, solicit ideas from them. This is how I work with campaign managers." Some consultants prefer a docile campaign manager and staff, even if they may be somewhat lacking in political aptitude. General consultants, with the approval of the candidate, usually seek unchallenged control over the entire effort, both the overall strategy and the specific tactics, leaving only the responsibility for implementation to the campaign manager. To most general campaign consultants, among them Lee Atwater and Charlie Black, control of the campaign is everything.

Of the leading consultants interviewed here, somewhat less dogmatic are the leading political pollsters. Most insist on having a campaign manager they can "work with," but rarely involve themselves in further staff selection. They want unlimited power to devise strategy, and a minimal role for the manager in this regard. As one pollster commented, "A manager should be the top administrator and nothing more." But although most pollsters insist on sole control over "ideas," they are generally less interested in the tactics and day-to-day affairs of a campaign.

A more distant approach is taken by most media consultants, such as Roger Ailes, Frank Greer, Ray Strother, and Bob Goodman, who decline to participate at all in internal campaign affairs. Said Ailes, "I refuse to dictate staff policy to the campaigns I'm involved in. Unlike other consultants, I define my role narrowly and stay within self-imposed boundaries." Ailes, like most media specialists, has little to gain from internal power politics, since he is only involved in the media angle of electioneering. A similar attitude is held by other media masters as well. According to the partners in Baily/Deardourff/Sipple, control over their aspect of the campaign – paid political advertising – is all that matters. Said John Deardourff, "It became clear that if you didn't control the advertising of a major campaign you didn't exercise control – period."[34] But fortunately for the media consultant, according to Matt Reece, most managers will capitulate rather than battle to the end. "I don't think the local manager has enough judgment to resist the temptation and the strong personalities that do great television."[35] In sum, almost every consultant is a dictator, but some demand more territory than others.

Along with the current trend toward specialization by professional advisors has come a need for candidates to hire more than one political consultant. Campaigns have begun to realize that, for example, it is not enough to buy or rent a couple of computers and hire a kid who has taken a course in computer programming and then think you have "computerized" your campaign. All the new technologies require individuals with specialized training, and acquiring their services can cost considerable money. Consequently, the latest entry into the campaign's inner circle is the fundraising consultant. According to the *National Journal*, only a few campaigns in 1984 reported hiring fundraising consultants, leaving the responsibility to the candidate, his supporters, and the campaign manager.[36] Yet only two years later, Keith Abbott, finance director of the Democratic Senatorial Campaign Committee, said, "Most of our [1986] candidates have one, two, three or even four [fundraisers] working for them in Washington."[37] The use of professional fundraisers is expected to grow rapidly in the coming election cycles, making the process for deciding campaign strategy even more complicated.

Since most campaigns can only satisfy one person's ego, it is, therefore, not uncommon for inter-consultant disputes to develop into outright rivalries. This can have a devastating effect, both on the candidate and the campaign. Warned Ailes, "If it's going to give the candidate ulcers to watch his consultants arguing with each other, you'd better keep him from the meetings." Said Robert Goodman, "In campaigns with too many consultants, it becomes more of a debating society. Too many ego clashes occur." It is also true that internal political rivalries inevitably breed external campaign chaos. As Strother wrote in his memo to Gary Hart about his 1984 campaign crew: "The personalities involved gave the campaign the feel of a new piece of chalk being scraped across a grade school blackboard. The participants used the press as sharp-edged tools to hack away at their enemies within the [campaign]."

Inasmuch as few consulting firms handle all aspects of electioneering, candidates employing more than one independent consultant are forced to accept the accompanying risk of internal disputes. Robert Goodman feels it was such a situation that may have cost Paula Hawkins her Senate seat in 1986:

Paula Hawkins had better ideas than a lot of people around her. There was one consultant in that campaign who dominated her mind and her soul, and was wrong almost every time. We tried to get around him, as did her other advisors, but we were beating our heads against the wall. I tried to speak to the candidate, but I was the new boy on the block, and this guy was just an overpowering salesman.

Roger Ailes described similar problems in the 1986 South Dakota Senate race of James Abdnor:

I should have won South Dakota. I should have been more egotistical in that race and not worked so cooperatively with the other consultants and the pollster. I should have just taken the lead. I took too much input, it got too confused, and there were too many people calling the shots. It was not Jim Abdnor's fault. He tried to sort things out, and did the best he could under the circumstances.

In reviewing his campaign a year later, Abdnor refused to blame internal consultant disputes for his defeat, though he did acknowledge his distance from the inner workings of his campaign: "I tried to be involved in the campaign process, but how much time could I put in? I didn't have the time to get back to the headquarters every hour. I was out on the campaign trail shaking hands." Campaign managers are too often unwilling, and candidates too frequently unable, to prevent unnecessary clashes between professional advisors.

The problem of internal consultant disputes has received remarkably little attention, even by political analysts with an interest in the study of modern campaign technology. According to political advisor Craig Shirley, most consultants are wary of publicizing personal or business disputes because at some future time they may find themselves working together on the same campaign. Nevertheless, observed Ailes, "There is a potential war brewing between consultants, because each of the major groups of consultants wants to have more control over the campaign." Each specialist invariably stresses the vital importance of his particular expertise in an attempt to receive the maximum financial allocation of campaign resources, necessarily at the expense of the other consultants. "As pollsters, we try to sell ourselves as people with no vested interest in the message delivery systems," claimed veteran Democratic advisor Bill Hamilton. "We only want what's best for the client on a cost-effective basis." Although Hamilton's remarks appear reasonable to an outsider, not all media advisors, direct mail specialists, and general consultants would agree with that analysis, and still fewer would graciously accept the directive of a pollster if it meant a smaller share of campaign dollars.

There is little debate among the various consultants, at least publicly, that it is in the best interests of the candidate and the campaign to have the "hired guns" work together as a team. "Political campaigns are a lot like war," maintained Squier, "in that we put aside personal differences and fight for a common goal." In practice, however, a spirit of compromise is often less evident. Most consultants see themselves as uniquely talented specialists who would be doing their clients a disservice if they were to concede at the first sign of resistance. "I should insist on having final say in strategy," said Goodman. "In the next elections, when it comes to media, I will." But pollster Harrision Hickman saw it from a different perspective. "If Robert Goodman feels this should be his new role, he's probably going to have trouble finding good pollsters to work for him. . . . If I am going to be held responsible [for winning or losing], I want the authority to sit at the head of the table and have a major role in the decisions." Said media advisor Strother, "When the pollster becomes the focus of the strategy team, the personality of the candidate and his human nature become buried and he becomes simply an issue-speaking machine." In that vein, pollster Bob Teeter advises his colleagues to "clearly differentiate when they are interpreting survey research data and when they are giving advice."

Yet there is still a growing number of "activist" pollsters who do not differentiate their responsibilities, and insist on personal involvement in areas other than survey research. One of them is Richard Morris: "I write the spots in some campaigns," he said in a 1984 interview. "Some of us give the media people draft scripts, some of us provide ideas."[38] But one media consultant interviewed for this book claimed he would quit a campaign before allowing Morris or any other pollster to dictate media strategy, to which pollster Hickman responded, "I will lie down on the railroad tracks to keep a commercial I believe to be harmful off the air." General consultants, to no one's surprise, are just as adamant. Declared Lee Atwater, chief political advisor to George Bush, "I won't get into a campaign unless I'm at the head of the table. If I've been asked to come in, and I accept, I'm going to come in on my own terms." Caught in the middle of this escalating battle is the hapless candidate.[39] As Richard Wirthlin noted, "Campaigns can be ruined, not by the candidate or by issues, but by the squabbling among the hired guns. That's a sad case but it does happen."

One way to solve some of the problems generated by competing advisors has been for the candidate to team up general consultants, pollsters, and expert specialists who like working together. This new team concept has had two major benefits for candidates who are dependent on outside advisors. First, it helps to limit tensions if compatible outside consultants are working together in a campaign. "It was fortuitous for Clements to have used DMI and us," said John Deardourff, "because Dick Wirthlin's office is just a block from here, and I'm able to run over there, and his people here, and everything tracks better." Second, it gives the professional consultants a form of quality control that has been lacking for some time. Most consultants will not recommend, or work with, individuals they feel are incompetent. "We know who we work with on campaigns," said Brad O'Leary, president of the American Association of Political Consultants (AAPC) and a leading Republican fundraiser. "I don't want to be in a campaign where somebody is ripping off the candidate, and I'll go up against that consultant if I know this is happening." Said Bill Hamilton, "Only in rare cases would a media specialist go off and do something wrong which hadn't been caught earlier in a strategy session with the other consultants." But another solution is offered by former National Republican Senatorial Committee (NRSC) Executive Director Tom Griscom, "A candidate does not need to have a room full of consultants to get the job done. Maybe the time has come when a pollster and a media consultant are all they need." Nevertheless, it is up to the candidate to determine the campaign roles that need to be filled with professional advisors, and then decide who will best fill them.

Most of the leading consultants agree that there are some in their business with only mediocre talent. "The number of consultants who are truly talented in both parties can be named on one hand," claimed Roger Stone, commenting that there are "a lot of practitioners out there who are good, honest, hardworking guys without much creativity and talent." Said John Deardourff, "There are a half dozen firms that have people who are of substantial stature and quality and whose advice is worth having. The others, I don't know." Consultants also acknowledge that misrepresented abilities, along with some unethical practices, can now be found in their craft. (See survey 2.5.) Many claim, however, that such practices take place to no greater or lesser degree than in other fields, and many believe the problem is exacerbated by the boom their business is currently enjoying. According to Harrison Hickman: "Misrepresentation is worse now than in the past, because there are more people out there who claim to be consultants. There are a lot

**Survey 2.5** *Do misrepresentation of abilities and unethical practices take place in the political consulting profession?*

|  | % |
|---|---|
| Yes | 88 |
| No | 12 |

more companies and people who are financially on the margin. They can't live off their record, so in order to survive they overestimate what they can do." Added political consultant Victor Kamber, "Over the years, there have been a lot of hacks in the business. . . . I think the mediocrity still exists in a number of people who have been around for a long time."

AAPC President Brad O'Leary, a proud and outspoken defender of professionalism in consulting, believes that consultant rip-off occurs primarily among consulting firms in their first cycle of business. "They won't survive into a second cycle with that kind of behavior because the other consultants on the campaign are going to make damn sure that these guys never get hired." Fundraiser Roger Craver blames candidate weakness for consultant misrepresentation and fraud: "It occurs more when the candidates are willing to retain a sycophant rather than a consultant. If they are looking for someone to make them feel secure in their paranoia, chances are they will end up with someone who is not very creative or not very honest." To veteran Democrat Matt Reece, both candidate and consultant are responsible for the continued misrepresentation:

All of us, including the new ones, sell magic; that's what the client wants to buy. He's not terribly aware of the elements of a campaign and what should go into it, but he's looking to win and he's looking for a magician. The trouble with being a magician in selling is that there is a tendency to overclaim, to reduce in the candidate's mind all the problems he is going to encounter.[40]

To Republican advisor Dave Keene, it is the candidate, not the consultant, who bears final responsibility for unethical campaign practices: "Candidates sometimes get desperate and are forced to choose whether to play it safe or go all out. I may be the one providing the choices, but it is their decision in the end."

Peter Kelly was particularly defensive against candidate criticisms of political consultants. "When candidates disagree with what the poll says, they'll claim it's inaccurate. When they agree with the poll, they'll think it's brilliant." But the candidates are not always wrong, and they can hardly be blamed for all consultant inadequacies. Particularly in the polling field, the quality of the consultant's work is largely dependent on the firm's employees. For example, the Democratic polling firm

Hickman–Maslin regularly requests that members of their staff meet the clients and attend early presentations to demonstrate the depth of knowledge and ability in their company. In contrast, Pat Caddell, once the wizard and guru of the Democratic Party, has more recently been criticized for being a "one-man operation," particularly after the departure of several key partners. In fact, the demise of Senator Joseph Biden's 1988 presidential campaign has privately been blamed on Caddell's lack of back-up in his firm. Said one consultant close to the situation: "Biden's not in the race any more, and Pat Caddell was one of the people writing the speeches [borrowing lines from speeches by British Labour leader Neil Kinnock and Robert Kennedy without attribution] that came under question. You figure it out." Added Bob Squier, not entirely in jest, "I have been Pat Caddell's friend and I've been his enemy. Being his enemy takes less energy."

With the advent of the desktop computer, it has now reached the point where anyone with a basic grasp of statistics and a creative mind can call himself a pollster. Richard Wirthlin alluded to this problem when he referred to the "fraud in polling," whereby pollsters will provide a campaign with surveys that have a professional appearance but are methodologically unsound – a problem that is beyond the abilities of some candidates to detect. Wirthlin explained:

A "9" typed on an IBM Selectric at DMI looks just like a "9" typed on an IBM Selectric of Joe Schlock who has never done any polling at all but hangs out his shingle as a pollster who happens to own an IBM Selectric. That is one of the things that makes it a very precarious decision for the candidate. How do you tell the difference?

Added pollster Peter Hart: "You go to some pollsters, and it's just a name on the door. They're hiring out for a sample, hiring out for phone banks, hiring out for their coding, hiring out for tabulation. They have no quality control, and the candidate is stuck paying everybody's overhead, and everybody's profit." Author Edward Schwartzman wrote in 1984: "Many survey firms are reliable, but some are not, some are incompetent, and some are simply thieves."[41] Brad O'Leary spoke of a major pollster whose numbers were consistently wrong because his sampling technique and questionnaire approach were methodologically unsound. "Is that unethical? No, it's not unethical. It's stupid, but not unethical." Another consultant, Tony Fabrizio, comically referred to this same pollster as "the Julia Child of polling; he throws artificial numbers into a microwave oven and bakes them." A similar though slightly less critical view of media consultants is held by media advisor Raymond Strother: "Consultants constantly promise things they can't deliver. Very seldom will a media consultant go in and say to a candidate: 'Here are the elections I lost. Look at those.' He ignores those completely, so in effect he is misrepresenting his product."

The high cost of hiring well-known consulting firms has also been questioned by many in the business. (See survey 2.6.) Media consultant Ken Swope directed his harshest ethical criticisms against the lofty fees demanded by some in his field. "I don't think people should be paid that much money simply because they are able to get it. If they got more publicity for making these obscene amounts [up to one million dollars in a California statewide race], the candidates would stop paying it." Some of the older general consultants, those who are less familiar with modern technology, "the so-called experts of campaign management, who have it all in their head," were criticized by pollster Lance Tarrance for overcharging. He added, "The campaign management consultants, who are not particularly skilled in media or research, are having a hard time keeping up with the changes, and therefore have a greater chance of not returning their dollars." Matt Reece, however, suggested that the knowledge of the general consultant about all the various campaign services and technicians, both good and bad, could save a campaign hundreds of hours and thousands of dollars. In fact, the only issue most consultants could agree on was the unlikelihood of candidate backlash. It does not seem imminent. Candidates eager to seek, or retain, public office recognize the current need for skilled professional guidance in running a modern campaign, and appear willing to pay the price to obtain it.

**Survey 2.6** *In general, are the great majority of political consultants worth the prices they charge?*

|  | % |
| --- | --- |
| Yes | 62 |
| No | 38 |

It is only recently that the field of political consultancy has emerged, spawned by the adaptation of technology to the electoral process. Thrust into the limelight and dubbed the "king makers" of the 1980s, today's political consultants have thoroughly transformed electioneering in America, merging the science of technology with the art of campaigning. The style and substance of American electoral politics will never be the same.

# 3

# The selling of the candidate

Mixing style with substance and imagery with reality, media consultants have developed a wide range of formats . . . both to inform and to deceive a television-addicted electorate.

Larry Sabato, author[1]

The technique in a good paid advertising campaign is to go with those lines of arguments, thoughts, beliefs and themes in which the public is already inclined to believe – or ready to accept. Even the slickest commercial only works when it stresses something that people already are inclined to believe. You cannot tell people on television that times are prosperous if it's 1932. They won't believe you.

Michael Barone, journalist

I love to do negatives. It is one of those opportunities in a campaign where you can take the truth and use it just like a knife to slice right through the opponent. I hate the kind of commercials that are just music and pretty pictures. The ones I like are those where you can really get at reality.

Bob Squier, media consultant

We have reached the point in political campaigning where a candidate's most important decision is not necessarily his stand on the issues but his choice of media advisor.

US Senator William Proxmire[2]

The rising power of the media consultants has caused a remarkable change in the American political campaign process. Since 1980, every major presidential candidate has had at least one media consultant on the campaign staff, nearly all Senate and House candidates in contested districts have purchased at least some television and radio time, and

Congress is replete with members that publicly attribute their election victories to paid political advertising. The average Senate or gubernatorial campaign currently produces and airs about twenty to thirty television advertisements, and in some states voters are seeing more political commercials than ads for Coca-Cola, Budweiser and even McDonalds. In this modern age of electioneering, television has surpassed radio and newspapers to become the most important mode of communication, and paid political commercials have become the key element in the process of winning elections. Television's contribution to political marketing has been truly extraordinary, and has empowered a growing number of professionals who now engage in a relatively new profession – the selling of a candidate.

The number of candidates turning over control of their campaigns, and therefore their political fortunes, to the gurus of media consulting grows with each election. Candidates have come to accept paid television advertising as the primary mode of interaction with the electorate. The reason is both clear and simple: it reaches every voter. According to 1980 government statistics, almost 99 percent of all American households had at least one television set. The average American adult watches more than three and one-half hours of television per day,[3] while the average American child upon reaching the legal voting age of eighteen has already watched 20,000 hours of television.[4]

It should, therefore, come as no surprise that television is frequently the most important source for election information. According to surveys by the Roper Organization, television was cited by the public as its favorite medium for obtaining information about political candidates. In national elections, television was ranked first by 75 percent of those surveyed, falling to 54 percent in statewide races, and 49 percent in congressional contests.[5] And according to Tony Coelho, former chairman of the Democratic Congressional Campaign Committee, 60 percent of the American public receives 100 percent of their news from television.[6] Almost nine out of ten Americans say they follow television reports about campaigns, and media information is almost always at the top of voters' lists of causal factors explaining their ballot decisions. A nationwide poll conducted by the Associated Press in November 1986 found that an almost equal percentage of the adult population considered television and newspapers as their primary source of information about candidates, with 42 percent naming newspapers and 39 percent naming television. The remaining 19 percent were divided among magazines, radio, and friends.[7] (Among younger people, those aged 19–34, TV was selected more often than newspapers.) A poll conducted by this author for Delaware Congressman Tom Evans, in 1982, asked voters which campaign media source most influenced their candidate preference. Television, according to the respondents, finished first, closely followed by newspapers – with radio and magazines a distant third and fourth.

Through the mid-1970s, the typical congressional or statewide candidate would allocate 5 to 10 percent of the campaign budget for a media "blitz" to be conducted, specifically, during the final days of the campaign. The commercials would be "cut" during the summer lull, and sent off to the candidate some time after Labor Day. Only the very sophisticated and wealthy campaigns had more than a single series of spots, and using paid advertising to respond to an opponent's paid advertising attack was then almost unheard of. These early commercials tended to be positive in nature. The candidate, seen walking along the beach and often with family, exuded social values and personal sensitivity, popular themes of the early and mid-1970s. By the late 1970s and into 1980, spots were being produced and aired on a weekly or biweekly basis. After the airing, the candidates would wait until the polling results, or their own intuition, indicated whether to continue with the set or request that new commercials be created.

The "back-'n'-forth" television campaign was first pioneered in 1982, by Missouri Democratic Senate candidate Harriet Woods. Hers was the first campaign to run a commercial that opened with a 10-second insert showing a brief portion of an ad run by her opponent, and which was then followed by her 20-second response to it. Four years later, the Ohio Republican Party purchased air time before, during, and after the local news to run its paid advertising campaign, which was a mock newscast attacking the Democratic governor. Not to be outdone, the Ohio Democratic Party bought air time – immediately before and after the Republican commercials – giving new meaning to the term back-'n'-forth. By 1986, statewide candidates for the Senate and for governor were spending an estimated 60 percent of their campaign war chests on TV advertising.[8] (See table 3.1.)

**Table 3.1**  *Political advertisement dollars spent on TV*

| Year | Amount ($ million) | % increase from previous election cycle |
|------|--------------------|------------------------------------------|
| 1970 | 12.0 | – |
| 1974 | 23.3 | 94 |
| 1978 | 57.6 | 147 |
| 1982 | 123.6 | 115 |
| 1986 | 161.6 | 31 |

% gain 1970–86: 1247%

*Source*: Compiled from Television Bureau of Advertising, Inc., TvB Report, "Political Advertising on Television"

Today, the most important political question no longer is whether to use television advertising, but how often, and how early in the election cycle it should begin. Commercials are now being aired more than a year in advance of the election, and it is not uncommon for candidates to initiate major expenditures for paid media long before most voters even become aware that an election is approaching. The first ad for a 1986 Senate incumbent seeking re-election appeared on 30 May 1985, featuring North Dakota Senator Mark Andrews – one and a half years before election day. North Dakota's other senator, Quentin Burdick, up for re-election in 1988, began his television campaign twenty-two months before voters could cast their ballots. The 1984 and 1988 presidential sweepstakes have been no different. In the earlier contest, by November 1983, several candidates had already broadcast fundraising films once, but none began a prolonged paid media campaign until January of 1984. Yet by November 1987, seven of the thirteen candidates were actively engaged in media efforts for the 1988 primaries and caucuses. "There are consultants to other campaigns who find it hard to believe we did it this early," said Tony Payne, media advisor to presidential candidate Michael Dukakis. "I find it hard to believe they are all going to wait until January."[9]

In actuality, it is often greatly to the candidate's benefit to be the first one on television, and this has led to longer and longer media campaigns. According to Democratic media consultant Robert Shrum, "The biggest advantage of going on the air early is that you can define the race. I'd rather have us define the race than the other guy."[10] According to a study by the *Washington Post*, fifteen of the nineteen GOP senators seeking re-election in 1986 were already advertising on television by mid-July of that year.[11] The media consultant to 1986 Missouri Senate candidate Kit Bond decided to be first to draw blood – six months before election day. "We wanted to draw [our opponent] out. We wanted to make her spend more money than she wanted to."[12] The immediate result was an eleven-point gain for Kit Bond. Just one day after winning the bruising June Republican primary for US Senate in California, candidate Edward Zschau had to face a barrage of negative advertising by his Democratic opponent, Senator Alan Cranston. Respected journalists Jack Germond and Jules Witcover described that race in their column: "Mr Zschau ordinarily would have had ample time to inform the voters about himself. But because the Cranston campaign, in its own ads, immediately gave the voters its version of who Mr Zschau is, the Republican candidate was stymied from the start."[13]

Although the length of the paid advertising season has grown considerably longer, the time between a candidate's commercials and his opponent's paid response has shrunk from months or weeks to just days or even hours. Key strategists in James Santini's 1986 Nevada

Senate campaign used their contacts in the television industry to acquire advance copies of their opponent's "attack" commercials several hours before they were to air. Within two days, Santini's media consultant had produced and begun to air a series of "counterpunch" ads for his client. It was not uncommon for both Senator Jesse Helms and Governor James Hunt, combatants in the 1984 North Carolina Senate race, to send a new video cassette of their commercials to every major TV station in the state, in response to the ad that had been run by the opposition no more than a few days earlier. The two candidates eventually ran about 7,500 commercials between them, averaging more than twenty-five a day during the campaign. In the 1986 Vermont Senate race between incumbent Patrick Leahy and challenger Richard Snelling, Democratic media consultant Ken Swope had the fastest turnaround of any advisor, producing commercials for Leahy that were in response to the opponent's attack even before the attack commercials had aired. According to Swope, "Snelling or his consultants would tell reporters what their client's next big issue would be, the reporters would run the story, and we'd have our reponse commercials even before they had finished producing their attack ads. Our commercials took the sting out of Snelling's attack before it had even been mounted." The ability to respond quickly to an opponent's campaign has become a major selling point of many consulting firms. Explained Bob Squier in authentic "media-speak," "If we make any claim at all, it is that we have fast turnaround. We really work hard at being in front of this business in terms of being able to understand when things have changed in a campaign, and be able to change with it – or even to cause change and then get ahead in terms of the back and forth."

Most of the seriously contested Senate races have now become "advertising battles" between competing candidates. The campaigns of the two congressmen seeking the Senate seat from Louisiana in 1986 typifies this. Each spent hundreds of thousands of dollars to bombard the state's television viewers with almost identical negative commercials. They opened with "1083" in large white letters stretching across a black background. In both candidates' commercials, ordinary looking people were asked by an unseen voice what 1083 meant. In both sets, the initial responses were humorous. Only the message was different. In Republican Henson Moore's commercials, the narrator explained that 1083 was "the number of votes Congressman John Breaux missed in Congress – one thousand eighty-three times he didn't show up for work." Breaux's look-alike commercial, in response to the one initiated by Moore, explained that 1083 was "the number of jobs lost in Louisiana every ten working days because of Republican policy Henson Moore promises to continue."

It is no longer uncommon for consultants to devise a campaign strategy that centers entirely on paid political advertising. In the 1986

South Dakota Senate race, for example, the average voter saw 300 commercials about the two candidates. The 30-second spot, and little of anything else, has now become the centerpiece for many campaigns. One election observer noted as far back as 1981: "The candidate's share of broadcast expenditures is significantly related to the candidate's share of the vote, even when the effects of incumbency are controlled for. Money spent on radio and television does affect the vote. . . ."[14] Maryland Senate candidate Michael Barnes even dropped his general consultant, media consultant, and pollster, and cut the salaries of his campaign staff so that he could keep his television commercials on the air. Most candidates have come to the realization that refusing to buy media time can lead to bitter disappointment on election day. Concluded political journalist Tom Wicker in 1986, "Candidates will not for long keep doing things that don't win elections."[15]

But why television and not radio or newspapers? Visual impact makes television stand out from other means of communication. Said Tony Coelho: "[People] don't care what you say. It's how you look." Studies conducted by leading Republican pollster Robert Teeter indicated that "80 or 90 percent of what people retain from a TV ad is visual. . . . If you have the visual right, you have the commercial right. If you don't, it almost doesn't matter what you're saying." Teeter, like many pollsters and all media consultants, pays strict attention to his client's television image, using research volunteers to study photos, video tapes, and recorded voices to determine what look and style would most effectively portray the client in a favorable light. For example, consultants have found that overweight candidates are presumed to be lazy and slow; hence Massachusetts Senator Edward Kennedy's infamous pre-election diets. Beards and mustaches, unless they are well-groomed and gray, provoke mistrust; women are perceived as weaker, softer, and more impulsive than men. Former Chicago Mayor Jane Byrne was perceived as less erratic and impulsive once she stopped wearing red dresses.

Through trial and error and extensive voter research, the leading media consultants have become well versed in the art of their craft, and have acquired sophisticated marketing skills that the typical candidate cannot match. "If you've got a candidate who comes across as bland, it helps to put him in a group," said William Feltus from Market Opinion Research. "If you've someone in a heavily Democratic district who comes across as a banker and country club member, shoot him in shirt sleeves." Media consultant Raymond Strother described the process he uses when a candidate's appearance needs to be altered:

Often when you are working with a candidate, you have to help him dress, help him speak, and on rare occasions, you have to explain to him how he should act in front of a camera. In one case, I had to bring in an acting coach because the person was so expressionless that I could have used a mannequin in his place and no one would have known the difference. He literally gave speeches where only his lips moved. He didn't even blink his eyes. We had to get some voice modulation and movement, so I had to bring in professional help.

In all probability, even the most technically proficient candidates lack the background and resources necessary to produce effective television advertising. Because it has become so crucial to electoral success, one of the most important decisions in a campaign is the selection of a media consultant. The candidate's search for professional advisors can be long and arduous, and probably no advisor is more difficult to choose than a media consultant. As with choosing other specialist consultants, claimed media advisor David Doak, "most candidates are not well informed consumers." Added Ken Swope, "Candidates should ask, 'If I hire you, are you going to be doing the work or are you so busy that you are going to have other associates in the firm doing my campaign?' That is one of the most important questions, *yet it is rarely asked.*"

Because major media firms can handle only a small fraction of the candidates seeking their services, they can be highly selective in the clients they choose to take on. "It's tougher in media to stay alive," said Republican advisor Roger Ailes, "because everything you do is so public. People don't blame the pollster for a loss. They blame the media consultant." Explained Strother: "I am very careful about prospective clients. If I don't think the candidate can communicate – I can normally tell this in the first four or five minutes – I will disengage. I won't allow myself to get involved with that candidate because it will be a hopeless task." Even personal wealth cannot buy the services of some media professionals. Despite the opportunity to earn almost one million dollars, media veteran Tony Schwartz rejected an offer of employment by New York Senate candidate John Dyson in 1986. While the candidate may be the one seeking a political advisor, in point of fact it is the media consultant, not the candidate, who decides whether to associate or not.

Many media experts have had previous extensive experience in either commercial advertising or television production, an asset they bring to the election process. President Reagan's 1984 re-election campaign gathered together a group of media all-stars from commercial advertising, dubbed "the Tuesday Team", to produce some of the slickest advertising ever created in a presidential race. One such member, Phil Dusenberry, the genius behind Pepsi and Apple Computer advertising, returned to politics in 1988 to assist the presidential campaign of Congressman Jack Kemp. However, some of the recent entrants to the field have been schooled more in politics than in media.

Professional media consultants are a talented, diverse lot, with their own unique idiosyncrasies. Political folklore has it that Roger Ailes, media consultant to Richard Nixon, Ronald Reagan, and George Bush, cannot complete a statement without including at least one four-letter word; that Bob Squier, with more clients in the US Senate than any other ad man, would rather die than attend a meeting in an office other than his own; that Bob Goodman, mastermind behind George Bush's rise to fame in 1980, creates his best campaign theme music in the shower. Some media consultants are extremely temperamental, some are flashy, and many have a keen sense of humor. Some make commercials that look more like 30-second movies, while others are less concerned with the production details. But whatever their personality characteristics may be, all appear, at least outwardly, supremely confident of their ability to produce results for their clients. Explained Ailes: "It takes an enormous amount of confidence in yourself to advise some guy about his career, his fortune, and his life, knowing if you fail, you've ruined him."

Squier likens his work to that of a dramatist:

Setting the media strategy is a lot like improvisational theatre in that we are trying to build a story that we don't know the ending of, with other characters on the stage which we don't know what they are going to say, all of this performed for an audience that is trying to figure out what in the world we are trying to do.

But Raymond Strother, Gary Hart's media advisor, believes much about media specialists is pure hype: "Candidate respect for media consultants is somewhat based on how many times they read about you in *Time* and *Newsweek*, how often they've seen you on television shows, and how many famous people you have represented. There are a thousand reasons why a person is elected, and a media consultant is one of those reasons – sometimes." Media consultant Frederic Papert agreed: "I don't want to spoil Bob Squier's new business pitch to any potential candidates . . . but there are limits to what even Bob Squier can do. . . . The candidate gets himself elected."[16] Concluded David Doak: "Many of the media consultants have convinced themselves that they are gurus who understand things better than anyone else. They probably don't. It's just the line they put out."

Frequently censured by the press for their (perceived) political power and ability to affect the outcome of elections (in the political world such criticism is akin to praise), many media consultants, particularly those at the top of their profession, are themselves harshly critical of their colleagues. Charles Guggenheim, the leading media figure of the late 1960s and early 1970s, now rarely works for candidates. "One reason I've dropped out of politics is that you begin to get the feeling that it doesn't make any difference if it [an advertisement] is good or not. I've seen too many campaigns won with awful material."

Most veteran political consultants blamed the inadequate commercial advertising or television training of many of the newer media consultants for the inferior quality of some commercials. Said John

Deardourff, "A lot of people who do not know much about the use of television have recently come into the media consulting business, and the quality of their production in a great many campaigns is abysmal – it's truly poor." Ken Swope added, "There are a lot of people out there who don't really belong in the business, because they have no experience. They don't know how to produce a good piece of film or video tape." Lyn Nofziger, political advisor and former White House political director, also criticized the new media entrants who, he claimed, mainly had financial gains in mind: "A lot of them get involved in the production of media because they make a lot of money that way. But they have very limited experience and very limited talent. As a result, candidates have a lot of bad media." Said Squier, "The idea of putting into the hands of a media firm three or four million dollars and your entire political career, and not knowing whether they really have any television experience, is just remarkable."

The media consultants, like other political advisors, are vulnerable to the peaks and valleys of election cycles. In an off-year, it is particularly difficult to secure enough work to retain and pay the media staff so as to maintain some continuity from election to election. Yet the cost of producing political advertising has remained more or less constant in the past five years, even with the increased sophistication in technology. In fact, according to Ailes, the cost of producing a 30-second political spot is still only about 10 percent of the cost of commercial advertising. The "paint brush" animation technique, which gives the effect of someone writing directly onto the television screen with a paint brush, once cost $15,000, but now costs only $600. Because consultants now take more care when filming spots, they have been able to reduce on-site costs by up to one-third of the 1982 price. Thus, although some particular costs have risen greatly over time, the average 30-second spot produced by Ray Strother that cost his firm $3,500 in 1982, cost $3,600 in 1986 – an increase well below the rate of inflation. He explained, "I want them to have very fine production, but I don't want them to have no money left to air the spots." Strother claimed to be attaining almost as much voter recall in 1986 at 450 rating points – each rating point corresponds to the number of viewers watching a particular television program, and is the basis for determining advertising rates – as he got in 1984 with 600 points, because of advances in technology. Several media consultants insisted their campaign commercials in 1986 had a greater impact on voter recall than in 1984, though to a lesser degree than Strother estimates. Frank Greer described his operation in a similar cost-effective fashion:

We have a staff of twenty people working around the clock. I have been here until 3:30 a.m. cutting spots, and then returned at 8:00 a.m. to record narration, and I will work late into the next evening as well. It seems like the prices are expensive, but for the kind of total effort and involvement we put in, we think it is a bargain.

Like others in the consulting field, the best media consultants generally have prices that match their reputation and the high demand for their services. (On occasion, though, commercial advertisers have been known to volunteer their services to like-minded presidential candidates.) At the outset, candidates are informed that media advertising is expensive, for no consultant wants to be associated with a client who cannot afford to pay. Nevertheless, consultants expect that, once a candidate views himself on television, the candidate will want to see – and will gladly pay for – additional material. Most media advisors charge separately for every conceivable aspect of their job (creation, design, production, and placement), and often there is an added general retainer fee, since the overhead costs are very high. Many candidates are quite willing to pay any price to secure the firm they think best able to provide a victory. "The more fees they pay, the more direction they take," claimed Strother. "Those that pay a lot of money are not going to refuse you, because they assume you know more about it than they do."

In addition, media consultants generally keep the 15 percent commission paid by the television and radio stations for the advertising time purchased. Bob Squier, for example, receives a $60,000 creative fee plus 15 percent from the "media buy," which can eventually reach one million dollars in states like California, New York, and Texas. David Garth often charges up to $25,000 a month plus commissions.[17] Since TV time is far more expensive than radio, it is also more profitable for the media consultant to encourage television over radio advertising.

It was easy for the early pioneers of paid television advertising to point to the string of candidates that had gained twenty-five to forty points in the polls, and won, because of good television advertisements. Candidates who saw it as a miracle technique were thus driven to television as the wonder tool that would assure them victory. The *Washington Post* commented on the "magic" of the advertising process in a 1986 article: "There is a rule of thumb in political advertising that two-thirds of viewers cannot remember a typical television spot the day after they have seen it. Every so often, though, an ad takes a life of its own. It reverberates for weeks. It triggers responses and the responses trigger counter-responses."[18] Not every candidate or political observer, however, so is enamored of the skills of the media consultants. Despite the high fees, "The marketing experts who sell their services to candidates . . . offer no warranties on their 'products' and no refunds . . . " said political journalist David Broder.[19] As former congressman and presidential candidate John Anderson noted, "Not every free-spending candidate can be transformed by a media maven into a winner."[20] And most candidates, unlike consumer products, cannot survive a failed marketing campaign.

While fees charged by media consultants may have made many of them wealthy, it is the exorbitantly high cost of air time that can bankrupt the candidates. The Federal Election Campaign Act attempted to keep costs under control by legally requiring television stations to charge their lowest unit rates for political advertising. The new regulation was temporarily effective, until even the lowest rates charged by television stations began to spiral upwards. A 30-second spot on *The Cosby Show*, the 1986–7 top rated program, is $30,000 in Los Angeles alone. *Dynasty* can cost up to $25,000 for a 30-second spot in Los Angeles, depending on the month in which it is aired. Small states do not have this problem. For the price of one *Dynasty* ad in Los Angeles, a statewide candidate in North Dakota, the cheapest media state in the country, can buy a television package that blankets the state's six stations for a week, making it possible for the average viewer to see one of his spots fifteen times. But in the more populous states where the rapid increase in advertising costs have been most noticeable, Senate campaign tactics are mostly concentrated on one of three goals, and sometimes all three: generating free television, radio, and newspaper coverage; raising money to finance paid commercials; and energizing supporters to go out and raise more money. In 1974, Senator Alan Cranston spent 23 percent of his $300,000 campaign budget on media.[21] By 1986, the Cranston campaign estimated that 64 percent of every dollar raised went toward the production and broadcasting of television commercials – about $6.4 million.[22]

Yet only in limited areas and rare cases has television advertising shown itself to be cost ineffective when compared with other forms of electioneering. "Individuals running for Congress often make the mistake of putting all their money into media," admitted media consultant Charles Guggenheim. "Where there is a small, confined constituency that represents only a small percentage of a mass market, it is often a mistake to use television." The New York City media market, for example, stretches over nineteen congressional districts in three states. Consequently, here it would take an inordinate amount of campaign expenditures to make any measurable impact. As Connecticut Congressman Stewart McKinney asked, "Who wants to be one of a herd? Who needs to pay $6,000 a minute for that!" California has fourteen media markets and seventy-five major commercial stations. Media analysts estimate it costs between $300,000 and $400,000 to buy enough television time so that the average California voter will see a single spot five times – the generally accepted minimum exposure for an ad to have any substantial impact.[23] New Jersey, one of the ten most populated states in the country, has no network affiliated television station within its borders, forcing statewide candidates to use both the New York and Philadelphia markets, a costly and wasteful endeavor, considering the small number of constituents as a percentage of the total audience.

Still, there are numerous cases where the mere act of putting ads on television, even in expensive and untargeted markets, has been crucial to the election outcome. The opponents (and some supporters) of New Hampshire Senator Gordon Humphrey saw him as a non-contender when he first ran for office, in 1978. He had no money, no name identification, and had never previously sought public office. But unlike his opponents, who refused to spend anything at all on TV advertising, Humphrey allocated almost 70 percent of his campaign budget to obtain exposure on expensive Boston television. Although only half of all New Hampshire voters watched television originating in Boston, Humphrey's commercials were still seen by a great many people who never saw any of his opponents on TV. Humphrey, like many of his Senate colleagues, won by exploiting the power of television. As former NRCC Communications Director Edward Blakely commented, "If I go on TV and my opponent doesn't, I'll win nine times out of ten."

It is virtually impossible to describe the "typical" political advertisement, because television advertising varies so widely in format. When campaign advertising initially began in the 1950s, many campaigns preferred longer advertisements that allowed more information to be presented. In the 1960s and 1970s, however, there was considerable use of minute-long commercials by statewide candidates. By the late 1970s, 30-second spots slowly began to dominate the airwaves, and are currently the most common commercial format. The old 5-minute commercials of the 1950s and 1960s have become too expensive to air, and are now primarily used for presidential candidates.

The latest trend in political advertising is the 10-second spot. Although the format usually limits the message to approximately twenty words, the 10-second advertisement costs about half as much as the standard 30-second commercial, which ad buyers say was 50 percent more expensive in 1986 than in the 1984 political season.[24] Using the same media budget, but running 10-second commercials in place of 30-second spots, can give the campaign twice the exposure in crowded primaries, where name recognition alone accounts for a significant percentage of the vote. Almost unheard of before 1982, "10s," as they are referred to in the trade, are so popular that many TV stations sold out their allotments early in the 1986 election season.[25]

Because of their brevity, most 10- and 30-second commercials employ gimmicks to capture the viewer's attention and interest. Humor, music, graphic designs, animation, all found in 30-second spots, are often used in the abbreviated 10-second commercial as well. Congressman Richard Shelby, in a tight race against Alabama Senator Jeremiah

Denton, developed a set of six 10-second advertisements that turned the election in his favor. In the middle of the screen was a picture of the smiling Denton. On one side was a large stack of dollar bills marked "Social Security;" on the other side, a small pile of bills marked "Denton's pay raise." In an instant, the money moves from the Social Security pile to the Denton's pay raise pile. "Again," the narrator says, "check the record." The same setup is repeated with five other issues. Jesse Helms used "10s" to damage opponent James Hunt seriously in the 1984 North Carolina Senate race. In his own voice, Helms rhetorically asked Hunt, "I support a balanced federal budget. Where do you stand, Jim?" And in another: "I oppose the Martin Luther King holiday. Where do you stand, Jim?" The repeated negative bursts against Hunt effectively shattered his favorable image, and contributed significantly to his defeat.

Some candidates still prefer the more conventional 30-second style, and even borrow themes and formats with a proven track record. "Every now and then I'll have a candidate come in and ask for the 'Gary Hart look,'" said Strother. "If they insist, I'll use it." Congressman Henson Moore, a candidate for the Louisiana Senate seat in 1986, not only borrowed the spirit of President Ronald Reagan's highly successful media campaign in 1984, but also took the signature line – "It's morning in Louisiana." New York Governor Mario Cuomo adopted another 1984 Reagan slogan, "Leadership that's working," in his 1986 re-election campaign. Democratic Senate candidate Thomas Daschle stole from the repertoire of Ronald Reagan (who stole from Jimmy Carter?) when he posed the question, "Are you better off today than you were six years ago?" Even in 1988, a campaign commercial for presidential candidate Jack Kemp began with a boy on a bicycle tossing a copy of the morning paper onto a front porch, just as a boy had done in a Reagan commercial, followed by a man running the American flag up a flagpole, again just like a Reagan spot.

Regardless of their length and style, all political commercials have a common goal – effective communication with potential voters. Ideally, a campaign's free media and paid media should mesh seamlessly, one reinforcing the other. With the professionalism developed in TV ads during recent elections, no medium offers a better means of communication than television. Although recent innovations in television advertising have blurred the once distinct styles of paid media, there still remains a number of well-defined techniques and formats for a typical, well-funded candidate to use. A decade ago, media consultants produced long, wordy advertising, occasionally interspersed with simplistic graphics or gimmicks. Today there are few rules, and some of the most successful political advertising has streched creativity to the limit in its use of unorthodox styles and techniques. The futuristic ads of the early 1980s, the "flip charts," "page wipes," and "revolving cubes," are commonplace today.

Political advertising on television has matured to the point where almost all campaigns use a predictable series of spots to achieve a variety of campaign goals. To faciliate an understanding of the style, substance, and purpose of television advertising in the election process, this author has divided political commercials into two major headings, *positive* and *negative*, with subclassifications under each, making it possible to recognize and classify nearly every ad produced in the most recent election cycle. The material that follows begins with the positive political commercials.

*The candidate recall spot*   The first obstacle faced by most candidates is overcoming low name recognition. It is universally accepted among consultants and their clients that television advertising has become the most successful means of quickly and effectively overcoming this hurdle. When Massachusetts Democrat Paul Tsongas ran for his party's US Senate nomination in 1978, he used clever advertisements centering on a small child's mispronunciation of his name. By using a child (always popular among voters) to create – and reinforce – favorable name identification in a crowded field of primary candidates, Tsongas was able to defeat better financed and, at first, better known opponents. Immediately after the primary, when name identification ceased to be a concern, that set of commercials was dropped in favor of more issue-oriented material. Republican Congressman Edward Zschau spent a sizeable proportion of his media budget in the 1986 California Senate primary, explaining how to pronounce (that is, remember) his name, a strategy that largely contributed to his victory over numerous competitors.

*The sainthood spot*   Frequently aired early in the campaign is a series of spots that are biographical in nature and devoted to celebrating the candidate's life story and accomplishments. The re-election campaign of Oklahoma Senator Donald Nickels produced a spot featuring his mother thumbing through an old family album as she talked about her son. "When Don was a boy, he showed great discipline and ideals" that gave him "the guts to stand up for what he believes." Texas Republican gubernatorial candidate William Clements appeared in several commercials wearing a Boy Scout leader's uniform, while voters were informed that he became an Eagle Scout when he was only thirteen years old.

*The traditional policy spot*   Once name recognition has been attained, the media consultant is then responsible for the construction of a positive image for the client. Using survey data, the media consultant (in cooperation with the pollster, the campaign manager, and the candidate) creates a series of advertisements that highlight particular issues or themes deemed most likely to increase public support. In as little as ten seconds, candidates promote their record of accomplishment along with vague proposals for new programs or solutions to old problems. Republican House incumbent Joseph Barton of Texas was portrayed in 1986 as the man who "fought for and got half a billion dollars, with millions more to come, money that will go towards educating our school children."

If the client is presentable, most media consultants will put the candidate himself on television (often referred to as the "talking head" spot) for greatest impact. The goal is to create, in the minds of the voters, a lasting favorable image, easy mental recall, and the association of the candidate with a popular theme or issue. New York Mayor Ed Koch was a media consultant's dream. His personality was perfectly suited for the rough and tumble world of New York City politics. Rather than employ images or gimmicks, media advisor David Garth just put Koch on television and let him do what he does best – talk about the issues:

My record in Congress is strongly pro-labor, but our municipal unions consider me anti-union. They don't like the fact that I want city employees to live in the city . . . that I want educators to account to the mayor for schools that don't teach . . . and that I don't want patrolmen to get two days off with pay for donating a pint of blood. . . . It's time we had a tough bargainer on our side of the table.

*The feel-good imagery spot*   Another weapon in the media consultant's arsenal is the imagery spot, a 30- or 60-second commercial devoid of all issues and substance. Its purpose is to appeal to feelings of American pride and community spirit, so as to link the candidate closely with the voters. A common method once used featured parades, marching bands, and flag-waving crowds of people cheering and waving to the candidate passing by. Today, such commercials are more subtle, and many give the impression of a travelogue, with strong emphasis on the landscapes and natural beauty of the particular state or community. In addition, some media consultants include original music and lyrics, specially composed to add originality and heighten the commercial's emotional appeal.

In the final weekend of the tightly fought Idaho Senate contest in 1986, the campaign of incumbent Senator Steve Symms pulled all his negative commercials off the air, choosing instead an ad that showed the candidate against backdrops of majestic mountains and amber waves of grain, with the campaign theme song's refrain, "I'm proud to be Idaho at heart," playing in the background. Not a single word was spoken in the entire 60-second ad. His opponent, Democratic Governor John B. Evans, ran commercials that treated viewers to images of the Sawtooth Mountains, lit up by the blush of dawn, or to the cascading Shoshone Falls, with a lone eagle soaring above. A song, done in Muzak melody, accompanied the images:

> Idaho, so beautiful
> So rugged, wild and free.
> Idaho, I want to see you be
> All that you can be.

Kent Conrad, running for the North Dakota Senate seat of Mark Andrews, was pictured against a backdrop of golden wheat fields, speaking of "a spirit in the people that says, 'Yes, we can.'" With the sun rising behind him, a smiling Henson Moore spoke directly into the camera: "In the early morning light, everything seems clean and new again. It's like nothing ever happened to spoil a sunrise. We in Louisiana share a wonderful life together." The imagery spot has become a standard item in the advertising campaign of most statewide candidates, both incumbents and challengers.

*The symbolism spot* Symbolism can be a powerful motivating factor in political advertising. More serious than the feel-good imagery spots and more emotional than the sainthood advertisements, symbolism commercials have a single, overriding theme that often attempts to motivate the viewer by using shame, disgust or some other negative emotion, although they are not negative ads. In the 1986 Maryland Democratic Senate primary, Attorney General Stephen Sachs and running mate Parren Mitchell, a leading black congressman, appeared in a commercial that featured the two clasping hands in slow motion as an announcer exhorted viewers to take advantage of an "uncommon opportunity" to vote for the Sachs–Mitchell ticket – at a time when racial tensions were increasing in the state. An even more powerful appeal was used in the Chicago mayoral election in 1983, when the campaign of Harold Washington used footage from the murders of both John and Robert Kennedy to illustrate "the occasions that most Americans are truly ashamed of." The ad ended with a scene showing white protesters hurling racial epithets and small projectiles at the black candidate – suggesting that Washington's defeat would be a victory for racists and an embarrassment for Chicago. The commercial enabled Washington to gain a small but critical percentage of white voters in his narrowly successful campaign.

*The testimonial* There are four types of testimonial ads. Candidates have often opted for the celebrity endorsement, filming well-known, well-liked personalities outside the political realm, in the hope that voters will transfer their good feelings for the star onto the candidate.

The most famous example is the popular movie actor who agreed to give a 28-minute nationally televised address on the eve of the 1964 presidential election, in support of Republican presidential candidate Barry Goldwater. Received by millions of conservatives with wild enthusiasm, that speech launched the career of then – private citizen and movie actor Ronald Reagan. In 1986, President Reagan was called on by dozens of candidates to appear in their commercials and address viewers. Actor Charlton Heston appeared in the commercials of several candidates, and in late 1986, presidential hopeful Pat Robertson used a page from the past when he enlisted Roy Rogers and Dale Evans in a $200,000 media campaign to drum up popular support for his White House bid.

A second testimonial format features the endorsement of respected politicians. Political endorsements are a popular vehicle, particularly for incumbents, and are used to demonstrate a candidate's power and clout in Washington. The 1986 Cranston Senate campaign in California shot a commercial highlighting Cranston's achievements in government, using testimonials from highly respected Senate colleagues like Edward Kennedy, Gary Hart, and Sam Nunn to make the case. Florida Congressman Claude Pepper, the oldest and one of the most popular members of Congress, gave Florida Senate candidate Robert Graham and numerous congressional hopefuls a boost in their campaigns by filming endorsement spots that began airing at a crucial point, just two weeks before election day. Graham's media consultant, Robert Squier, claims that a perceived relationship with a popular politician can be worth as much as five percentage points.

One of the oldest and, historically, most effective TV testimonials is called the "man-on-the-street" (MOTV), designed to demonstrate support for a particular candidate among "average" voters. Individuals appear on screen for several seconds, praising the candidate's character, policy positions, leadership or some other attribute. Unknown to the home viewers, however, is the fact that nearly all MOTV spots employ preselected individuals, such as friends of the candidate or loyal party workers, and are not a random selection from the populace. Of the media firms included in this book, only one, Bailey/Deardourff/Sipple, offered that they actually used random selection for man-on-the-street spots.

The format for the fourth and newest testimonial resembles a "mini-docudrama," in which a single individual recounts for the audience how the candidate, singlehandedly, improved the quality of life for the speaker and the community in general. Consultant Robert Goodman, who claims authorship of this format, first used it in the 1984 re-election campaign of Mississippi Senator Thad Cochoran. In 1986, Mark Andrews, a Goodman client, ran a commercial featuring a mother with a crippled child. Praising Andrews for setting up a rural health program, the mother says, "Until Mark Andrews introduced his CARS program, Ellie and I would take the train to Minneapolis for the necessary treatments. Thirteen hours each way. It was brutal." Another Goodman client, Henson Moore, also featured grateful constituents. A teacher whose school burned down tells of Moore's promise: "'Don't worry, I'll get the money to build a new one,' he said. 'And he did.'"

*The image alteration spot*　One of the most difficult tasks in electoral politics is to alter or eliminate a negative impression of a candidate. This is particularly true for incumbents. Media consultants are often called on to remake a candidate's image to save him from defeat. It can take weeks of strategy and the use of every tool, gimmick, and technique available. A candidate's age, health, residency, length of political service, voting record, and many other facts about him can be used by opponents to discredit his candidacy in the minds of the voters. At the same time, although it cannot always work miracles, television advertising can also be used to blunt such attacks, and has allowed candidates, in the words of Charlie Black, to "out-shout any negative press coverage."26 By doing so, it has turned electorally marginal candidates into senators, governors, and congressmen. It has also turned many an ordinary media advisor into a political "guru."

No candidate in the history of politics has, thus far, spent as much money, per voter, on television advertising as West Virginia Senator John D. Rockefeller IV. Successfully tagged with the label "carpetbagger," a charge almost impossible to refute because of his New York roots, Rockefeller was defeated in his first attempt for governor, in 1972. In the subsequent race four years later, his campaign blanketed the state with television advertising, a first for West Virginia. This time, the sheer number of television commercials and his constant references to his association with the state successfully eliminated his previous carpetbagger image. He spent $9 million of his own money, most of it on television, to win re-election in 1980, and another $13 million in his successful campaign for the US Senate in 1984, again depending on lengthy, expensive media blitzes to provide him with votes. In fact, in the 1980 and 1984 campaigns, Rockefeller set new standards in media saturation by advertising on television stations well outside West Virginia, including some as far away as Washington, DC. Never in the history of electioneering has a candidate gone to such great lengths to have his television advertising seen by as many potential voters as possible.

Altering the elitist image of Kit Bond, a Missouri Senate candidate in 1986, was only a matter of filming the candidate in a checkered sport shirt, speaking directly to sympathetic voters, instead of addressing impersonal crowds in a business suit. (During a trip to a Missouri state fair where Mr Bond, formerly a lawyer, was going to film some campaign commercials, the candidate took off his dress shirt and tie in the car and put on a homespun, meant-for-television plaid shirt – with the price tag still visible on it.)

Often, the key component in changing a candidate's image is simply the tag line at the end of a political commercial. When polls showed that Iowans disliked Washington politicians and were more likely to support for political office a local Iowan farmer than someone in any other occupation, 1980 Senate candidate Charles Grassley adopted "A man of the soil. Chuck Grassley – He works for Iowa" as the tag line for every campaign commercial. The gimmick removed the tarnish of his having been in Congress, and identified him instead with what Iowans respected the most.

A candidate's age can be a major campaign issue, particularly when the candidate is considerably younger or older than the opponent. In recent years, television advertising has emerged as the only effective outlet for alleviating voter doubt or concern about a candidate's ability to govern. Many voters initially thought North Dakota Senator Milton Young (1974) and South Carolina Senator Strom Thurmond (1978) were too old to represent their respective states effectively, leading their opponents to turn the election into a referendum on their ability to govern. But Young and Thurmond turned the debate to their own advantage, using television advertising to show Young splitting a block of wood with a karate chop and Thurmond sliding down a fire station pole, both of them more active than many people twenty years their junior. The strategy was simplistic, yet the sight (repeated day after day) of these men engaged in strenuous activities muted the age issue, and thus insured their victory.

The controlled environment of television advertising allows a campaign to address difficult issues without the possibility of any unforeseen, and potentially dangerous, variables which might occur in a press conference or a news interview. Yet television has also created a sense of immediacy among voters, who have grown to expect, if not demand, that serious allegations be answered promptly. Candidates that refuse to respond are no longer considered innocent until proven guilty. While campaigning for the 1980 Republican primary, New York Senator Jacob Javits chose to ignore repeated charges (including several paid political advertisements) by his opponent that he was too old and his health too poor for him to merit re-election. Instead of defending his health, Javits stressed his lengthy Washington experience. Post-primary polling indicated that the age issue scared away thousands of voters that would have otherwise voted for Javits, and cost him the nomination. Elderly Washington Senator Warren Magnuson, aware of the Javits results, chose a different tactic to convince voters of his capabilities. Stressing his leadership position in the US Senate, Magnuson endeavored to make age an advantage. "I may be old," concluded Magnuson in his television advertisement, "but the meeting doesn't start until I get there." However, television does not require, and often does not reward, the direct approach. Like Javits, Magnuson lost.

There are some images that even the best crafted television advertising cannot erase. "In the history of the United States, we have had twelve Presidents who previously served as generals in the Army," began a commercial for former Secretary of State and presidential candidate Alexander Haig. "In the history of the United States, there have been eight wars and not a single one of them started when a former general was President." Haig directly addressed the concern of many Americans about military figures in politics, but it had no effect on his public standing. Former Deleware Governor and multimillionaire Pete duPont knew that any attempt by his presidential campaign to deny his wealth image would appear phony, so he refused to shed his usual shirt and tie for his campaign commercials. Instead, he appeared in full color, with the other candidates shown in small black-and-white photographs. The stark contrast was visually effective, but duPont continued to fare poorly in public opinion polls.

If there is a single trend apparent today in political marketing, it is the increasing proportion of negative political advertising. Going on the offensive – attack politics – is becoming more common because, while vicious and distasteful, its effectiveness cannot be denied. Candidates, like Senator George Mitchell, former chairman of the Democratic Senatorial Campaign Committee, agree: "[I'm] afraid negative advertising is being used because it works."[27] Two telling demonstrations were provided in 1986, one by a leading media consultant and the other by a US senator. John Deardourff, media advisor to Pennsylvania gubernatorial candidate Bill Scranton, was instrumental in his client's decision to forego negative advertising in the final two weeks of the campaign. Said Deardourff at that time: "It is still too early to tell whether this will affect the campaign one way or the other. It may either change the direction of major campaigns in the future, or it may prove the validity of negative advertising."[28] Deardourff's candidate lost. In the second instance, former National Republican Senatorial Committee Chairman John Heinz, two-term senator from Pennsylvania, said just days before the 1986 election, "If we retain Republican control of the Senate in spite of the wave of some of the most vicious, negative advertising, it will prove negative advertising isn't the answer."[29] His party lost eight seats and control of the Senate. For many candidates, negative advertising has proven to be the answer.

Even though some consultants prefer the terms "comparative" or "issue-oriented" to describe negative advertisements, the purpose remains the same – to discredit the opponents to such a degree that the voters will reject their candidacy. Many consultants believe there is a certain dissatisfaction level, where enough voters have such an "unfavorable" impression of the candidate that he cannot hope to succeed. In 1985, Stuart Rothenberg, director of the Free Congress Research and Education Foundation, described the most effective method for reaching that level: "To defeat an incumbent, a challenger who is employing a negative contrast with his opponent must do so in strong enough terms and with enough repetition and volume to make the voters first uncomfortable with the status quo, and then willing to support someone else."[30]

Negative campaigning is not new to the political process. Early politicians were renowned for their vicious personal attacks on some politicians now revered in history, George Washington for one. From the mid-nineteenth century through the elections of Franklin Roosevelt, it was common to hear blatant falsehoods being spread by opposing candidates. Accusations of corruption, dishonesty, and even illegitimate children and treason were disseminated in pamphlets or from the stump. Candidates were also easy prey for the sharp pens of the day's cartoonists and satirists. But from the late 1940s onward, political opponents were more likely to trade occasional jabs rather than bludgeon each other to death. Although television advertising was used by an increasing number of candidates through the 1960s and 1970s, negative advertising was not particularly prevalent. It was generally believed that attack advertisements were a high-risk tactic, prone to backfire, and for a time the closest any candidate got to a negative advertisement was to pronounce himself superior to his opponent. Rarely did a candidate use paid political advertising to challenge his opponent on specific issues. Negative advertising did not become commonplace until the current decade. As Charles Guggenheim noted, "There has always been nastiness in politics, but the floodgates are open now."[31]

Not only has the use of negative ads increased, but their style and substance has been radically altered in the most recent election cycles. "Since the dawn of political advertising on television," wrote the *Washington Post* in 1986, "it's been a rule of thumb that the best way to attack is with surrogates, that the candidates' hands should be kept clean."[32] However, according to a recent viewer reaction study by William Feltus, head of the Washington office of Market Opinion Research, if the candidate puts his face on camera, "the credibility of the attack goes way up."[33] According to pollster Edward Mellmon, studies in research psychology indicate that people process negative information more deeply than positive information. "When we ask people about negative ads, they'll say they don't like them. But that's not the point. The point is that they absorb the information."[34] Paul Maslin, Democratic pollster and advocate of "comparative" politics, believes that people actually want more information – even if it is negative:

Here we had this brand new tool, television, it was so potent that we got duped into thinking that if we just showed a candidate with his jacket off and flashing a nice smile, that would be enough. Now I think we're finding more and more that the electorate wants a choice; they aren't going to make decisions until they have seen comparative information.[35]

It is quite obvious that as election day approaches, negative advertising increases. Nevertheless, a *New York Times* study in August 1986 found that voters in eleven of the thirty-four states with Senate elections had already been exposed to some form of attack advertisements from one candidate or both – seventy days before the election.[36] According to Deardourff, candidates feel they "can't afford to sit back and wait until the first punch is thrown." Bob Squier agreed: "There are some campaigns where, although you are a front runner, you look at your numbers and you realize that the election could move away from you very quickly. You may have an undefined opponent who could define himself in a way that could be very tough on your candidate, so we decide to define him ourselves." Some campaigns feel there is no alternative but to use negative ads. As the campaign manager for Republican Senate candidate Ed Zschau remarked to reporters, "We found that our positive ads had no impact at all, so we switched."[37] Another important finding of the Feltus study was that roughly 50 percent of all Senate advertising in 1984 was negative or comparative, and that the ratio was surely higher in 1986.[38] By contrast, only 5 percent of commercial advertisers use comparative information. Successful 1986 Senate candidates Alan Cranston (California), Richard Shelby (Alabama), and Wyche Fowler (Georgia) used about 80 to 90 percent of their TV time to run negative commercials against their opponents.[39] Several other successful Senate candidates in 1986 had equally high negative ratios.

Former Senator Thomas Eagleton, who chose to retire in 1986 rather than face another difficult re-election campaign, blamed the consultants, not voter behavior, for the rise in negative campaigning. "It's getting worse every year – the inevitable result of the increasing pre-eminence of television in the election process. The campaign people try to squeeze the most impact they can in 30 seconds, and that usually means a slam on the other person."[40] Nevertheless, Eagleton did not disagree that negative advertising, and little of anything else, has propelled unknown candidates into the lead against better known opponents and even well-established incumbents, and that a major reason for the growth of negative advertising is its success in elevating challengers into office. "A challenger who does not attack during the campaign has little chance of ousting all but the most incompetent or corrupt incumbent," concluded Stuart Rothenberg.[41] In August 1986, Alabama Senator Jeremiah Denton held a 25-point lead over Congressman Richard Shelby, but after two months of Shelby's unceasing negative spots, that lead had shrunk to just seven points. On election day, Shelby defeated the incumbent by less than 1 percent, ending his campaign as it had begun – negatively. Said Shelby's media consultant, "These ads are the reason we have been able to close the gap."[42]

Incumbents have a significant advantage in name recognition, fundraising, and other aspects of campaigning that can lead to re-election. Challengers are, therefore, forced to find other forms of leverage to increase their chances. The logic of politics usually requires the challenger to use any means available to point out what is wrong with the status quo – and to blame it all on the incumbent. Political scientist Gary Jacobson suggested that, "In the search for campaign issues, challengers are necessarily opportunists. It is a matter of exploiting the incumbent's mistakes – neglect of the district, personal lapses, a string of 'bad' votes. . . ."[43] Challengers are often unable to generate enough free publicity to lure the incumbent into battle. Negative advertising is, therefore, often the only way to force the incumbent into battle, even if it is only to deny the malicious allegations of the challenger.

According to interviews with leading consultants, when incumbents are forced to use negative advertising, it is often a sign of perceived vulnerability. Candidates, particularly incumbents, are usually hesitant to respond to negative advertising with negative advertising. These same consultants also acknowledged that the number of incumbents they encourage to turn to negative advertising grows with each election cycle, and they explained why. In the past, the first rule of incumbency was to ignore your opposition. At a 1984 NCPAC candidate training school, leading pollster Arthur Finkelstein advised the participants, "Why give an unknown opponent free publicity!" But when challengers, particularly statewide candidates, have sufficient funding and are using their campaign cash on effective campaign advertising, they rarely will remain unknown for long. It is no longer difficult for most Senate candidates, through television advertising, to achieve a threshold of recognition at which voters begin to take notice of their campaign and message. Today, well-funded challengers, using paid political advertising, can compete with the incumbent on a more equal footing than was possible a decade ago. Consequently, it is now to the incumbent's advantage, particularly when the challenger appears to have significant financial backing, to define the race (that is, the issues and personalities involved) before the challenger does. Said media consultant David Doak on the eve of the 1986 elections, "If you don't use negative ads, and your opponent does, it's a sure way to lose." Hence the rise of incumbents using negative advertising.

As with the positive campaign spots, negative advertising can also be broken down into several distinct categories.

*The general negative spot*  The most common theme of a negative ad, particularly among challengers, is the opponent's record of service. A candidate's controversial votes while in office, statements to the press or to public audiences, are all fair game, and especially so in modern politics. Although usually straightforward, most commercials of this type generally end with a hook or twist, the "tag line," in an effort to catch the viewers' attention and increase recall. When James Santini, formerly a Democratic Congressman, announced his intention to seek the Nevada Senate seat in 1986 as a Republican, no one criticized his opponent, Harry Reid, for running attack commercials that ended with the tag line, ". . . now a Republican, at least until November." Santini later responded with a, "Now that's dirty, Harry," ad campaign. Oklahoma Congressman James Jones tried tapping the emotions of angry farmers by highlighting his opponent's vote against emergency farm credit, yet ended the ad with humour: ". . . And finally, I'll have more time each day to work on Oklahoma's problems. Because I won't need one of these." Jones, almost completely bald, then switched on a hair dryer.

While voters in Pennsylvania listened to a lengthy discourse of senator Arlen Spector's "record," they also watched a bust of the Senator crumble into pieces with the announcer remarking that he was "not all he's cracked up to be." During this ad's run, Spector's opponent gained fifteen points. In North Carolina, where voters had endured a bitter $25 million negative campaign waged by Senator Jesse Helms and Governor James Hunt in 1984, the attack ads in the 1986 Senate race had almost an apologetic tone. "I just hope it's a clean campaign," says a woman in an ad for Senator James Broyhill. "They're both nice people." But the ad then goes on to attack Broyhill's opponent, Terry Sanford, as a tax-and-spend liberal.

When the individual under attack is mainly an adminstrator with a less defined record, such as a big-city mayor or a state governor, media consultants have more leeway to be aggressive. The commercials are often more creative, and the attacks and tag lines more vicious. "Can the man who drove Pittsburgh to its knees put Pennsylvania back on its feet?" became the media slogan for Republican gubernatorial candidate Dick Thornburgh in his successful 1978 battle against former Pittsburgh Mayor Pete Flaherty. Thornburgh's media consultant designed a series of hard-hitting spots, hammering away at his opponent's questionable performance as mayor of Pittsburgh, and frightening voters from other areas of the state into voting Republican. The press, and some in the public, severely criticized the Thornburgh campaign for what seemed an excessively tough approach, but survey data confirmed its effectiveness in swaying undecided voters away from Flaherty. A similar hysteria (and outcome) was whipped up by the 1987 re-election campaign of Philadelphia Mayor Wilson Goode. More than

90 percent of Goode's paid media was designed to blacken opponent former Mayor Frank Rizzo's reputation. One particularly harsh ad assailed Rizzo's tenure as "a mayor out of control. . . . He tore our city apart once. . . . Can we afford Frank Rizzo again?"

*The flip-flop*    One of the oldest negative formats in television advertising scours the opponent's voting record and public statements, and then goes on to present a series of the apparent inconsistencies, preferably on controversial or embarrassing issues. A sequence of five 10-second spots dramatized Illinois Senator Charles Percy's political shift from moderate to conservative, in 1984, by asking where he stood on Social Security, the B-1 bomber, and other issues, while viewers saw a check written in a box labeled "yes" – and then again in another marked "no."

The major flip-flop innovation in 1986, however, was in the individuals who employed this style of commercial. Almost exclusively utilized by challengers up to then, no candidate invested more time and money in negative advertising, and the flip-flop style, than incumbent Senator Alan Cranston in that year's California Senate race. Cranston unleashed a barrage of negative commercials against opponent Edward Zschau the day after Zschau's victory in the Republican primary. Called "flip-flop updates," they featured two photos of Zschau, one facing left, the other right, with the words "Zschau vs. Zschau" superimposed between them. The ads contend that Zschau voted two different ways on aid to the Contras, South African divestment, nuclear test bans, and several other controversial issues. They struck a nerve, and helped Cranston to a 20-point lead in the polls. Throughout the summer and into the fall, the Democratic candidate never let up, continually hammering away at his opponent's credibility. In one particularly clever ad, the Cranston campaign parodied a television mail-order "greatest hits" advertisement, complete with song titles scrolling up the screen while the gravel-voiced narrator makes the pitch. The titles included "Zschau Bop Flip-Flop," "Yes, No, Maybe," "Say Anything," and "How Many Times can a Man Change his Mind?" The Cranston ad, which concluded, ". . . on November 4th, the Zschau song and dance comes to an end," was specifically targeted at younger voters who had been trending toward voting Republican. It proved very effective as a last-minute criticism of Zschau, without causing much backlash against Cranston's own candidacy.

*Compare and contrast negative*    In the 1960s and 1970s, most negative adverstising was of the compare and contrast variety, clearly illustrating, in a matter of fact manner, where a candidate and the opponent disagreed on various issues and in philosophy. Despite the current trend toward personal attacks and exaggeration, a large percentage of negative advertising is still legitimately comparative. Specific issues or votes are listed on the screen while an announcer informs the viewer of each candidate's position. An ad for North Dakota Senate candidate Kent Conrad claimed, "While one candidate was voting to cut Social Security, the other was working to keep Social Security from being taxed. While one candidate was voting to cut wheat prices, the other was advocating policies to raise farm commodity market prices."

South Dakota Democrat Tom Daschle went a step further in his successful 1986 race against incumbent Senator Jim Abdnor. Daschle's media consultant was able to film both candidates covertly as they spoke before a gathering of farmers at the South Dakota State Fair. A commercial was then produced with actual clips of the two candidates and their contrasting viewpoints on the farming problem. The carefully edited spot made Daschle appear better equipped to handle agricultural issues than Abdnor. "That advertisement may have been the most important reason for my defeat," Abdnor concluded after the election.

*Not-on-the-job*   First used by S. I. Hayakawa in his successful battle against incumbent California Senator John Tunney in 1976, and later by the National Conservative Political Action Committee to defeat entrenched Nevada Senator Howard Cannon in 1982, the attendance record of incumbent legislators has occasionally been the focus of negative advertising. In a particularly ingenious series of ads during the 1984 elections, Kentucky Senator Walter Huddleston, a supposedly safe incumbent, was defeated by a long-shot but gutsy challenger named Mitch McConnell. Although leading his opponent by forty points in most polls, Huddleston was unseated solely because of a pair of commercials, among the most original and effective in political history, both featuring a pack of barking hound dogs and a rustic farmer. The first spot shows the leashed dogs pulling the harried farmer along as he carries a photograph of the missing senator. The agitated farmer pauses several times to ask various passers-by "Where's Senator Huddleston?" A Huddleston look-alike starred in the second spot, which was aired several months later. The Huddleston look-alike is seen racing down hills and right through a coffee shop in a desperate attempt to keep ahead of the farmer and the hound dogs. The commercial ends with the Huddleston look-alike stuck up a tree, dogs barking below, and the vengeful farmer exclaiming, "We've got you now, Senator Huddleston."[44]

In a less humourous vein, Pennsylvania gubernatorial candidate Robert Casey criticized opponent William Scranton, son of a former Pennsylvania governor, for missing a large number of meetings of public organizations over which he presided, including the Pennsylvania State Senate: "They gave him the job because of his father's name," said the ads, "The least he could do is show up for work." In 1986, a year of political innovation, Richard Shelby criticized Alabama Senator Jeremiah Denton, not for being absent from Washington, but for being absent from Alabama. The narrator claimed that Denton "comes home rarely . . . tells us he's too busy to see us . . . get's angry when we ask him why. . . . What could Senator Denton be hiding from?"

*Negative-on-positive*   The 1986 election cycle saw the emergence of campaign commercials themselves as a popular subject for campaign commercials. Since television has come to dominate the election process, it was only a matter of time before the candidates and their consultants would realize that even an opponent's campaign commercials were targets for attack. In particular, commercials that claimed an opponent's commercials to be inaccurate proved to be very effective at destabilizing and discrediting the opponent's campaign. A brief commercial by Robert Graham, discrediting a claim made in a Paula Hawkins commercial, all but destroyed her credibility on an issue closely associated with her campaign: "Paula Hawkins has claimed that in 1982 she met with Chinese leader Deng Xiaoping about stopping drug exports from China. Now we have learned that two of Hawkins's own aides admit the meeting never took place. . . . If the people who work for Paula Hawkins now say they don't believe her, how can we?"

*Negative-on-negative*   There is an unwritten rule that when a candidate resorts to extreme negative advertising, he had better be prepared to face a similar barrage of attacks. Sooner or later, an offending ad is repackaged by the other side as an object lesson about the character flaws of the attacker. Thus, a common characteristic of negative advertising in general, and negative-on-positive in particular, is that it usually yields an even more negative response: "negative-on-negative." Such races are interesting to watch from a technological perspective, as new levels of creativity are often set, but voters tend to be less than impressed with attacks, counterattacks, and counter-counterattacks.

Three 1986 Senate races clearly illustrate the back-'n'-forth nature of negative advertising. The most expensive race took place in Florida, where incumbent Senator Paula Hawkins accused Governor Bob Graham of lying about her voting record on drugs, and he accused her of distorting his record on crime. In the Hawkins ad, while the screen shows a silhouette of a couple watching Graham's negative commercial, the announcer reads:

There's an ad on TV that tells us who the real Bob Graham is. It is so false, you wonder why it was allowed on the air. He tries to make it seem that Paula Hawkins opposed money for the Coast Gaurd and for drug education. Those statements are false. . . . Now if Bob Graham is trying to make Paula Hawkins look soft on drugs, *on drugs*, what in the world will he do next?

The Graham ad that the Hawkins campaign referred to had questioned her votes on several pieces of legislation that contained many items, among them funding for the Coast Guard and for drug education programs. Graham's commercial had presented a narrow, biased view of Hawkins's record, which her campaign sought to exploit.

The campaign of Harriet Woods, Democratic Senate candidate from Missouri, came upon a farming couple whose mortgage on their farm had just been foreclosed by an insurance company on whose board sat Republican opponent Kit Bond. Thinking he had found the key to victory, Woods's media consultant Robert Squier edited interviews with the couple, including a scene where the couple broke into sobs while talking about their lost dairy herd. The three-part set of commercials met with the full approval of the candidate.

Bond's campaign team was initially crushed by the powerful ads, but after completing several focus group interviews that indicated a degree of voter distaste for the harsh attack, a strategy was formulated to criticize the Woods campaign for "gutter politics" and to encourage critical articles about the commercials in the news media. In a subsequent interview with a local reporter the farming couple were quoted as saying, "I kind of felt like we had been used [by the Woods campaign]." Bond's staff, masterfully, had the article distributed across the state. The growing outcry against Woods was enormous, and she responded by firing her media consultant. Bond's media consultant then produced the first of several negative-on-negative spots, featuring critical news clippings about the Woods commercials. "Almost as sad as a family losing its farm," said the announcer, "is a politician using their pain for political purposes." By using the press clippings to make the point, and not Bond himself, the damage was enormous.

The Woods camp then produced an equally harsh response ad: "He couldn't take the truth about his ties to a company foreclosing on family farms," read the narration. "So, Kit," the ad concluded, "we're going to fight your mud-slinging with a political tactic you might find amazing. It's called the truth." Still later, the Bond campaign ran negative, man-on-the-street (MOTV) testimonial ads, complete with a comment from one woman who called Woods, "a little bit of a mudslinger," and another who claimed, "I haven't heard anything positive [from her yet]." After facing intense criticisms for her ads, Woods retaliated by using actual excerpts from Bond's ads to accuse him of distorting the facts and misrepresenting her advertisements. In the end, Bond was victorious.

But the viciousness of Missouri was mild in comparison with the 1986 Wisconsin Senate race. When Senate Democratic candidate Edward Garvey accused incumbent Senator Robert Kasten of "drinking on the job," in reference to the Senator's arrest for driving while intoxicated, Kasten responded by airing a commercial that began: "What would you think of a candidate who pays thousands of dollars to someone who impersonates a reporter and spreads lies about his opponent?" and accused Garvey of a "return to Watergate politics." Garvey had indeed hired a professional investigator, who falsely identified himself as an independent reporter so he could snoop into Kasten's legal and financial affairs. The bad publicity undermined Garvey's candidacy far more than the drunk driving charge hurt Kasten. Garvey's response, a television commercial that said, "The question for Wisconsin is Bob Kasten, and the answer is no," was received poorly by the public and press. In fact, the charges and counter-charges caused the *Wall Street Journal* to write, "The fog is thick on Lake Michigan but not as thick as the mud being slung in this state's Senate race."[45] In the end, Kasten's campaign was highly successful in actively responding to his opponent's negative advertising.

*Defensive-negative*   Consultants have also learned how to turn some negative advertising against their client into a plus for his campaign, but in a more passive fashion than the strict, negative-on-negative style. There are a number of cases in which negative advertising has actually benefited the maligned candidate, and where defensive-negative advertising has fostered a "sympathy vote" for the attacked candidate that otherwise would not have existed. William Scranton, 1986 Pennsylvania gubernatorial candidate, received nationwide publicity for his decision to abandon negative advertising, and sought to capitalize on this attention with an ad that said: "Win or lose, there will be no more negative ads from my campaign. Mudslinging is not leadership. I intend to give you the kind of campaign, the kind of leadership you deserve." He had thus set himself on the high road, while at the same time implying that his opponent, who refused to modify his own attacks on Scranton, was a mudslinger.

Two other examples of candidates adopting defensive-negative strategies were Ken Kramer and Tom Kean. Kramer, the 1986 Republican candidate for US Senate in Colorado, built an entire campaign around his poor media image, complete with TV ads admitting his inability to make a slick TV commercial. These "not slick, just good," ads were designed to gain sympathy following attacks by his more photogenic opponent, Congressman Tim Wirth.

Tom Kean, the leading contender for the New Jersey Republican nomination for governor in 1981, became the focus of negative advertising by several of his opponents. Since it was impossible to refute every charge made by every opponent, Kean counterattacked with a generic defensive-negative commercial specifically designed to encourage a sympathy vote in favor of his candidacy – and making him look like the underdog fighting against a multitude of "mud-slinging" enemies. As the audio portion of the ad described, in emotional terms, the unfair treatment Kean was receiving from the other candidates, the visual showed piles of mud being slung at, and eventually covering, a full-screen picture of Tom Kean. The commercial ended with the mud slowly disappearing, Kean's face gradually reappearing, and the announcer declaring that all charges against Kean were false and so the slate had been wiped clean. The ad was passive in that it did not name names or deal with any particular charges, but it was, nevertheless, effective in blunting the negative advertising of his opponents.


*The-hit-and-run*  Just as candidates will attempt to identify themselves with individuals who are popular in the eyes of the public, they will also attempt to identify their opponents with unpopular people − a sort of anti-endorsement. Often, the unpopular person is entirely peripheral to the election. One of the major strategies behind hit-and-run advertising, and the reason why it is often saved for the final days of a campaign, is to prevent an opponent from responding properly to the allegations before voters go to the polls. An extreme example in 1986 was South Dakota Senator James Abdnor's criticism of his opponent, late in the campaign, because he had invited actress Jane Fonda to testify before a House Agriculture Committee hearing. Fonda, the advertisement said, "has been identified with more radical causes than almost anyone in America." Said Abdnor in defense of the ad, "This lady has not exactly been a positive force for America. She deserved that." The public apparently agreed. Abdnor gained almost ten points in the public opinion polls during the telelvision life of the Fonda spot.

In a similar attempt in the 1986 California race, Republican Ed Zschau ended several commercials with the line: "Alan Cranston consistently opposes the death penalty. Maybe that's why he doesn't oppose Rose Bird." Rose Bird, who was chief justice of the state Supreme Court, had overturned every death penalty conviction that had come before her. She was also the most unpopular political figure in the state, and so the Zschau ad sought to tap into the intense public feeling against her. One of North Dakota Senator Mark Andrews's ads sought to link his opponent with unpopular Senator Edward Kennedy by featuring the endorsement of his opponent by a noted left-wing publication, *The Village Voice*: "a voting guide for liberals," the ad said, whose purpose is to secure a Democratic-controlled Senate which would "guarantee that Teddy Kennedy will be the next chairman of the Senate Judiciary Committee. ... Let's not give New York or Massachusetts another senator." In the 1988 Republican presidential primaries, candidate Jack Kemp produced an ad in which a full-face color portrait of former Democratic President Jimmy Carter magically metamorphosed into George Bush − much like Lon Chaney turning into the werewolf − while the announcer compared Carter's attack on Kemp's economic policies to that of George Bush.

Although often overlooked by political journals and the press, particularly in this decade, there are numerous candidates who, with the assistance, if not encouragement, of paid media consultants and pollsters, have inadvertently managed to destroy their own candidacies by the improper use of television advertising. "Television is not a neutral medium," claimed a leading Republican pollster. "It can help, but it can also hurt. We've run into cases where candidates have spent over fifty thousand dollars on a single ad, and every time it ran, they actually *lost* support." Even some of the most respected (and expensive) advisors have been accused of producing material damaging to their own clients, though their candidates often have no one to blame but themselves. Former political media consultant Charles Guggenheim singled out (it is not uncommon for media consultants to criticize others in the profession) the previously described 1986 Missouri senate race. Said Guggenheim about his equally renowned colleague: "Bob Squier is not a political novice, yet he practically destroyed his candidate out there. Why didn't he know better? Why didn't she [Harriet Woods] know better?"

Most pollsters surveyed for this book routinely pre-test attack ads written for their clients. Some pollsters even post-test ads as well, by arranging for selected viewers to watch the ad on television at home, then phoning them a few days later to probe their recall. Consultants agree that commercials considered by voters to be in bad taste can undermine even the most credible and well-organized campaign, regardless of whether the opposition wages a counterattack. Yet current testing techniques still cannot prevent the occasional self-damaging attack advertisement from slipping through. Negative advertising has by no means been developed to the stage where it entails no risk to the user.

What was probably the most infamous and self-damaging commercial of the 1982 elections occurred in the highly charged California Senate race. Used by Governor (and favorite) Jerry Brown against opponent Pete Wilson, it featured controversial pro-nuclear freeze advertisements that overtly resembled those used by Lyndon Johnson against Barry Goldwater in 1964. Both the audio and video switched from a nuclear bomb explosion to the earnest face of a young boy who pleaded, "I want to go on living." The commercial ended with a female voice saying, "Jerry Brown supports a nuclear freeze. Pete Wilson doesn't. Vote for Jerry Brown, as if your life depends on it." Voter resentment against this obvious and crude emotional pitch caused Brown's popularity to drop sharply immediately after the airing of the advertisement, and its run had to be prematurely cut because of the massive voter backlash. Brown's election momentum had been shattered, and he was never again to lead his opponent in the polls.

A similar situation manifested itself in the Tennessee Senate race where Robin Beard's strong challenge to incumbent James Sasser was dealt an early and fatal blow after Beard ran a particularly foolish negative advertisement. An actor dressed to look like Fidel Castro thanked "Senor Sasser," shown lighting a Cuban cigar with American currency, for supporting foreign aid, particularly aid to countries friendlier to Castro than to America. But voters in Tennessee were unmoved and unamused, and Beard found himself under sustained attack for the commercial. Sasser capitalized on Beard's blunder, drawing attention to the ad at every possible occasion, and coasted on to a landslide victory.

Personal attacks can pack a powerful punch, but they can just as easily knock out the proponent of the attack as the opponent. A personal attack directed at a popular incumbent by a relatively unknown and underfinanced candidate for New York governor in 1986 did the individual far more harm than good. Republican Andrew O'Rourke, campaigning against Governor Mario Cuomo, ran a commercial that began: "An apology to Emperor Cuomo. We apologize for disturbing you with our invitation to debate. We only thought that since Presidents Reagan and Carter and Ford took the time to debate the issues with their opponents, you would, too. But we were forgetting they were only presidents. And you have already elevated yourself a good deal beyond that." The financially starved O'Rourke campaign had less than $100,000 with which to air the commercial, and according to the *New York Post*, "Campaign people generally believe four times that much money is needed to make a dent in the public consciousness."[46] Yet polls conducted shortly after the running of his commercials showed there had been movement in O'Rourke's support – downwards. Among those who had not seen the commercials, 10 percent held a favorable view of O'Rourke, while 18 percent had a negative impression. But among those who had seen the commercial, only 7 percent had a favorable view of O'Rourke, compared with a noticeably high 26 percent who viewed him negatively.[47] As Cuomo's campaign manager said in response, "We believe from the beginning that O'Rourke's campaign made a basic tactical error by airing such purely negative commercials. It looks to us like a classic case of an individual . . . attacking someone whom the voters hold in high regard."[48]

Richard Snelling, the Republican Senate candidate from Vermont in 1986, was not restricted by the financial limitations that faced O'Rourke. His campaign advisors were among the best in the business, and his attacks on his opponent were far more issue-related. Yet, his loss, like O'Rourke's, was also of landslide proportions. Snelling, former Vermont governor, saw whatever hopes he had for victory dashed by a series of negative spots against incumbent Patrick Leahy. It is one of the rare examples of a sophisticated, well-planned, well-orchestrated strategy that, nevertheless, quickly backfired. Snelling's media team pre-tested, using the latest techniques, several potential new ads before a small group of undecided voters. The ads, focusing on Leahy's attendance and voting record, were no more negative than those that had been prepared for other Senate candidates that year. However, several members of the pre-test group were so offended by what they saw that they notified the Leahy campaign, which immediately called a news conference and denounced the ads before they had even been aired. Leahy quickly put defensive negative ads on the air that countered the charges, and effectively made Snelling the "bad guy" in the Vermont race. "I don't know about the other states," Leahy said later, "but in Vermont, negative ads hurt [my opponent] more than they did me."[49]

Poorly detailed research and improper execution can be disastrous in efforts to tinker with a candidate's image – even in positive spots. Attempts to alleviate a perceived character flaw may backfire by drawing attention to another. Elizabeth Holtzman, Democratic candidate for US Senate from New York, had a high name recognition level, strong grassroots activity, and a rather stable base of support, in her 1980 bid. However, surveys indicated trouble ahead; many voters believed her cold and aloof, and not compassionate or caring. Unsure of how to improve voter perceptions, Holtzman's campaign consultant took her off television for a full month, ignoring a cardinal rule of modern politics that negative perceptions cannot be changed without heavy and controlled television exposure. When her commercials finally reappeared, she was photographed in large, empty rooms or cold, marble hallways, and almost always was alone. The attempt to portray Elizabeth Holtzman as a hard-working congresswoman only served to reinforce her image as a loner. Thus, instead of altering negative perceptions, Holtzman's media reinforced them. Her support began to slide gradually, and she lost by less than 1 percent on election day. Her consultants made the wrong commercials for the wrong person at the wrong time.

In the 1982 New Mexico Senate race, a negative campaign commercial by the incumbent cost him the election, while it also signaled to voters that a candidate's commercials were a legitimate news item as well as a campaign tool. Harrison "Jack" Schmitt, one of only two incumbents defeated that year, watched in panic as his lead over opponent Jeffrey Bingaman dwindled to single digits by the final month of the campaign. Schmitt launched two decidedly negative commercials, attacking Bingaman's record as state's attorney general and suggesting he was soft on crime. The press tends to give credibility to incumbent statements, but also demands significant substantiality. The evidence behind the charges was weak, and Bingaman fought back masterfully in the press by turning Schmitt's tactics against him. According to

Bingaman's consultant, Les Francis: "For eight or nine days the newspapers and television news shows contained stories about the controversy, the nature of the ads, and our response. . . . Schmitt mishandled the situation terribly; first he said the ads would be pulled; then he kept them on."[50] Bingaman reversed a mid-October seven point deficit and pulled ahead in the final week of the campaign. When the public was questioned as to which side it believed in the controversy, 51 percent chose Bingaman and only 13 percent picked Schmitt. More importantly, the crucial undecided vote which Schmitt needed to secure his victory now went over to the Bingaman camp.

Since the 1982 election, a battle has developed between consultants and the press over the efforts of campaigns to stretch, bend, and twist the truth in their paid advertising. "We are propagandists, not reporters," said Republican media consultant Roger Ailes. "We get paid to show our candidate's strong points, not his warts."[51] When criticized for producing "misleading" advertising in the 1986 Florida Senate campaign, consultant Charles Black responded, "Are we obligated to give all the background? Of course not. You can't say it in thirty seconds."[52]

The increase in negative campaigning, along with the cries of "distortion" and "foul" emanating from candidates, consultants, and voters alike, has resulted in an effective demand for more factual evidence to support paid political advertisements. In the *Miami Herald*, Florida's largest newspaper, eleven of the seventeen stories (between 21 September and 20 October 1986) about the Senate race focused on the ads by the two campaigns and on their advertising specialists.[53] Said a television reporter attached to the CBS affiliate in Miami: "I feel amazed and embarrassed when the coverage of a major Senate race is reduced to an examination of their television ads."[54] An examination of hundreds of news clippings from the 1986 election lends credence to the argument that the print media do not recognize the subtle differences in negative advertising, yet have been remarkably effective in reporting distortions in political advertising. According to Democratic media consultant David Sawyer, "You try to put an unsubstantiated ad on TV and in 48 hours the press will be all over your case."[55] Concluded veteran consultant William Roberts, "The press blows the whistle [on the candidates] pretty fast when they are wrong or making errors in what they are saying. Most now take great pains to do their advertising accurately."

Not limited to scrutinizing negative advertising, the news media have often challenged the legitimacy of positive spots as well. When the Paula Hawkins campaign ran an advertisement that featured President Reagan personally meeting with the Florida senator in the Oval Office, and strongly suggested he had agreed to approve a cost-of-living increase for Social Security recipients only after a personal plea from

Senator Hawkins, the *Miami Herald* ran a description of the commercial under the headline: "Spot doesn't tell the whole story."[56] The newspaper noted that the cost-of-living increase had been approved two months before Hawkins and Reagan had met. In a subsequent episode, Hawkins's spokesman admitted he could not back up the claim made in a TV commercial about the senator's role in stopping drug trafficking from China. The acknowledgement was featured in numerous press stories, and the media's hyperbole later became the focus of opponent Robert Graham's final attack commercials. "Hawkins' commercial may have violated Senate regulations," was the headline of another *Miami Herald* article, which reported that her campaign had spliced video footage of Hawkins debating on the Senate floor.[57] Senate rules prohibit any use of television or radio recordings of floor debate for political purposes. "Bob Graham won because Paula Hawkins lied about meeting with Chinese officials," claimed Raymond Strother. "Graham was elected because his character was solid and she appeared less than substantial and less than honest."

Opponent Graham was himself not spared the media's eagle eye. A letter from the commandant of the United States Coast Guard requesting that Graham "immediately withdraw" a campaign commercial that showed Graham talking with Coast Guard personnel found its way on to page one of the *Miami Herald*.[58] The Graham commercial had sought to identify the apolitical but popular organization with Graham's candidacy. Despite the official request and the surrounding publicity, the commercial continued to be aired. Envisioning the future, media consultant Robert Shrum predicted: "The press will become the independent arbiter of [advertising] disputes in a campaign."[59]

Press concern with political advertising has not always pleased the candidates. Said California Senator Alan Cranston in an interview with the *Washington Post*, "A few weeks ago, I did a series of press conferences laying out my position on education. It got no coverage. But I guarantee you, if I'd thrown a few bombs at my opponent's TV spots, it would have."[60] With all the fuss about television advertising, it has become difficult even for the candidates themselves to talk about important issues. Florida Senate candidate Bob Graham was equally critical: "If you read the stories, all that is being written about is 30-second TV spots. This whole race is being defined by 30-second spots. . . . It's a very frustrating commentary."[61]

Radio advertising, often overlooked by candidates concerned with newspaper or television coverage, has also grown in sophistication and voter impact over the last decade. Demographically easier to target than television or newspapers, radio has the advantage of being a completely segmented medium, allowing the candidate to pitch a particular message to a specific voting group. It is, therefore, potentially more cost effective and certainly much cheaper. Thus, the 30- or 60-second radio spot has become a powerful weapon in politics, particularly for those candidates without large budgets.

At one time radio was a major component of campaign strategy, but it lost influence following the 1968 election. According to pollster Bill Hamilton, the rating services for radio were not as accurate as they were for television, hampering consultants wishing to target a particular audience. Also, station managers were often uncooperative in allowing political campaigns to buy only "drive-time" slots, 7:00 a.m. to 9:00 a.m. and 4:00 p.m. to 6:00 p.m., when radio has its greatest audience. However, media consultants have recently developed a strictly technical approach to radio advertising, further defining it with each passing election. Democratic media consultants Ray Strother and Frank Greer now recommend that their candidates spend a significant percentage of their budget on radio advertising, primarily because it has again become a segmented medium.

In 1972, George McGovern's presidential campaign became the first to target "rock and roll" radio stations. Hoping to capitalize on the newly passed constitutional amendment granting 18- to 21-year-olds the right to vote, he sought to encourage the pool of millions of first-time, youthful voters to support his candidacy. This early attempt at differentiating radio listenership has developed into a science, with more than a few consultants claiming to be experts specifically at placing radio ads. In 1986, Michigan Republican Bill Lucas, in his successful bid to become the first black person to obtain his party's nomination for governor, used black radio stations to encourage black Democrats to vote in the Republican primary, all the while appealing to black pride. Yet his commercials on white radio stations consistently downplayed the race issue. Candidates have to be careful, when segmenting their campaign, to avoid saying something to one group that contradicts a statement to another group. This danger – being caught in a contradiction – is often present in campaigns that rely heavily on radio advertising. Louisiana Senate candidate Henson Moore, in a commercial that was aired only on black radio stations, attacked opponent John Breaux for twice voting against declaring a national holiday on Martin Luther King's birthday. Yet Breaux did vote for the holiday in 1983, the year that it passed, while Moore had opposed it on every occasion. Breaux's public denouncement of Moore's commercial received wide publicity in the black community, and also undermined Moore's credibility among white voters.

Since radio commercials can be created, produced, and ready to air in less than a day, they give the candidate and his consultant the flexibility to respond quickly to changing events or outside forces. It is not uncommon, in the 1980s, for a statewide campaign's strategy to include the development of a different series of radio commercials each week, the focus of each set determined by the latest polling data or an important news item, thus ensuring that the advertisements are both timely and effective. This strategy is nearly impossible to carry out on television because of the lengthy preparation time and the amount of money each commercial requires. Candidates themselves have also "rediscovered" the benefits of radio advertising. In a 1986 press conference, New York Governor Mario Cuomo told the journalists present: "Don't flatter yourself that you're the best way to reach the public, because you're not. I'm probably better off with the 10-second on radio, because those are my words. When I talk to you, they're your words."[62]

In addition, radio has been effective in building name identification and favorable impressions for candidates who might otherwise have had difficulties on television. When Andrew Young first ran for Congress in a predominantly white Georgia district, he used radio extensively to build support. Emphasizing his message and not his race, Young surprised observers by winning the district. A decade later, John East decided to challenge the incumbent senator from North Carolina in what all agreed would be a very tough race. East had never run for office and had an even greater handicap – being a polio victim who was confined to a wheelchair. Using radio extensively, East was able to reach the people of North Carolina without raising doubts about whether he was physically fit to serve. Radio advertising made the difference in his narrow election victory. In an age where visual appearance has become a deciding factor in politics, radio provides the forum and the opportunity to address the issues and speak to the voters in an atmosphere where visual appearance is irrelevant.

But as with television, the major trend in radio advertising is in the direction of negative politics. Recent studies by several major polling firms have concluded that negative radio advertisements cause a significantly smaller and less intense backlash than negative television spots, because radio does not give the viewer a visual image to pair with the tough words. According to Roger Ailes, "Radio conjures up words, but it does not attach a face that adds both a wanted impact and an unwanted backlash. It does not provide the listener with someone to hate."

A recent example of a campaign using radio instead of television to send a negative message was the 1986 Vermont Senate campaign of Patrick Leahy: "Oh boy, it's going to get knee-deep around here. Dick Snelling has hired some famous direct tricksters to foul up the airwaves with a big-bucks, political smear campaign. . . . Do we really have to go through this in quiet, sensible, beautiful Vermont?" A simple television commercial was also produced, with roughly the same voice-over and a single black-and-white photograph of the senator that twisted and turned as the announcer spoke, but it was never aired. Radio had proved highly effective (and less costly) in presenting Leahy's message to the public, and the minimal additional impact that television could have provided was unnecessary. John LeBoutillier, because of his highly negative media campaign that depended heavily on radio advertising, won an upset victory in a 1980 Long Island congressional race against incumbent Lester Wolff. In one radio commercial, a speaker softly ticked off a list of foreign cities his opponent had visited, while "airline lounge" music played in the background. The ad was effectively designed to attack Wolff on an uncontestable issue (traveling at taxpayer expense) without whipping up anti-LeBoutillier sentiment.

Newspaper advertising is considered the least effective medium for swaying voter opinion. Most consultants have concluded that the impact of a newspaper advertisement is almost negligible, even among voters who claim to read newspapers "always" or "often." According to media consultant John Deardourff, newspapers have lost their position as the most credible source for political information, and this shift of public opinion has limited the success of print advertising. Said Congressman Harold Volkmer after Handgun Control Inc. purchased full-page ads attacking him in every daily newspaper in his district: "They're out of step. . . . It helped me; it didn't hurt me."[63] Said conservative political consultant Arthur Finkelstein, "Newspaper ads are only read by your supporters, your opponent's supporters, and the political in-speak people," those people whose lives are in some way attached to the political world. Fellow experts agree that most people skim read, chosing only those articles that catch their eye. According to media consultant Frank Greer, political advertisements go unnoticed by the vast majority of a newspaper's readership, and of those that happen to glance at an advertisement, less than half take the time to read it. Moreover, the percentage of readers who can recall any given point, even among those who claim to have read the advertisement, is surprisingly small. Concluded Bill Greener, former director of operations at the Republican National Committee, "I've tried to buy repeat pages, page domination, every theory known to mankind, and it becomes very expensive for the impact you get."

Nonetheless, there have been some effective newspaper advertising efforts. In the overwhelmingly Republican state of Idaho, party nominee David Leroy saw his support drop dramatically after a sportsmen's political action committee placed several full-page ads that criticized him for not being a sportsman, nor owning a hunting license. In outdoor-oriented Idaho, this revelation fatally wounded his campaign. On the same day that President Reagan arrived in Colorado to campaign for Ken Kramer, his opponent, Tim Wirth, took out full-page advertisements to highlight four major bills that his Republican opponent had voted against, but which President Reagan had signed, implying that the conservative Kramer was not a strong supporter of the president. "Welcome to Colorado, Mr President," the ad began. "It is indeed an honor to have you here. While you are here you might ask Ken Kramer a few questions . . ." To add an additional twist, Wirth concluded the ad by telling Reagan, "I truly look forward to working with you as a US Senator." Kramer, who had been leading in several statewide surveys, lost the election by less than 2 percent.

Candidates still use newspaper advertising effectively to announce particularly important stages in their campaigns, thereby ensuring at least some press coverage. According to Democratic pollster Bill Hamilton, "Some candidates, particularly on the Democratic side, are forced to buy newspaper ads if they want to get the paper's endorsement."[64] Nevertheless, newspaper advertising is decreasing in both use and importance. As Finkelstein concludes, "If you want to communicate to the politicians, take out a newspaper ad. If you want to communicate with the voters, use radio and television."

Describing the most recent innovations in television advertising, the *Washington Post* wrote: "The candidates themselves had been almost [uninvolved] players in the change. The big roles were played by their hired strategists, media advisers and pollsters."[65] However, interviews with a wide variety of consultants qualified the validity of that statement. A few, like Congressman John Rowland, have little involvement in the creation of their campaign advertisements. "I never saw our ads until after the election," he admitted. "My object was to shake a thousand hands a day. At the end of the campaign, if I was sitting in the office watching TV commercials, I would not have been out at the factory gates, the grocery stores, or the bowling alleys." But most candidates are preoccupied with their (and their opponent's) image, particularly in the television spots, and, to the disdain of some media advisors, are often personally and energetically involved in their production.

One of the more obscure aspects in the candidate–consultant relationship concerns the disagreements that can occur, and nowhere in politics are the disagreements more emotional than in those over television advertising. To avoid major disputes, most political advertising firms have a set procedure for the production of commercials. First, the media consultant will submit a concept for approval, followed by the rough copy and then the finished copy. After an agreement is reached, the commercial is shot, and shortly thereafter the candidate receives a rough copy of the spot, and finally the finished advertisement. The process can be terminated at any stage, and it is apparent that this method of procedure tends to reduce consultant–candidate misunderstandings. Media advisor Edward Blakely considers the internal marketing of his commercials, that is, selling them to the candidate, to be the most difficult task a media consultant undertakes in a campaign. "We are not gods," he emphasized, "and if I am writing copy for a candidate, there may be factual or stylistic corrections that have to be made. But I try to make them think they are part of the process – even if this is just a public relations tactic." Added Raymond Strother:

Sure my candidates will argue with me on occasion. I'll argue with them right up to the limit where it makes them angry, but then I'll do it their way. But I will let them know that if it is done their way, I am not responsible for it from that point. It scares the candidate, but that's what I must do, because I know more about it than they do.

In the end, the media consultants usually have their way. Said Roger Ailes: "When we first sign up with a candidate, we always get a lecture that we can't do negatives. But when the polls tighten up, the candidate says, 'Smack that guy – call him a communist. We've got to get him.' I just wait, and eventually they come around to my point of view."

Asserting independence from the media consultant can often be a matter of both pride and principle for some candidates. Paula Hawkins agreed to run a set of commercials, then changed her mind and instructed the consultant to produce new spots, accepted those spots, but then changed her mind yet again and rejected the second set of commercials. Harriet Woods, an extremely independent candidate, began airing pro-choice abortion advertising four weeks before election day, because she "wanted to be sure people understand her position in her own words."[66] Pollster Harrison Hickman, whose firm polled for Woods until a disagreement in strategy led to their voluntary departure, told Woods "it would be risky to raise that issue," but the campaign ignored his advice and went ahead with it anyway.[67] Her refusal to accept expert advice, and the final election result (she lost), did not pass unnoticed by other candidates. In the end, most candidates are prepared to defer to their paid advisors and the strategy and tactics recommended, even when those tactics involve high risks. But all maintain at least some degree of independence. Concluded Frank Greer: "Every candidate in some way defines the message of the campaign. Some accept what I recommend and rarely change a concept, rarely change even a word. Others come up with creative ideas on their own and have a lot to say about their message."

Disputes aside, most candidates are satisfied with their paid media campaign, and many even praise their advertising publicly. "You've got to see my ads," said proud and jubilant Boston Mayor Kevin White during his re-election campaign. "They are powerful."[68] Boasted Arkansas Senate candidate Ray Thornton at a press conference, "We've got some television spots that are really going to do it for us."[69] Some candidates even attempt to focus public attention on their paid advertising. In the 1980 Iowa presidential caucus, Ted Kennedy told crowd after crowd to watch his ads on television because "That will tell you why it is we're running for president and what some of the important issues are."[70]

Most candidates also apparently accept that what is disseminated from their campaign is their responsibility and not that of the consultants. And although it may not appear so to outside political observers, candidates often refuse to adopt negative strategies or use vicious rhetoric against their opponents. Bob Squier's favorite pro-negative campaign line, "If the opposition will stop lying about us, we'll stop telling the truth about them," does not work with all candidates. Despite the negative advertising that does appear, there are thousands of other spots produced by media consultants that will never get to the voters – on orders from the candidates. In fact, most media consultants admitted often having considerable difficulty in convincing their clients to go negative. When Pennsylvania gubernatorial candidate William Scranton announced two weeks before election day that he was cancelling all negative radio and television spots against his opponent, he declared that the campaign had degenerated into a "back alley brawl."[71] He later added that "I felt the campaign was being sucked down a road I didn't want it to go."[72] But despite the tremendous surge of favorable publicity surrounding his decision, Scranton still lost the election. In a similar situation, Helen Bentley hoped to capitalize on favorable publicity when she challenged her opponent, veteran Maryland Congressman Clarence Long, to join her in dropping all negative ads from the campaign. He refused, and the contrast between Bentley's positive and Long's negative advertising probably put her over the top. "It was my decision," Bentley emphasized later. "I was tired of the negative, but I knew he wasn't. We caught him napping."

In other well-documented campaign incidents, 1986 California Senate candidate Edward Zschau vetoed a radio commercial for being "too snide" in attacking his opponent's tax votes, and willingly retracted a characterization of his opponent as an "apologist" for the Soviet Union when a reporter asked him about it.[73] Zschau also rejected a National Republican Senatorial Committee commercial featuring a very unflattering photograph of his opponent. "I thought it was really in poor taste. I wouldn't use it," he said later.[74] When Ned Ray McWherter sought the Democratic nomination for governor of Tennessee in 1986, he was widely regarded as the favorite. However, strong negative advertising by an opponent shrank his lead dramatically, and his pollster and media consultants urged him to respond in kind. McWherter refused, suggesting in an interview that he would rather lose the primary than win with negative commercials. "I want to finish this campaign with style and class," he said. "The difference between me and my consultants is that I live in the state."[75]

A similar disagreement between candidate and consultant occurred in Florida, where Democratic Senate candidate Robert Graham refused to air negative advertisements until late in the campaign. According to Graham pollster William Hamilton, "He ran his own race. He really wanted to run the idealized, democratic election campaign, with nine debates and the whole thing. We [the professional advisors] were more cynical. We wanted him to take her on."[76] It is impossible to determine the actual percentage of commercials rejected by candidates for being distorted or too critical, but it is clear that candidates are generally quite careful about what they allow on the air.

Nevertheless, there are a number of candidates willing to go on record with varying degrees of support for negative advertising. Some have defended their use of negative advertising as retaliation to their opponent's negative commercials. A few candidates who publicly denounced negative ads then began using them again. Though the reasons may differ, in the heat of the campaign, the act of running negative ads is more important than the reasons. "If I was 35 points behind, I wouldn't change my tactics," claimed North Carolina Senate candidate Terry Sanford. "I am running a campaign for what I stand for. I am telling people to look at me."[77] Yet in the closing days of the campaign, Sanford began running ads telling voters to "take a closer look" – not at Sanford, but at opponent James Broyhill. In a televised debate between Roy Romer and Ted Strickland, Colorado guber-natorial candidates in 1986, Romer announced that he "would like to end all these negatives right now." He held out his hand to Strickland and said: "Let's shake on it – no more negative advertising from either side. We can do it with one handshake."[78] Strickland, accusing Romer of dishonesty and hypocrisy, refused the handshake. Romer then refused to give up his negative ads unilaterally. Colorado Senate candidate Kenneth Kramer blamed his negative advertising on his opponent: "Tim [Wirth] started it. I was forced to run negative ads in self-defense."[79] As Jim Abdnor concluded following his electoral defeat in 1986, "When people are emotionally involved in a campaign that is on the rocks, a lot of things can overtake better judgment. When you get mixed up in mud, you get mud back."

Some candidates, like former Florida Senator Paula Hawkins, feel no remorse about negative ads. "That's the way the game is played today," she said. "Florida is a television state, and we're a television campaign."[80] When Helen Boosalis, a contestant in the 1986 Nebraska gubernatorial race, complained about opponent Kay Orr's tough ads, Orr responded sharply, "This is not a [cooking contest] bake-off."[81] North Dakota Senator Mark Andrews told the *Washington Post* his attack ads are "what's changing the campaign momentum around," (less than two weeks before he was defeated by under 1 percent of the vote).[82] Reportedly, the reason why the 1986 Texas gubernatorial campaign, noted for the string of negative commercials by both Mark White and William Clements, became so viciously negative was that "the two candidates really hated each other."[83]

No longer can candidates simply select a media consultant and then sit back and wait for the votes to come pouring in. According to practical politics author Edward Costikyan: "The 1980s candidate must do more than hire a media man who won some recent election. The candidate must master the basic tools of communication and be able to distinguish between commercials that are all image and those that resonate the underlying ideas that stimulate voter response."[84]

Quite clearly, the complex relationship between the candidate and his media specialist can be affected by the emotional stress of the campaign. Important to maintaining this relationship on an even keel is the degree of trust the candidate has in the media advisor. But just as important is the ability of the candidate to understand and appreciate the skills of political marketing. Candidates who can successfully communicate their message to a responsive electorate are the winners. Media consultants can create and produce, but it is the candidate who has the final word – and the final responsibility. Not even modern campaign technology can remove a candidate entirely from his own campaign.

# 4

# The party's just begun

The centralized element of [national] Republican fundraising gave them an advantage in allocating money to particularly needy, close races; thus the Republicans, partly through their edge in centralized resources, were able in 1980 and 1982 to win the lion's share of close contests.

Norman Ornstein, political scientist[1]

Nobody notices that we now have a 90 million voter list, that we will mail 18 million pieces of mail, or make 10 million phone calls, and conduct ballot integrity programs in key states, or that we have registered two hundred thousand more voters in pivotal areas. We have again taken a major role in helping our candidates get elected.

Bill McInturff, Director of Party Development,
Republican National Committee

Throughout much of the 1970s, academics and politicians alike were ringing the death knell for the national political parties. But as the statements above graphically illustrate, the national party organizations have more recently experienced a resurgence in viability, influence, and involvement. Their traditional roles of selecting candidates, coordinating patronage, and serving as a link to the electorate have since given way to non-allocable services, coordinated expenditures, and fundraising. The road back from insignificance has not been without its setbacks, failed programs, and the occasional dissatisfied "beneficiary." But for candidates and campaigns in the 1980s, the revitalized party has only just begun.

From the end of World War II to the mid 1970s, the primary purpose of the two national party organizations was to turn out the base party vote nationwide, leaving most other tasks to state and local leaders. Throughout the 1960s, many of the most talented political

115

tacticians were attracted to the national party organizations in the hope of landing an important job in a presidential race or a major statewide contest. But as the power, prestige, and effectiveness of the consulting industry began to explode in the late 1960s and early 1970s, the flood of talent to the national parties slowed to a trickle. Individuals who otherwise would have sought employment with their party were, instead, being recruited by budding consulting firms, or even forming their own. The parties were slow to change, failed to adapt to the new environment, and were remiss about acquiring and utilizing the new techniques in campaigning. As veteran consultant Robert Squier explained: "Both political parties were negligent in understanding the new technology and putting it to use. They allowed entrepreneurs like myself to flourish. The parties should have taken our place in that technology."

The national party organizations also saw their influence diminish with the growth of television electioneering, requiring specific expertise that the unprepared parties were unable to provide. According to former Republican National Committee (RNC) Communications Director Gordon Wade, "Television permit[ted] the attractive, well-financed candidate to appeal to broad masses of voters," thereby reducing the need for volunteers and grassroots electioneering, as well as the party's ability to select and influence its candidates.[2] Top-heavy with old fashioned field organizers, the two national party organizations were ill prepared to deal with new technology in the changing electoral environment.

The Democratic and Republican parties faced this life-threatening dilemma differently, due primarily to the lack of foresight within the leadership of the national Democratic organization. The Democratic National Committee (DNC) decentralized itself, handing much of its remaining power and responsibilities back to the state party organizations or to the rising new breed of talented political advisors and consultants. The Republicans, on the other hand, embraced the new technology as the best hope of closing the gap between their candidates and the Democrats on election day.

That gap had never been wider than in the 1974 election. "The party was decimated by Watergate," said former RNC Communications Director Ed Blakely. "Fundraising was abysmal; there were bodies all over the place. But out of the ashes, some good started to happen." Wade listed the party shortcomings following the 1974 Republican debacle: "We analyzed the problems of party organization . . . poorly defined responsibilities; inadequate or nonexistent goals; poor techniques. . . ."[3] They were neither minimized nor ignored by subsequent party leaders, contrary to past party practices (and to those of their Democratic counterparts). Under the subsequent RNC national Chairman, former Senator Bill Brock, and the newly chosen National

Republican Congressional Committee leader, Congressman Guy Vander Jagt, the national Republican organizations enthusiastically underwent a fundamental change in their activities and responsibilities, eventually placing the organizations at the cutting edge of the new techniques.

It was decided that the most important priority was fundraising. "Without money, you can't do anything," recounted Blakely, "and all our resources were spent raising money. They almost let everybody go in the national headquarters just to raise money." The new emphasis on money and services pleased Republican candidates back home, and this was not lost on the national party. According to former RNC Political Director Bill Lacy:

One of the reasons why technology was so widely accepted in the Republican party is because we have been the minority party. We have had to do more aggressive, future oriented, technically oriented things to win. The Democrats haven't. They can afford to lose a certain percentage of traditional support of virtually any campaign they're involved in.

Moderate success in the 1978 election cycle encouraged the Republicans to experiment further in 1980. That year's Republican landslide had two effects. The importance of a strong national political organization had now been re-established as a key element in Republican victories. But the very people who had masterminded and supervised the Republican victory of 1980 were suddenly in demand to fill positions in the newly elected administration and the now Republican-controlled Senate. Although this paradox went largely unnoticed by outside observers, the brain drain induced by the Republican successes in 1980 created a serious vacuum in the national party organization, rendering it void of experienced political operatives in 1982, and leaving the field organization in the hands of many individuals with only limited political experience. According to RNC Field Director Ed Brookover, it was not until the 1986 election cycle that the three sister organizations, the Republican National Committee (RNC), the National Republican Senatorial Committee (NRSC) and the National Republican Congressional Committee (NRCC), had matured to the point where all three had a deep level of experienced staff and field personnel.

Viewing their 1980 disaster with great alarm, the national Democratic organizations began to reverse their decentralization process, adopting many of the new campaign techniques already standardized by their Republican counterparts. In a speech to the Democratic National Committee in 1981, fundraiser Roger Craver told his audience, "There has come a chorus of Democratic voices urging a close examination of the party's basic tenets and new emphasis on nuts and bolts, such as effective direct mail fundraising, computerized voter targeting, and more extensive polling." This was probably the first time in their

**Table 4.1** *Spending by the national parties ($ million)*

| Cycle | Republicans | | | Democrats | | |
|---|---|---|---|---|---|---|
| | Total expenditures | Coordinated expenditures[1] | Direct contributions | Total expenditures | Coordinated expenditures[1] | Direct contributions |
| 77–8 | 85.9 | 4.3 | 4.5 | 26.9 | 0.4 | 1.8 |
| 79–80 | 161.8 | 12.4 | 4.5 | 35.0 | 4.9 | 1.7 |
| 81–2 | 214.0 | 14.3 | 5.6 | 40.1 | 3.3 | 1.7 |
| 83–4 | 300.8 | 20.1 | 4.9 | 97.4 | 9.0 | 2.6 |
| 85–6 | 254.2 | 14.3 | 3.5 | 62.7 | 6.4 | 1.6 |

[1] "Coordinated expenditures" are monies spent by the parties on behalf of their candidates, and are in addition to contributions made directly to candidates' campaigns. They are limited by law, and are allowed only in general elections.

*Source:* FEC Press Releases: 24 April 1980, 21 February 1982, 3 December 1983, 5 December 1985, 31 May 1987

history that the Democratic party leadership were told that "nuts and bolts" now meant direct mail, computerization, and survey research, instead of the literature drops and door-to-door canvassing that most candidates had come to expect from the party.

In accordance with Craver's advice, the most sweeping change was the dramatic shift to direct mail fundraising, a well rewarded decision that eventually paid for the Democratic party's entire modernization process. According to former Democratic party Treasurer Peter Kelly, the Democrats never thought seriously about direct mail until the 1980 election. "In 1980, the RNC raised $30 million in direct mail; we raised only $2.5 million. While we were struggling to pay off old debts, salaries, and still come up with $3 million for the presidential race, the RNC was able to spend money on everything." The new strategy reaped immediate dividends, increasing the national party donor list from 25,000 to 250,000 by the end of 1982.[4] Yet despite the new emphasis on direct mail, the disparity in fundraising between the two parties is still clearly evident. Thus, the national Democratic organizations have been severely restricted in their ability to provide expenditures for their candidates similar to those of the Republicans on behalf of their candidates. (See table 4.1.)

According to Democratic consultant Bob Squier, "The Democrats are still probably five to eight years behind in direct mail technology in terms of list development and sophistication. The Republicans have been so far ahead for so long that they have been able to experiment and innovate a lot more approaches." Kelly was considerably more critical. "That's not better direct mail technology. That's just a plain absence of commitment and hard work on the part of the Democrats." Nevertheless, in 1986, the Democratic Congressional Campaign Committee and the Democratic Senatorial Campaign Committee, which had both been continually hampered by financial problems, finally emerged as valuable support organizations for their candidates, a fact acknowledged by present political leaders in the two parties.

Many of the current strategies and practices used by the national party organizations can be traced back to rewrites of election law made in 1979. Said Common Cause President Fred Wertheimer about the FECA and its 1979 amendments:

There was a big argument at the time of the campaign finance laws that they left no room for the parties, that the new laws would destroy the parties. In fact, the parties are playing a much bigger role today than they were before these laws. These laws have enhanced the role of the political parties in the campaign process.

By the late 1970s, Congress (and many in the academic community) had come to feel that volunteer activities had been curtailed too drastically as a result of the 1974 and 1976 election law amendments.

(See chapter 1.) To rectify what it perceived to be a flaw in its earlier legislation, Congress passed the 1979 FECA amendments that gave parties the right to develop and encourage "generic contact" (solicitations by the party that do not specify any individual candidate) through "non-allocable" services, a Federal Election Commission phrase to delineate party programs and activities that: 1) do not count against a party's legal contribution limit to its candidates, and therefore 2) do not need to appear on a candidate's FEC report. Non-allocable services could take two forms: either "party building" or "volunteer intensive." Thus, the national party organizations were given the opportunity to pursue, with unlimited expenditures, both party building and volunteer intensive programs without fear of violating any election codes.

The FEC determined party building activities to include voter registration, voter list development, ballot integrity (an election day effort to insure that only *qualified* voters cast ballots), and get-out-the-vote (GOTV) mail and phone banks (locations where a multiple number of phones are used by volunteers to identify likely supporters), all of which could be done with unlimited funds as long as the party only advocated itself (that is, the entire slate of candidates). Since 1980, both national party organizations have employed the party building portion of the FEC ruling to influence elections in tightly contested statewide races. However, because of their party's superior financial condition, the Republicans have had significantly more opportunities to institute and perfect the various party building services, on behalf of their candidates.

A second, and more controversial, aspect of the 1979 amendments and FEC interpretation has only recently come into play in the electoral process, though its impact can already be measured in millions of dollars. It is now legal for the national party organizations to send out any number of direct mail packages endorsing a candidate so long as they are clearly marked as being paid for by the party organization, authorized by the candidate they are intended to support, and – most importantly – so long as volunteers have had a significant part in the process of getting the package delivered to the voter. That is, as long as volunteers played an important role in the letter's delivery, by folding, stuffing, labelling and stamping the piece, then the direct mail packages can be entirely paid for by the national party organizations. If not volunteer intensive, it then falls into the category of a coordinated expenditure, which will result in some cost to the candidate. In 1986, for example, the standard bulk rate was 10 cents a letter. However, the national party organizations receive preferential non-profit status, which allows them a 3 cent deduction. In addition, both parties now have facilities which allow them to sort by zip codes, and in many states even by postal carrier route, at a rate of 5.1 cents per letter. Thus, the national parties can, through coordinated expenditures, conduct a direct mail campaign on behalf of a candidate, and save his campaign almost 50 percent in postage costs. However, if the direct mail program is volunteer intensive, as defined by law, the national party can pick up the entire tab.

Bill McInturff, director of party building for the RNC, estimates that about 11 million dollars were spent in non-allocable activities (including some party building programs) by the three national Republican organizations in 1986, much of it in the final week of the election to increase the Republican turnout. The Republican National Committee alone put $4.1 million into voter list development and get-out-the-vote efforts in twenty-five targeted states.[5] In the four days preceding the election, the national party called 3.1 million voters previously identified (through registration data or earlier phoning) as Republicans or Republican supporters. Another 2 million voters received a prerecorded message from the President by computerized phoning, urging them to vote. This was backed up with a "blizzard" of mail in the final week, stressing the importance of the upcoming election. The national GOP also briefly ran a set of generic TV and radio ads targeted at the 18- to-24-year-old vote in selected states.[6]

Former Democratic Congressional Campaign Committee Political Director Thomas King admits that his party spent only a fraction of that amount in 1986, though they did attempt a less well-funded vote drive similar to that of the Republicans. The DNC targeted sixteen states at a total cost of $1.2 million.[7] About 2.4 million calls were made in addition to the 2.2 million letters sent to registered Democrats. Said DNC Political Director Jeffrey Ely: "I think we are competitive in states where we are active."

As McInturff concluded, "The FEC has provided a small loophole that we have driven a caravan of trucks through. We take the laws very seriously. We understand exactly what we have to do to comply with them, but we take advantage of every loophole." Said Bill Lacy: "It is not technology that is bringing the parties back, it's the non-allocable expenditures. A consultant can provide you a massive influx of non-allocable resources that can only be expended, according to law, by the political parties." The most important consultant-related loophole is in the field of polling. During the first six months of 1986, the NRSC spent over $600,000 on surveys in states with close Senate races.[8] Under the "depreciation" allowance clause, which reduces the value (that is, the price the candidate must pay) of the poll by 50 percent after fifteen days, and even more if the national party organization waits sixty days or longer, much of the polling information was then transferred directly to their Senate candidates at sharply reduced cost. Thus, these various clauses and loopholes have restored the position of the national party organizations in the campaigns of their candidates, even in this new age of consultants and modern campaign technology, a position most political scientists in the 1970s assumed to be gone for good.

Even with its strong financial base, the Republican National Committee and its sister organizations are not able to assist every House and Senate candidate. Though the committees initially decide from twelve to eighteen months in advance which states and districts are going to be targeted, the party continually updates its assessments as new information comes to light. Districts that once looked promising may be dropped because the GOP has been unable to field a credible candidate, while some races are added if polling data and other information indicate increasing vulnerability in a Democratic incumbent. According to Ed Brookover, former RNC Field Director, a September announcement that the national GOP organization would not contribute large amounts to the campaign of New York gubernatorial candidate Andrew O'Rourke because of his lagging efforts was a clear signal to political observers that the party no longer regarded the race as winnable. As Brookover concluded, "By the end of the election cycle, there are really few surprises. The Democrats know which races we have targeted, and we know whom they have targeted. The candidates know as well."

Unlike the financially strapped Democratic National Committee, the RNC has gone "high tech," even in its field operations. During the 1986 election, every member of the field staff had a personal computer, primarily to speed communications between national headquarters and the representatives in the field. Each member of the field staff was required to submit a weekly report to Field Director Brookover, analyzing the progress of targeted campaigns. This process, first instituted on a small scale in 1982, became an established part of the RNC routine in 1986. The three national Republican organizations also offer high tech schooling for their party's candidates (with separate courses for incumbents and challengers), campaign managers, and finance directors. According to the late Congressman Stewart McKinney, who had been trained in an incumbent candidate school, "They work you very hard, sometimes to midnight or 1:00 a.m., but they are very, very professional."

The National Republican Congressional Committee has rightly earned the respect of its candidates – and their opponents – for its expert advice and services. Ten years ago, author Robert Agranoff wrote that as the "technological sophistication of campaigning increases, candidates are turning elsewhere for technical assistance and funds, for access to the mass media depends not on party, but on skills and money."[9] A decade later, consultant David Keene explained why the political climate had changed: "The new freshmen are grabbed by the campaign committees, which are on the leading edge of the technology, and are given all the support they need. Because they are younger, they tend to believe more in it, and the committees have put together for them what amounts to a political machine in the modern age." NRCC Executive Director Joseph Gaylord concurred: "What we try to do is develop a presence with the incumbents so that they will rely on both our expertise and the talent we have available to help them."

The NRCC's "board of directors" consists of the Republican members of the US House of Representatives, and it is therefore not surprising that the Congressional Committee is, first and foremost, an incumbent-oriented operation. In 1986, the NRCC added, for the first time, an extensive incumbent field organization. Five field representatives began working with the incumbent legislators in early 1985, in an effort to shore up support in their districts. Incumbent survey research was also conducted, for the first time, in the 1986 election cycle, and a crew of finance people were put on the NRCC payroll to help incumbents raise money. As a result, the NRCC was able to reduce from forty-five to fifteen the number of vulnerable House seats, causing the Democrats considerable difficulty in recruiting high quality challengers against many of the Republican incumbents. The NRCC's campaign skills and value to its incumbents were borne out when Republicans lost only six House seats in an off-year election, compared to twenty-six in 1982.

But the benefits of the NRCC are not reserved for the most senior members of Congress only. On the contrary, freshmen and sophomore representatives are even more likely to receive NRCC assistance. As Congressman Guy Vander Jagt, chairman of the NRCC, told *Congressional Quarterly* before the 1984 elections, "I think the old axiom still holds that the most vulnerable time for congressmen is in the first election, and if you miss them on the first election, it gets more difficult to beat them. ..."[10] The NRCC is selective in providing institutional support for its incumbents, and only those vulnerable members of Congress who appear weak and in the greatest potential danger of defeat will be given maximum committee funding and full access to all committee services.

The NRCC also allocates a significant portion of its time and budget to candidate recruitment, in the effort to find strong congressional candidates to challenge Democratic incumbents, particularly in marginal districts. Eight full-time field coordinators spent months scouring the country for quality challengers, while the Washington staff were holding a number of "recap" meetings with the previous year's losers to reconsider their campaigns and discuss possible strategy for 1984. This system was widely regarded as an important factor in limiting Republican losses in 1982 and 1986, when the historic off-year election trends would have suggested a much greater Republican defeat.[11]

To challenger candidates unsure of their strategy or tactics, the

Congressional Committee can be of great help, serving as "general consultants" for those campaigns that have none. Field staff will be sent into their district, armed with polls, opposition research, and a detailed voting history of the district. A strategy statement will be prepared, submitted to the campaign manager for comment, and then presented to the candidate. From interviews with party officials it is apparent that candidate input and willingness to implement strategy recommendations vary; thus, the candidate–party relationship is, in effect, not dissimilar to the candidate–consultant relationship. Republican David Christian, challenging a potentially weak incumbent in Pennsylvania's 8th District in 1984, was presented with an entire election strategy, expertly prepared by the NRCC and fully approved by his staff. Yet Christian never felt comfortable with the battle plan, and on the stump continually ignored NRCC advice and his own staff's recommendations. His campaign never really got off the ground, and eventually was removed from the NRCC list of targeted races.

But ultimately most candidates do accept NRCC advice. "The NRCC had to convince me that my campaign should start negatively," said New Jersey Congressman Dean Gallo after his successful upset victory over an entrenched incumbent in 1984. "I almost vetoed the strategy, and we went with it despite my apprehension. It was a wise decision because it brought the election to the attention of the public." John Hiler chose not to hire a consultant in his 1980 congressional campaign, a decision he did not regret: "The NRCC were our consultants. We had someone from the NRCC come in starting in July, and we took advice from him. I'd say we had a very good relationship. In fact, I ended up hiring that person as my administrative assistant after the election."

The NRCC has also been a saving grace for cash-starved candidates in search of quality, but inexpensive, television advertising experts and equipment. In coordination with its sister Republican organizations, the NRCC opened, in 1978, a cut-rate media warehouse where a candidate could obtain professional script writers, producers, and editors. According to Edward Blakely, former communications director of the RNC, "We looked around and found that there were a lot of our congressional candidates who could not afford the higher priced media agencies that produced political advertising. We decided that this would be an important service to offer them." Only eight candidates took advantage of the new facilities in the first year, but its success convinced the NRCC to search for new ways to assist its candidates in gaining paid media exposure.

In 1979, the NRCC devised an extensive, and costly, program in which six students would be selected for a six month political advertising school, trained in the techniques of campaign advertising, examined and graded, and on successful completion of the program would be placed on the NRCC staff at a salary of about $1,500 per month. About fifty candidates received advertising assistance from the student media producers: each was responsible for eight campaigns, though some eventually did more and others less. According to Blakely, the program was a failure. "It is hard to take someone just out of college, throw them out in a campaign alone, and have them have any credibility with the candidate. Time after time there were conflicts." Many of the candidates (about 40 percent, according to Blakely) reacted negatively to the program, and in some cases the candidate refused NRCC help and went elsewhere instead.

Although the media school was disbanded following the 1980 elections, the media production service expanded dramatically in 1982, aiding ninety-two GOP candidates with the partial production of 180 television advertisements and other media services, such as the purchase of increasingly expensive air-time, an otherwise potentially unaffordable campaign necessity. "Full service" assistance (that is, copy creation, on-location shooting, production and editing) was also given to twenty candidates in 1982, and twenty-five candidates in 1984, at an estimated value to the fortunate candidates of from $60,000 to $90,000.[12] The latest video hardware and digital video effects, along with a top-of-the-line character generator – the "bells and whistles of television politics" – were made available, for the first time, in 1984. The communications division was also upgraded in 1984, with almost double the personnel of 1982. Although restrictive finances forced the NRCC to cut back on the number of full service clients in 1986, more candidates nonetheless used NRCC media facilities than in any other election cycle in history. Blakely estimated that about 125 Republican congressional candidates had at least some contact with the NRCC media center, prompting him to comment: "More and more candidates want to use the service, but more and more have to be turned down. We can't do everybody, and that's because there are more and more people getting elected who then talk about how great the service was. It's word of mouth." Thus, by providing advertising expertise, minimizing creative and production costs, and occasionally subsidizing media time, the NRCC has been providing an invaluable election service to its candidates, relieving them of some of the excessive costs faced by their opponents.

The National Republican Senatorial Committee (NRSC) has clearly been the most successful, and envied, national party organization in fundraising. Unlike its sister organizations and the Democratic counterpart, the NRSC is the only national party organization with the resources to fund every candidate under its jurisdiction up to the maximum amount allowed by federal election law, which ranges from $102,800 in the smallest states to $1,720,861 in California.[13] "I knew from the beginning that we would have full NRSC financial backing," said New Hampshire Senator Gordon Humphrey about his 1984 re-election campaign. "Not only did they contribute their maximum, but they also encouraged their donors to send contributions directly to our campaign, and that substantially exceeded our expectations." Direct mail specialist Bob Odell continually stressed the remarkable impact of this capability: "In 1980, Paula Hawkins won the Republican primary in somewhat of an upset. But the day after, she had all her dough, the maximum allowed by law, and that's one hell of a stack of cash. No one had to make a phone call. It was there. Bingo." According to former NRSC Executive Director Tom Griscom, "The greatest asset we offer our candidates is our financial base. The key to our committee was the extra money we could provide a campaign."

Because of this, and coupled with the additional resources available to their candidates that are financed by the committee's superior fundraising base, the NRSC has, deservedly, been given much of the credit for the success of Republican Senate challengers in 1980, and for returning Republicans to office in the 1982 and 1984 elections. Nevertheless, the narrowing technology gap between the Republican and Democratic committees did play a major role in the inability of the NRSC, despite its superior financial resources, to protect its 1986 incumbents.

Not content with its cash advantage, the NRSC has also employed additional money for research and development in other directions. They maintain a special "combo" account to pick up Republican senators' office expenses, such as newspaper subscriptions, photographs, television tapes and transmissions, and other costs. Through August 1986, the NRSC had provided about $800,000 to its senators, an amount which also does not count against the NRSC's contribution limits.[14] A second edge, available only to Republican senatorial candidates, is the organization's research capabilities. Using a highly trained and motivated investigative staff, the NRSC compiled extensive and detailed reports on the political and personal life of every 1986 Democratic challenger. The material was so comprehensive, and of such potential value to its Republican candidates, that the Democrats questioned the methods used to gather the information, while NRSC employees refused to discuss their methods at any length. In the only documented case of impropriety (the Senate race in Alaska), the committee got into trouble when one of its researchers, completing background information on the Democratic contender, was caught misrepresenting himself as an aide to that candidate during phone calls to the candidate's former employer. Although it generated bad publicity for the NRSC, the Republican candidate was not affected, and won easily.

Among the primary NRSC electioneering advances demonstrated in the 1986 election cycle was a unique, intensive analysis of their own candidates. Voting and attendance records, contributor lists, fundraising figures and any additional and relevent personal statistics or facts were compiled by the NRSC research staff and analyzed by professional consultants. Each candidate then received a model of the likely campaign strategy of his opponent. Knowing their own strengths and being able to anticipate the opposition, the Republican Senate candidates were better prepared to respond, and, at least in theory, were in a stronger position to defend their voting record. In addition, the NRSC created, and currently operates, an ongoing data bank that studies voter reaction to the full scale of television advertising, from simplistic candidate awareness commercials to the most negative attack spots. They also had consultants on retainer to advise their candidates how best to reach black voters through radio and newspaper advertisements, how to deal with organized labor, how to design computer software for campaign finance reports, and how to prepare for televised debates. As Republican fundraiser Bob Odell said, in responding to a claim by some social scientists that the rise of modern campaign technology and the consultant has caused a corresponding decrease in the importance of the national parties in the elections of their candidates: "The operation of the NRSC is awesome. I've never seen a more committed, resource laden, a more willing political organization in the United States. The last time I saw anything like it was in the 1960s."

Recently, the most significant technical improvements by the national Republican organizations have occurred in the area of nationwide list development. The marriage of modern political direct mail technology with the computer has created innovations in analyzing, tracking, and characterizing voters on a grand scale, resulting in the computerized national mailing list. Individual names, along with any potentially useful data available, are gathered from voter registration lists, local and state party organizations, or even from state motor vehicle departments, and placed on a single, computerized master list at the Republican National Committee headquarters in Washington.

The process for obtaining these lists is straightforward. For example, the national Republican organizations combined to give the Pennsylvania state GOP organization $350,000 in 1985 to hire people to solicit donations by telephone, producing 35,000 new Republican donors as of October 1986.[15] The proceeds paid for the state party to compile a sophisticated computer list of all 5.7 million registered voters – a list which could then be combined with neighborhood information from census files and phone numbers. The RNC also bought the addresses of 1.7 million members of the military from the Pentagon, and then sent the appropriate lists to state and local party organizations for use in their electioneering and distribution of applications for absentee ballots. As of November 1986, the RNC had over 60 million voter names on computer tape, a feat as yet unsurpassed by any political organization anywhere. The voter registration roles for thirty-seven states were computerized in time for the 1986 elections, and in early 1988 Chairman Frank Farenkaupf expected to have all fifty states on line by the evening of 15 August 1988, the nomination date for the next Republican presidential candidate.

However, much of the significant Republican advantages in the early 1980s have been erased by the adoption of equally sophisticated campaign techniques within the national Democratic organizations. Said former RNC Political Director Bill Lacy, "In terms of raw technology, there is no difference between the parties. In the ultimate quality of the technology available, there is no difference." Former DNC Treasurer Peter Kelly suggested that the Democrats may even be ahead in some areas. "Our hardware and software were purchased in 1984. Some of theirs was purchased in 1976 and before. Of course it's been upgraded, but it's still older than ours." Many of the Democratic gains were achieved by copying the strategy of their Republican counterparts. To quote a candid Anthony Coehlo, Chairman of the Democratic Congressional Campaign Committee: "I'm not afraid to tell people that I've studied what the Republicans have done. I've taken their book, looked at it, reviewed it, thrown away the pages I didn't like and amplified on those I did. I don't see any point in re-inventing the wheel."[16] Republicans also played a role in the gains of the Democratic organizations. Former NRSC Director Thomas Griscom adds, with more than a hint of disgust:

I was really not pleased to read several stories, back in September, outlining everything we were going to do about turnout, from what kind of message it was going to be, what it was going to say and how many people it was going to go to. It was signaling to our opponents what we were going to do, so they could plan on it. This bothers me.

The process of learning from each other's successes and failures is routine in party politics. "What we do is public knowledge," suggested Edward Brookover, RNC Field Director during the 1985–6 campaign election cycle. "The Democrats have watched what we do, and they have copied it. We are not a corporation like Coca-Cola, with a secret formula that nobody can find out about."

For the Democrats, much of the 1980s has been spent repairing strained relations with their candidates. As mentioned earlier, the Democratic party was considerably slower than the Republicans to adopt the new campaign techniques, and because of their poor financial condition, the Democratic organizations were not able to give large sums of money to their candidates. DNC Political Director Jeffrey Ely observed that even in 1986, "it was difficult to get candidates to accept the fact that the party could be helpful." Some veteran incumbents had even refused to acknowledge that the new campaign technologies actually existed. As media consultant Robert Squier asserted, "Democrats had to be dragged kicking and screaming into the twenty-first century. You had a lot of curmudgeons who have been around for a long time."

Nevertheless, the national Democratic organizations now play a major role in the elections of their candidates. In 1982, only five state Democratic parties had up-to-date computerized voter lists. Early in the 1986 election cycle, the DNC decided to target states where they expected close Senate or gubernatorial contests, and focus on fundraising and get-out-the-vote efforts in those races. By election day, thirty-five states had computerized voter lists, state-of-the-art computer hardware and software, and a direct mail program that was in place and raising money.

According to leaders in both Republican and Democratic campaign committees, the most significant difference between them in the area of candidate assistance is clear: Democratic activities are severely more limited as a result of budgetary constraints, though even this gap may be shrinking. (See table 4.2.) Republican congressional candidates, in particular, receive more than three times the funding in direct contributions and coordinated expenditures from the national party organizations that their Democratic counterparts do, though the disparity has lessened somewhat since 1982.

According to DSCC Executive Director David Johnson, "We have not caught up with the Republicans in terms of what we offer our candidates, because that is a function of fundraising. In 1984, we raised $9 million and they raised $83 million. This is an enormous disparity." As political scientist Norman Ornstein observed: "[The Democrats] began the campaign trying to raise enough money to overcome the GOP advantage and to protect their major asset – strong and solid incumbents. The Democrats, as a result, could not devote resources to a wide range of GOP [held] districts."[17]

The same situation existed in 1986 as well. In contrast to the NRSC, which had so much money that it had to search for ways to spend it, the DSCC had only about $5 million to give to competitive races, less than two-thirds the maximum allowed by law.[18] According to DSCC Chairman George Mitchell, his organization was only able to marshall its resources to target sixteen races in 1986, compared with maximum funding for every GOP senatorial candidate.[19] In several closely contested Senate races, among them California, Alabama, and Florida, Republican candidates received the maximum party contributions allowed by law, while the Democratic hopefuls received only a fraction of the amount. In Florida, the NRSC earmarked $750,000 for Paula Hawkins, but the DSCC managed only slightly more than half that amount for Robert Graham.[20] All this should change, however, in the 1988 elections. As of 1 January 1988, the Democratic National

**Table 4.2**   *Direct contributions/coordinated expenditures by the national parties to their House and Senate candidates ($ million)*

| Cycle | Senate | | | House | | |
|---|---|---|---|---|---|---|
| | Coordi-nated | Direct | Total | Coordi-nated | Direct | Total |
| *Republicans* | | | | | | |
| 77–8[1] | 2.6 | 0.7 | 3.3 | 0.8 | 3.8 | 4.6 |
| 79–80 | 5.5 | 0.7 | 6.2 | 2.4 | 3.8 | 6.2 |
| 81–2 | 8.7 | 0.6 | 9.3 | 5.5 | 5.0 | 10.5 |
| 83–4 | 6.8 | 0.07 | 7.5 | 6.3 | 4.2 | 10.5 |
| 85–6 | 10.1 | 0.8 | 10.9 | 4.2 | 2.6 | 6.8 |
| *Democrats* | | | | | | |
| 77–8[1] | 0.4 | 0.5 | 0.9 | 0.5 | 1.3 | 1.8 |
| 79–80 | 1.2 | 0.5 | 1.8 | 0.3 | 1.1 | 1.4 |
| 81–2 | 2.4 | 0.6 | 3.0 | 0.8 | 1.1 | 1.9 |
| 83–4 | 4.4 | 0.5 | 4.9 | 1.8 | 1.3 | 3.1 |
| 85–6 | 6.6 | 0.6 | 7.2 | 1.9 | 1.0 | 2.9 |

[1] Congressional/senatorial campaign committees only.

*Source*: Compiled from FEC Press Releases: 24 April 1980, 21 February 1982, 3 December 1983, 5 December 1985, 31 May 1987

Committee has already pocketed numerous healthy donations, including a contribution of one million dollars from Joan Kroc, widow of the McDonald's Corporation founder. And the DSCC has found itself in a considerably stronger financial position in comparison to the 1985–6 election cycle.

To determine its "high opportunity" races (those seats currently held by the other party, but where the Republican candidate is highly vulnerable), the national Democratic organizations have adopted targeting methods and criteria similar to those already in use by the Republicans. But because of their financial situation, the Democratic Congressional Campaign Committee (DCCC) and its sister organizations allocate their funds with great caution, delineating several crucial hurdles that a candidate must clear before money can be passed on to that campaign. This represents a major departure from past party practices:

In prior years the money raised by the DCCC was distributed first to Democratic incumbents, with each incumbent certain to receive some money regardless of his or her vulnerability. In 1984 Coehlo decided that the limited resources demanded a change in strategy: The money should be used more directly to protect vulnerable incumbents and to boost potentially successful Democratic challengers.[21]

It was Coehlo's belief that the DCCC could provide additional resources in close elections only if it ceased providing funds to candidates assured of re-election. In accordance with the party's new policy, the candidate must now demonstrate a strong financial base, the campaign must have completed a comprehensive survey of voter attitude, and the DCCC has to be convinced that the incumbent is at least somewhat vulnerable. Finally, the candidate must present a detailed plan of how the party funding will be spent. According to then DCCC Political Director Tom King: "No candidates will get five thousand dollars if they are going to buy a million potholders. If they have a large overhead, they are not going to get our money. If they are paying for things that make sense, like direct mail, phone banks, get-out-the-vote operations, TV, radio – that's fine with us."

Because of their limited funds, the Democratic organizations lack the extensive polling data available to the Republicans, and this hampers Democrats' ability to monitor daily developments in the various districts. According to DNC spokesman Terry Michael, since 1981 the DNC has conducted only one national poll and a series of focus groups at a cost of about $125,000. The RNC, by comparison, spends an average of well over $70,000 a month on polling and focus group research. Whereas the NRCC was able to track in about fifty-five congressional districts in 1986, and the NRSC in seventeen states (eventually reduced to twelve in the final two weeks before the election), the corresponding Democratic organizations had to depend in large measure on the candidates themselves to complete this activity.

Party observers consider the Democratic tracking program to be about two election cycles behind the Republicans in extent and sophistication. Said NRSC Executive Director Tom Griscome about his Democratic counterpart, "[DSCC Executive Director] David Johnson would say to me, 'You know, I don't have all the sophisticated tracking the Republicans do. I just have the public surveys.' My response was to say, 'David, you may be lucky. Every night, I go home knowing exactly what we look like, and some nights it ain't very good.'"

Moreover, unlike the NRSC and the NRCC, the corresponding Democratic committees do not keep consultants on retainer, though they often pay for their services on a race by race basis. Said DNC Political Director Jeffrey Ely:

It is a daily battle to fight off the urge to hire consultants with their various schemes and plans, many of which sound very good. But if you have limited resources like we do, you have to take the attitude that the plan has to be extraordinarily helpful before we can buy into it. We just don't have the funds to do it.

Democratic candidates are thus denied an important continuity that can get lost in the shuffle as the election approaches. This may also account for the problems the Democratic party has, periodically, with its consultants. Ely candidly admitted that even in 1986, the relationship between the two was often strained: "There were cases where the consultant wouldn't cooperate with the party. It all comes down to our lack of a track record, the lack of a relationship between the party, the candidate, and the consultant. So Democratic consultants have a history of doing things on their own." However, for the first time in its history, the DCCC began to pay consultants in 1986 to prepare comprehensive public opinion surveys on behalf of selected candidates, and consultant involvement, paid for by the national Democratic party organizations, is expected to increase with each election cycle.

Individually, Democratic congressional candidates are not told which pollster to use as a prerequisite for funding. Instead, candidates are given a list of reputable, loyal party pollsters, with an occasional recommendation if there is something unique that the candidates might otherwise not have known, and then they are left to decide which one suits them best. Tom King was quick to point out this major difference between the philosophies of his organization and that of the Republicans on the issue of consultants: "The candidate is putting his life on the line. He deserves to make at least a couple of decisions. One of them is who does the race. We don't say who you have to use. Republicans do that, but we don't." But to Bob Squier, this approach was chosen more out of fear than from a desire not to interfere with their candidates: "The campaign committees, particularly on the Democratic side, are so afraid of injuring the feelings of the political consultants that they stand way back, treating the entire field of consultants as if they are basically alike." Squier strongly disapproved of this party policy because it forces candidates, many of whom are political novices without much understanding of modern campaign technology, to determine the subtle differences between consultants.

Recently, in another technological breakthrough, the DCCC has fully automated its political operation, providing the party with instant communication capabilities with most of their House candidates. Using a newly designed system called the Bulletin Board, the DCCC now can acquire late-breaking information on key issues and immediately transmit the material by computer to the various campaign headquarters across the country. Internally, the DCCC went from twelve computers in 1984 to over seventy computers in 1986. This new computer capacity has encouraged House candidates to bring their campaigns "on-line." According to King, "We went through fifty of our key races and only one didn't have some sort of computer capacity. With our new computers we can finally give our people the advice necessary to become a modern campaign."

The Democratic Congressional Campaign Committee has gone through remarkable growth in other ways as well. It has increased its staff by almost 900 percent since 1981, with a total of seventy people on the payroll for the 1986 election, including five field personnel added in 1986, compared to none in 1982. Direct mail grew from $60,000 in 1981 to $10 million for the 1986 cycle. The enlargement and modernization of the entire DCCC operation represents, both nationally and at the individual candidate level, a significant advance for the Democrats, who were in danger of lagging far behind their Republican counterparts in both campaign hardware and software. "[Chairman] Coelho has juiced up the DCCC so much, got it going so fast, that the next period will see some consolidation. We have growing pains now, but we will be a well oiled machine by 1988," King predicted.

The Democratic Senatorial Campaign Committee also became fully automated in 1986. That is, every list – financial, voter, and data base – was computerized for immediate access and handling. "We don't have any typewriters in this office any more," claimed DSCC Executive Director David Johnson. For candidates, the major change in the DSCC has come in its direct involvement in their campaigns. The DSCC, a young organization created in 1980, had originally been incumbent oriented. However, with the dramatic improvement in its fundraising capabilities, it spent much of its time and resources in 1986 on Democratic challenger races. There was far more "hands-on" involvement than at any time in its brief history. According to Johnson, "We were in touch with our campaigns daily, sometimes two or three times a day. We were tracking candidates better simply because we had more money and more experience." This close candidate–party involvement was important when the DSCC sought to assist its candidates in exploiting the weakness of their Republican opponents. In fact, it was a DSCC field decision to employ phone banks on behalf of its candidates in seven marginal states, to hammer away at the Republican incumbents for their stand on the Social Security issue. A bold move, it has been credited with several Democratic upsets on election day – six of the seven targeted Republicans were defeated.

However, the DSCC does not try to control its candidates' campaigns to as great an extent as the DCCC. "We are not in the business of micro-managing campaigns," claimed Johnson. "We think the best person to decide how to run a race is the candidate." However, Johnson did acknowledge that the DSCC does inquire how its candidates would spend party contributions before such allocations are made, and that the final decision of the DSCC to provide funding can depend on the use to which the candidate plans to put the money. And despite Johnson's claim of official consultant impartiality, there was one notable exception in 1986 with the Louisiana Senate campaign of John Breaux, in which the DSCC managed to create near-havoc by its unsuccessful attempt to convince the candidate to fire one media consultant and hire another.

The DSCC and its sister organizations were also heavy users of the new Harriman Communications Center, a state-of-the-art TV and radio production facility owned and operated by the DCCC, and located in the basement of the Democratic party headquarters. Initially paid for by leading Democratic activist Pamela Harriman, widow of former presidential candidate and New York governor Averell Harriman, to provide Democrats with the same facilities already available to Republican candidates, the Harriman Center does not offer full service assistance. Rather, it provides camera crews, sound recording, and video tape editing to the campaign while leaving the script and other creative aspects of paid advertising to the candidate and consultant. Its primary objective is to stretch the production dollar, leaving the candidate and campaign in a better position to get their message on the air after the spots are completed. In the 1984 election cycle, about 600 radio and television ads were produced, at a saving of about $800,000 to the candidates and Democratic committees. The usage and savings were even greater for Democratic candidates in 1986. But Tom King most emphatically does not want to see the Democratic party in the media business. "Every race is an individual race, not a cut and paste situation. We don't have the time, and we can't do all the races that would need us. The candidate should have someone else to rely on."

The Democratic National Committee experienced a new vigor in 1986, as it rapidly accelerated its rebuilding efforts. The structure, emphasis, and appearance of the DNC was radically altered in the effort to regain candidate confidence and return party influence to Washington, DC. Said Jeff Ely:

The DNC had come to feel that they had gotten out of the business of electing Democrats and had gotten into the business of fighting about rules, doing those things which made us appear like we were a party out of control. Now we talk about the sensible things needed to win campaigns – doing the training, building the technology it takes.

Public relations were only the first step. After losing a large number of close races in 1980, 1982, and 1984, the DNC decided to concentrate on the traditional get-out-the-vote (GOTV) program, but using the latest campaign techniques to get Democrats to the polls. Although more limited in scope than the RNC efforts, the DNC was able to match Republican technical sophistication for the first time in areas where both were operating get-out-the-vote programs.

The DNC also instituted a program in the 1986 election cycle that would upgrade the capabilities of the state party organizations to assist their candidates seeking office, an operation that should be fully in place by election day, 1988. Fundraising experts were brought on and sent to key states early in the election cycle, to design an individualized, computerized program for obtaining voter lists and raising money. Another DNC representative followed later to translate the computerized fundraising program and provide easy candidate access. In those states that had a fundraising program in place by early 1986, the average amount raised was more than half a million dollars by election day. According to Ely, "These states were very appreciative of what we did. In the other states, we could only apologize for not having enough resources to provide greater assistance."

Perhaps the most important change in the DNC, however, was in its campaign structure. This change was the final elimination of ethnic and special interest coordinators (Republicans had done away with them years ago). Instead of targeting voters by race, religion, color, sex, or national origin, the country was divided into four regions, each with a regional coordinator who was assigned twelve or thirteen states. There were also eight field staff hired by each regional coordinator, the first time that the DNC used field personnel – yet another break with tradition. As Ely characterized the new philosophy of the DNC:

We used to be geared to serving constituency groups. Now we are geared to improve the nuts and bolts of the party, working with state party organizations on a daily basis to help make their jobs easier. Elections aren't won by building networks of constituency groups. They are only won by reaching a wider number of voters, and this can only be done with modern campaign technology.

Although the Democrats are unable to allocate the same amount of funding and resources as the GOP to a like number of candidates, nevertheless their sizeable field organization, recent computerization, and increased reliance on quality consultants are rapidly closing the technology gap with the Republicans. The Executive Directors of the DSCC and the NRSC both agree that those candidates who end up targeted by the Democrats do receive roughly an equivalent amount of money and services to that received by their Republican opponents. Tom King declared: "The Democrats have come of age technologically. If you give me an equal amount of money, and an equal playing field, I'd run as a Democrat." Added Ely: "It used to be that if you went to a candidate and said you were from the Democratic National Committee, they'd send you back where you came from. Now they are glad to see us." DCCC chairman Tony Coelho was particularly popular on the

1986 campaign trail because he dispensed checks from the committee to the candidates at nearly every stop.

The dramatic leap in the technology and expertise available from the two national party organizations is also occurring in other areas of electioneering. The proliferation of political action committees has actually given the parties a new role, increasing – not diminishing – the parties' contribution to the election of their candidates. Pollster Lance Tarrance suggested that the Republican party, and to a lesser extent the Democratic, has converted itself into a "super PAC – on the one hand a money machine, and on the other a repository of campaign expertise." In the conventional manner, both the DCCC and the NRCC send out PAC bulletins every month in an attempt to draw in more dollars for their candidates. "It's an elegant little system," suggested national syndicated political columnist Michael Barone. "They tell PACs which races are serious and which are not; which challengers have fallen down and which have not. PACs do listen. It's wonderful." In 1984, the Democratic incumbent from Indiana's second congressional district was targeted by the national Republican organizations, who pumped $80,000 in cash and services into the race. Corporate PACs, following the Republican lead, threw in another $85,000. But in 1986, the district was no longer targeted, the national Republican organizations gave only $1,000, and with two weeks to election day, not a single corporate PAC donated to the campaign.[22] Where national Republican money goes, corporate PAC donations soon follow. Once the national Democratic organizations have made a contribution, the doors are opened for labor funding.

In addition, the two national parties now have PAC experts on their payrolls to assist their candidates in directly obtaining PAC funding. According to an RNC PAC liaison specialist, "We give a challenger or open-seat prospect a list of every PAC that exists. From there, we try to determine which committees will have a philosophical affinity for the candidate, and find out whether the PAC has an interest in the candidate's district."[23] In every candidate packet distributed to all Democratic House challengers is a list of the major PACs which have historically been pro-Democratic. The PACs are divided into seven categories for easy reference. The list includes the PAC's name, address, and phone, the name of the PAC president, and also a specific contact person so as to facilitate communication and contributions. Even as PACs have become more technically efficient (and as candidates have improved their ability to communicate directly with PACs), PACs have not weakened the involvement of the national parties in the campaigns of their candidates.

However, there are limits to what the national party organizations can achieve for their candidates. "We don't make or break candidates," admitted former RNC Field Director Ed Brookover. "The edge we provide may just be able to take the candidate from close to across the finish line." Election results in the past two decades have shown that the national parties can provide the greatest edge, particularly to their marginal candidates, in those years when the public desires a change. Again, according to Brookover, "The public has to be ready for a national issue. We can't just make something up." But in election cycles where national issues already exist, the parties have proven their effectiveness in exploiting the national mood of the electorate, and reinforcing public perceptions to gain more votes for their candidates than they would otherwise have received. In close congressional elections, the vast resources available to the national party organizations have often provided targeted candidates with the margin necessary for victory in closely contested races.

Of the past ten elections, only three saw a net change of at least twenty-five House seats from one party to the other. In each of those three elections, there was either an overriding national issue or a frustration that was exploited by one of the national party organizations, much to the benefit of their candidates. The Democratic National Committee, for example, was successful in turning Watergate from a condemnation of President Nixon into an indictment of the Republican party, which led to a Democratic landslide in the 1974 congressional elections.

The first election that featured an extensive paid media campaign by one of the political parties on behalf of all its candidates was in 1980. After experiencing limited success with its "America Today" paid media campaign in 1978, the Republican party was eminently successful two years later in using television commercials to turn the Iranian hostage affair and other failures of the Carter administration into a national referendum on the Democratic party. In a major decision which broke with precedent, the leaders of the RNC, NRCC, and NRSC agreed to pool resources to create a single, well-organized, well-funded institutional advertising campaign. As Edward Blakely, head of broadcasting services at the time, said later, "Up to that point, the three committees had been very competitive. It would have been easier to achieve an arms agreement with the Russians than to see such cooperation happen at that time." Republican candidates across the country willingly and enthusiastically campaigned on the same issues and slogans in a concerted effort to demonstrate party unity. Not since the 1964 Goldwater debacle (see chapter 5) had a national party organization so successfully orchestrated a nationwide campaign. To quote a *Congressional Quarterly*: "The GOP blanketed television screens all over the country with the message that Democrats had controlled Congress for a quarter-century and that House Speaker Tip O'Neill was an obese, ageing, unresponsive political boss. Virtually all Republican challengers hammered home the same message, professionally scripted for them in Washington."[24]

Republican candidates were not consulted during the creation of the media campaign, though they were advised of its contents before the commercials were released for airing, and were offered the option of having the spots pulled from their area. The 11 million dollar national media effort, "Vote Republican – for a change" was a major factor in electing large numbers of Republican congressional and senatorial candidates. According to Blakely, "They were attack ads, but they were done with humor and taste, and they rang true. It added 3 or 4 percent to the average House candidate. When you realize how many Republicans won by fewer than 3 percent [about fifteen], it was very effective." In addition, the commercials greatly improved the fundraising climate, allowing the three committees to provide direct cash contributions to candidates they were not initially able to target.

Taking a cue from the GOP, the Democrats successfully used the subsequent recession and economic hardships to swing the 1982 elections back to their party. The "It isn't fair – it's Republican" media campaign enabled the party to associate dislike of Reaganomics with incumbent Republicans. This tactic yielded significant electoral gains on the congressional level in those areas where the commercials were aired. But according to Republican Blakely, "Some of their spots were devastating, but our greatest luck was that they didn't have the money to air those commercials effectively." The Democratic advertisements were made available to the party's candidates, who were then encouraged to raise the money (as there were no alternative funds for this) to air them whenever finances allowed.

However, the 11 million dollar counterattack with the "stay the course" message probably saved the Republicans from even greater losses. In this century, the party in control of the White House has lost forty-five House seats, on average, in the first off-year election. The Republicans lost only twenty-six. According to Burton Sheppard, "It is a generally held view that the 1982 election showcased the Republicans' ability to use superior financial resources to minimize Democratic gains – in short, to distort the electoral outcome despite the macro forces favoring the Democrats."[25] The common element in the 1974, 1980, and 1982 campaigns was a clearly delineated and publicly accepted national issue.

There were no such national issues or themes in the two succeeding elections, and consequently, the swings in House party membership were relatively slight. The national GOP organization attempted, somewhat unsuccessfully, to make the 1984 elections a referendum not just on President Reagan but also on the Republican party. Fourteen million dollars was spent on the "Vote Republican – for the future" media effort, but its impact was limited. Although radio and magazine advertising were added to the television component, it did not move votes. While the American public was clearly willing to cast its vote for the incumbent president, to a great extent they rejected the party message. Reagan's coat-tails were shortened, and Republican gains in the House were limited to fourteen seats.

In 1986, the Republican party tried again to fill the political void by making the drug problem a national issue. However, it failed for two reasons. First, the public did not view the GOP as having a monopoly on the anti-drug crusade; and secondly, few voters perceived drugs to be a partisan issue. Late in the campaign, the National Republican Senatorial Committee began airing radio ads concerning the conservative social agenda, aimed primarily at younger voters and born-again Christians in four targeted southern states. "Ever think about what's important to you?" the commercial began. "It's probably simple – a steady job, a healthy family, and a personal relationship with Christ." But these ads were dropped after only one week, following protests from leaders of the Jewish community. Republicans lost in all four states where the ad was aired.

A debate still simmers in both political camps over the effectiveness of national media efforts in electing their candidates. "If it works, everybody takes credit for it. When it doesn't appear to work, everybody gets demolished," says RNC Party Development Director McInturff. "Our belief is that national media helps carry an umbrella under which our candidates can run." The RNC claims that where Republican commercials were played heavily, survey results show they did improve the Republican climate, and therefore added to the vote totals of their clients. When asked by disgruntled candidates to prove the usefulness of national media efforts, the RNC used survey research to compare the generic Republican vote in media markets where its commercials were heavily played with those where they were not. There was a small, but consistent, percentage point difference. Nevertheless, according to McInturff, "Most of our candidates would still prefer to see our tangible cash in their own campaigns."

The issue over media effectiveness conceals a deeper and potentially more explosive problem. As the national party organizations become more important and acquire new ways to flex their political muscle, they will inevitably begin to usurp the independence and decision making power of their candidates. In fact, it has already occurred. For the first time since the adoption of the FECA in 1971, House Republican candidates, in 1982, found themselves in near rebellion against the election strategies of the national party – and helpless to do anything about it. The initial advertising campaign, "The Democratic last will and testament," had the early support of House incumbents, though complaints soon arose. "Incumbents like something if they are told to like something," claimed Blakely. "When the commercials were first shown, they all liked it. But when they found out the White House didn't like it, you could see the mood change." The "last will" commercial was quickly pulled from circulation, though Blakely insists, quite openly, that "the candidates had nothing to do with the decision to pull the commercial." A number of congressional incumbents later went to the RNC requesting that they remove the subsequent "stay the course" media campaign from their area because they felt close identification with President Reagan might cost them the election. As former White House Political Director and Reagan–Bush Campaign Director Edward Rollins acknowledged, "I didn't think 'stay the course' was a good slogan. I don't know of anyone who liked it except for the NRCC campaign people and some of their pollsters."

The Republican party found itself in a difficult situation, since its media buys are 40 percent national (with the same commercial airing at the same time on every network affiliate) and 60 percent spot (referring to each single, targeted media market). It was possible to pull individual commercials in the spot markets, but the only way to change the national buy was to pull every one of the commercials. After intense deliberation, the party organizations decided to ignore the complaints of its candidates, particularly in the northeast where unemployment and dislike of Reaganomics was high, and maintain the national campaign. According to a high ranking RNC official, "One candidate screaming in North Dakota does not change the fact that everyone else in America may see and like the commercial" – the national Republican organizations attempt, as best they can, to placate disgruntled candidates, but they are unwilling to change a strategy they believe will help the vast majority of candidates at the expense of a few. As McInturff concluded: "When you are running a national party, you are asked to make decisions about not what helps every single candidate but what helps the large majority of candidates. There is no important decision you can make that will keep 100 percent of your candidates happy."

Regardless of national themes or demonstrated party successes, some candidates are simply unwilling to accept the advice provided by the national party organizations, preferring instead to trust local experts or their own intuition. Sometimes party advice is simply ignored. Said Brookover: "We spend a lot of time digging deeper into polling numbers to learn what our candidates' weaknesses are, even when they are leading. But some candidates just gloss over it, telling us, 'We're still ahead. What are you worried about?'" According to Republican media consultant John Deardourff, even NRSC Chairman John Heinz preferred to use costly outside consultants rather than free "in-house" advisors in his re-election campaigns. "He never used the services of the NRSC when he ran. Did Heinz want a field man from the NRSC coming into Pennsylvania telling him how to run his campaign? No."

Similarly, while both parties claim an increased role in the campaigns of their candidates, both also acknowledge that their new involvement has not always met with the approval of every candidate. "The Republican party has been treating congressional races as if they were miniature presidential races," suggests dissatisfied Congressman Mickey Edwards. "You win not by tying into the grand march of history but by concentrating on the individual, unique aspects of each district."[26]

Most incumbents are reluctant to speak out publicly against the national party organization, but high level administrators in the campaign committees admit that a large body of their candidates have opposed significant interference (that is, involvement) from Washington in their campaigns. According to Tom Griscom, "When incumbents consider a strategy that may backfire, the rule is that they don't tell us until after the fact. Then they'll call and say, 'What can you do to get us out of this mess?'" Although staff members at the RNC refused to list the 1986 races which least welcomed national party involvement, Ed Brookover did venture that Republican candidates who took their advice did better than those that didn't: "Some of our candidates lost because they made some basic assumptions that were just plain wrong. We tried working with them during the campaign but some of them just didn't change. They lost precisely for the reasons we told them they would lose." Tom King concurred: "Some candidates won't listen to us, so we have to beat it out of them – or withhold money. You've got to be tough. They're not going to win if they don't listen to us, to be quite honest."

In many ways, the incumbent Republican senators who faced re-election in 1986 typified the recurring conflict between an increasingly informed and involved party apparatus and its clientele. Many had been swept into office in the Reagan–Republican landslide of 1980, without much direct support and encouragement from the national party organizations. Although the RNC and its sister organizations had advertised heavily nationwide, benefiting all party candidates, they did not strongly target states like Alabama, Florida, and Georgia (among others) because they had not elected Republican senators in many years. Many of the newly elected senators, although successful, continued to hold a grudge against the national party for its lack of confidence and support in their battle to unseat entrenched incumbents. In their 1986 re-election battles, several were openly hostile to offers of advice and assistance from Washington. According to Edward Brookover, "Some of our candidates were saying to us, 'Who are these bozos who told me I couldn't win in 1980 and why should I listen to them now in 1986!' There was probably some validity to that statement," Brookover said, "though we hoped they would feel differently."

Consequently, the NRSC is somewhat reluctant to dictate electoral strategy to its candidates. The organization is in constant contact with incumbents when Congress is in session, and they maintain daily communication with the various campaign headquarters, yet their strategy is very much "hands-off." Former NRSC Executive Director Tom Griscom defined the limits of his committee's current involvement in the day-to-day affairs of their candidates when he said: "I don't think it is our role as a national committee to go in and dictate to thirty-four Senate races, to tell them, 'Here's your little package – jump in. This is what you have to do.'"

Clashes between candidates and the national party organizations are not limited to Republicans. Former DCCC Political Director Tom King has similar difficulties with his incumbents. "It's tough to tell an incumbent who has won ten times in a row that the way he has won in the past might not work this time." Many challengers, and even more incumbents, have become hesitant about outside involvement in their campaigns. When the DSCC tried to force 1986 Louisiana Senate candidate John Breaux to hire a new media consultant, Breaux refused, and his campaign staff continuously bickered with national operatives over strategy and tactics. That media consultant, Raymond Strother, remained with the campaign, and guided the candidate to victory in the subsequent election. It is clear from interviews with party leaders and political consultants that some candidates are not anxious to trade autonomous decision making power for a few "pearls of wisdom" or some extra dollars in the bank.

On occasion, though apparently less frequently than in the past, a candidate may receive poor advice from the national party. A prime example of this was the 1986 California race pitching Republican Congressman Edward Zschau against incumbent Democratic Senator Alan Cranston. Following the advice of an ill-informed individual at the National Republican Senatorial Committee, Zschau spent the first crucial days following his bruising free-for-all primary on vacation, rather than immediately focusing on his opponent. It was assumed by the Republicans in Washington that Cranston would not begin attacking Zschau for several weeks, so as to save his funds for the expensive statewide media blitzes in September and October. But instead, Cranston immediately released a barrage of negative advertising that caught Zschau unprepared (he had just fired his media consultant). This action gave Cranston the opportunity to regain the momentum, to launch an unanswered political attack, and to double his lead in the polls – a lead which had previously been shrinking. Zschau was needlessly put in a defensive position, and this cost him crucial dollars, as well as time, in a desperate effort to recover lost ground. His narrow defeat (49 percent to Cranston's 51 percent) would most likely have been averted had he rejected the advice of the NRSC, remained on the campaign trail, and immediately after the primary come out swinging against his opponent.

A highly touted NRCC gimmick in 1986 to discredit Arkansas Congressman William Alexander also backfired on his Republican opponent. To draw attention to Alexander's many international trips at taxpayer's expense, the NRCC conducted a lottery to award a free trip for two, anywhere in the world, to a lucky Alexander constituent. But the winners turned out to be staunch Alexander supporters who publicly defended the congressman – and greatly embarrassed the Republican opponent.

But the greatest error by any national party organization in 1986 was one that fatally damaged one of the Republicans' best candidates and probably cost them a crucial Senate seat. The Republican National Committee announced in September that it would conduct a "ballot integrity" program designed to justify challenges of voters in heavily Democratic precincts in those states where close elections were anticipated. According to RNC political director William Greener, "The targeting was not based on gender or race or age; it was based on vote performace."[27] However, in Louisiana, a federal judge issued a preliminary injunction against the Republican effort, claiming that the Republicans "had singled out the blacks, and as such, [the attempt] was not in good faith . . . "[28] Democratic party officials immediately attacked the program, claiming that it was "the latest attempt by Republicans to disenfranchise minority voters with abusive tactics that skirt the edge of the law."[29] Although not involved, or even consulted, by the RNC, Republican Senate candidate Henson Moore saw his lead evaporate after the scandal broke, and he eventually lost by a 53 to 47 percent margin to Democratic opponent John Breaux. This author interviewed the pollsters and media consultants for both candidates in the race: each one credits the negative publicity surrounding the GOP ballot security plan as playing a significant role in Moore's defeat. "It didn't help, I'll admit that," concluded Brookover.

Clearly, the national party organizations have already learned from their 1986 successes and failures. Future targeted races, particularly those involving incumbents, will probably see more "hands on" activities by party operatives. The greatest change may come in the NRSC. No longer will candidates receive full funding and coordinated expenditures with few or no strings attached. According to Griscom:

I think we need more direct contact with our campaigns. If we are going to track, I'd want to know two months ahead of time what is going on, day in and day out, rather than finding out when it is too late. If our role is to be hands-on, then we will need more input into what's happening. We will need somebody inside the campaign.

Added Brookover, who, as 1988 NRSC political director, has brought a new philosophy to the committee: "It's not that we want to run their entire campaign. It's that we really do have people here who care about their party, and they spend twenty-four hours caring about nothing else. And we have learned something."

The national parties have also learned that today's skilled professional consultants are essential to modern electioneering, and moreover, that the campaign techniques they provide have not destroyed the parties but have strengthened them. The brief period of extreme candidate independence from the national party organizations in the 1960s and 1970s has proven to be the exception, not the norm, in American politics since World War II. Despite the fears and pronouncements of many political scientists – and even some candidates and consultants – the rise of professional campaigners has actually supported the resurgence of party power in Washington. In fact, according to 1986 RNC political director William Greener, "There are any number of projects that would never have been attempted, much less achieved, without the involvement of the consultants the RNC utilized."[30] Not a single staff member in either party was condemnatory of the role of consultants, or even attributed a decline in party influence to them. Several had actually worked as political consultants before coming to the national parties. Pollster Lance Tarrance did not find this fact at all surprising: "Many of the general consultants who had worked their way to the top have migrated to one of the campaign committees. They have brought with them some of the statewide technical innovations and are trying to develop a more universal pattern for their party's candidates." Rather than compete with the political consultants, the national parties have recognized their expertise and adopted their skills to benefit party candidates. A majority of Republican consultants agree. (See survey 4.1.)

The parties have employed sympathetic consultants to train party personnel in modern campaign technology, and with their institutional framework, the parties serve as "library" and "resource bank" for both consultants and candidates. Attempts to establish an institutional memory, to avoid having to gather statistics, research, and the like, election after election, have proven increasingly helpful to candidates

**Survey 4.1** *How important are the national party organizations in the elections of their candidates: very important, somewhat important, or of little or no importance?*

|  | Total (%) | Republican consultants (%) | Democratic consultants (%) |
|---|---|---|---|
| Very important | 41 | 65 | 7 |
| Somewhat important | 38 | 25 | 57 |
| Little or no importance | 21 | 10 | 36 |

with limited political resources. Their programs contribute, in large measure, the the success of their candidates, and inasmuch as the parties also provide services that might otherwise be unaffordable to its candidates, they confer a significant financial benefit as well.

In the final analysis, there is just so much assistance the national parties can provide their candidates. According to Brookover, "Without strong candidates, we will lose elections. There is only so much make-up you can put on somebody. There is only so much the parties can do." Griscom concurred: "Nineteen eighty-six shows us that everything we had cannot take the place of the candidate, the type of campaign that they run, the organization that they have, and their ability to deliver a message." Yet the harsh words of one political consultant are surely no longer appropriate. Years ago, Richard Viguerie told a reporter that the Republican Party "is like a disabled tank on the bridge, impeding the troops from crossing to the other side. You've got to take that tank and throw it in the river."[31] A more appropriate commentary came from Blakely when he listed what national party organizations can do for their prospective candidates: "If I were trying to recruit you to run as a candidate, I would say, 'Look, we'll provide you with full funding, we'll give you double coordinated, our field guy will be in three times a week, and we'll do your advertising for you. There are a lot of benefits I can now offer if you were to run.'" Blakely's opinion is held by a majority of the leading political consultants *in both parties*. (See survey 4.2.)

**Survey 4.2** *Overall, is the importance of the national party organizations currently increasing or decreasing?*

|  | Total (%) | Republican consultants (%) | Democratic consultants (%) |
|---|---|---|---|
| Increasing | 60 | 65 | 53 |
| Decreasing | 23 | 10 | 41 |
| Stable (response volunteered) | 17 | 25 | 6 |

The national party organizations are more influential, more powerful, and of greater benefit to their candidates than at any time since the passage of the 1974 Federal Election Campaign Act. They have protected many vulnerable incumbents, provided the necessary additional resources at critical times for numerous victorious challengers, and served as a laboratory for the development of new electioneering techniques. But ultimately, it remains for the candidates to decide whether to avail themselves of what the parties have to offer in the 1980s; and candidates know that even with modern technology the national parties still cannot perform miracles.

# 5

# Politics through the mail

The fact is that direct mail is technically neutral. Whether or not the cause or candidate succeeds depends far less on the talent and inside manipulation of the direct mail experts than it does on the acceptance of the ideas and issues by the American electorate.

Roger Craver, fundraiser

I know candidates who will spend hours with some loco-yoko group representing some damn thing that controls all of twelve votes, spends half a day getting there, half a day getting back, twenty minutes shaking hands and then doesn't have time to look at a direct mail letter going out to 150,000 households. They're insane.

Bob Odell, fundraiser

Direct mail is probably the least understood and most maligned of the recent innovations in electoral politics, yet it is the one aspect of political technology on which most, if not all, of the others depend. Candidates today, faced with raising millions of dollars under a restrictive federal law that limits individual contributions to $1,000 per candidate per election, have been forced to turn to a new generation of political technocrats, the direct mail specialists. Political fundraising has become a technician's game, and direct mail has provided the vehicle for obtaining the funds necessary to run a political campaign. Yet some of the greatest innovations in direct mail have actually come with regard to gaining votes rather than raising money. An entirely new breed of consultants has begun using the letter as an advertising tool, directing carefully crafted messages into the homes of probable voters. As this decade draws to a close, candidates have come to realize that electoral success and direct mail success are closely related.

The first extensive, organized use of direct mail in a national

146

campaign occurred during Woodrow Wilson's administration, when the Democratic National Committee devised a letter solicitation program that resulted in about 300,000 contributions. In the late 1930s, the American left used direct mail fundraising to provide operating capital for various "New Deal" style private programs and organizations. Dwight D. Eisenhower became the first national candidate from the Republican party to rely significantly on direct mail, raising about $1.5 million from 300,000 contributors.

More recent direct mail history is rather unusual among modern campaign technologies in that its candidate-practitioners, who were most successful in fundraising at the presidential level, were considerably less successful in attracting votes. The campaigns of Barry Goldwater in 1964 and George Wallace in 1968 depended heavily on direct mail, inasmuch as the candidates appealed to an easily identifiable segment of the population, thus enabling the campaign to target, and effectively devote its efforts to, those people most likely to give money. Goldwater was, in fact, the first presidential candidate to claim more than half a million financial contributors, who were responsible for almost $6 million in donations. But he failed to get the votes from the population at large.

It was George McGovern's 1972 presidential race that many campaign experts credit with bringing direct mail into the modern age of electioneering. Like Goldwater and George Wallace before him, McGovern was able to obtain significant financial support from large numbers of small contributors. But McGovern was the first presidential candidate to plan systematically a sophisticated direct mail effort, which eventually brought the campaign over 600,000 contributors and $15 million in contributions.[1]

An important stimulus to direct mail came in 1974, when Congress passed an amendment to the Federal Election Campaign Act (FECA) which limited personal political contributions to $1,000 to any one candidate in any one election. According to fundraiser Bruce Eberle, "When they came out with the FECA laws, they made direct mail crucial, an almost essential vehicle of any campaign, even if it was not the sole source for funds. The days of fat cats were over." Candidates who had relied on a few wealthy backers for support were suddenly faced with the necessity of spreading the financial burden over a broad number of contributors. Campaigns that received numerous small donations had now been put on equal footing with those receiving a few large contributions. Thus, the FECA was the catalyst that forced all candidates to look for new ways to generate campaign contributions. Many had no choice but to turn to direct mail.

By 1976, most major candidates entering the presidential election process used direct mail, at least to some extent. More than one-third of Jimmy Carter's private contributions came in response to direct mail, a surprisingly high figure considering that Carter was not attempting to appeal ideologically to the more extreme elements of the Democratic Party.[2] On the Republican side, nominee Gerald Ford, using direct mail, raised $2.6 million, surpassing his more conservative Republican opponent, Ronald Reagan, who preferred television solicitations to direct mail appeals.[3] By 1980, however, the Reagan campaign had come to rely more heavily on direct mail, with about 50 percent of Reagan's funding in the early stages of the primaries coming from mail solicitations.[4] Now, no presidential candidate can hope to raise sufficient funds without an extensive direct mail effort. Some, like 1988 presidential hopeful Jack Kemp, are even prepared to go into debt in order to finance a major direct mail campaign.

More recently, of the approximately $16 million that the Reagan–Bush re-election campaign raised in 1984, $11 million – more than two-thirds – came through the mail.[5] Incumbent senators and congressmen use direct mail routinely to maintain support in their constituencies. Senate and gubernatorial challengers have been somewhat slower to adopt direct mail as a primary fundraising technique. In 1986, about three-fourths of all Republican Senate candidates used direct mail fundraising on a major scale, though the percentage was smaller on the Democratic side.[6] However, nearly every statewide campaign, and the majority of congressional candidates, have since discovered, and are currently using, direct mail technology to at least some degree.

The present process of choosing a direct mail organization is comparatively simple. A team of consultants from a general, multi-program direct mail firm will meet with the candidate or campaign staff (usually including the manager or finance director), and together they determine whether it will be mutually profitable for both the campaign and the firm to engage in fundraising mail or voter persuasion mail. Some companies go a step further. Bruce Eberle requests that each new client make a presentation to his firm's employees, in an effort to establish a close working relationship. It has become crucial that this first exploratory meeting take place very early in the election cycle. "Otherwise," according to Roger Craver, "a successful multi-step direct mail campaign is improbable. Generally, we recommend that candidates allow at least eighteen months to develop a full program."

Since the more established firms tend to have a long list of clients, it is usually necessary for House and Senate campaigns to be assigned an overall account executive who handles the various packages as they are produced. Provided that both the campaign and the direct mail firm are satisfied with each other and with the business arrangements as well, then a contract is signed and the direct mail program begun.

Once the firm receives the go-ahead from its client, it will proceed to create the copy for the letter, which is then approved, or revised, by the candidate or the candidate's agent. Direct mail letters are all different, although as with television advertising, they fall into predictable categories. Among the most effective are those in which the potential contributor is asked to donate a specific amount to provide a specific service. In the 1986 Florida Senate contest, the Hawkins campaign implored contributors to "Keep Paula Hawkins on TV," listing the price for airing 30-second commercials in various markets and then asking to which particular TV shows donors wanted their advertisement money to go. In a similar approach, Roger Craver likes to send potential donors, by Federal Express (an overnight mail delivery service) a copy of the actual proof of a political advertisement, along with a note indicating its cost and a request that a check be sent at once – in a Federal Express return envelope included in the package. Another popular format is the "confidential memo," which informs "insiders" of campaign strategy, and warns that if a contribution is not sent immediately, the campaign may not meet its goals. Brad O'Leary is fond of the invoice technique, in which the direct mail envelope and letter inside are designed like a genuine invoice. Potential donors are told that they *owe* a specific amount to a candidate, and are instructed, not asked, to forward that amount immediately. Added O'Leary, "The gimmick works, but it brings a whole lot of heat with it. A whole lot of people will bitch like crazy that you sent them an invoice. You'll also get twice as much money as you would get in a more normal mailing."

Perhaps the most common approach is the "Dear Friend" approach. Signed by a well-known politician or celebrity, these "personal" letters are produced by the thousand, although every attempt is made to have them appear as though the signatory wrote each one. The "dear friend" salutation is often scratched out and the name of the donor penned in by a piece of high tech equipment. The psychological tone used suggests to the reader: "We intended to send everyone a form letter, but you're special and we know you're special."[7] Sometimes a short "handwritten" note is added to suggest authenticity. There is a clear sense of urgency in every direct mail letter, a new crisis to overcome. And of course, each contains an urgent appeal for money.

It is the candidate who generally provides the research and documentation that goes into a direct mail letter, although many direct mail firms will assist in this if necessary. However, obtaining a signatory to the letter, which is often the most important piece of the direct mail package, rests entirely with the candidate. The final steps include determining which voters will receive the package (by creating, through purchase or rental, a mailing list) and supervising its production and distribution.

The direct mail firm will frequently test the fundraising potential of a particular package (the copy, mailing list, or both) or test a series of mailings at critical periods during the election cycle. The importance of this procedure cannot be overemphasized. According to Roger Craver,

"The best direct mail package in the world is worthless if sent to the wrong mailing list. If there is any 'science' in direct mail, it rests with the way in which mailing lists are drawn up." Most fundraisers have adopted the one-sixth method of testing (that is, addressing the package to one-sixth of the entire donor file and then evaluating the response) before mailing to the balance of the donor list. The tests are generally completed in a period of less than three weeks so as to keep the results reliable and minimize the effect that a change in current events and issues might have on the tested package. A direct mail package will be used until the candidate or his agent decides that it is no longer profitable. The entire process is repeated with each new package developed. In the more expensive or more complex races, several different fundraising packages will be mailed on the same day to similar segments of the same list, to test which appeal will work best for the client. A growing number of candidates are even retaining a direct mail firm months after the election, either to pay off debts or to continue building funds for the next campaign.

Direct mail fundraising efforts revolve around two kinds of mailings: "house" and "prospecting." Since all candidates begin their political careers as non-incumbents, their initial direct mail campaign must first begin by prospecting for donations, a process that often starts as much as two years before election day. A list of potential donors whose characteristics the campaign or the direct mail firm believes will make them most likely to respond to the candidate's particular appeal is compiled from various sources. Generally, individuals with a previous history of contributions to other like-minded candidates are initially sought, though wealthier campaigns may expand that list to include those with similar employment, religion or other matching characteristics. Appeals to prospective contributors tend to be emotional, evoking strong images in regard to issues that are often controversial in nature. According to Bruce Eberle, "Sometimes rules of grammar are broken, but always with a purpose." Simply stated, the key to successful prospecting is to motivate the readers, using whatever words or symbolisms it takes to move them to contribute. Thus, in prospect mailings the tacit rule among direct mailers is that there are no rules: anything goes in the pursuit of profit.

Those who eventually do respond and donate are then included in a campaign's "house list," consisting of individuals who have shown a commitment to the campaign and may be willing to give again in the future. The donor's name, address, and telephone number (if it was provided), the amount donated, and a record of past donations are all fed into a computer so the campaign will have data on the background and donations of each contributor. This then allows the direct mail firm to classify each house list mailing according to the size of the contribution, date of the latest donation, and the frequency of gift giving. The house list is programmed for continuous mailings, sometimes as often as every four to six weeks as the campaign approaches completion. The ultimate goal of any direct mail effort is to build an extensive and reliable house list that will yield significant sums with each mailing.

A frequently overlooked aspect of the direct mail fundraising effort is the "production," which is the actual package received by the prospective contributor. In 1981, author Larry Sabato divided the typical direct mail piece into five categories: 1) the letter, 2) the additional enclosure, 3) the contribution card, 4) the return envelope, and 5) the carrier or mailing envelope.[8] The components that make up the overall direct mail package have, for the most part, remained much the same since direct mail first became widely used in the 1970s.

However, over the past five years significant innovations have greatly altered the appearance, form, and style of the typical package, and have modernized it far beyond what practitioners might have imagined a decade ago. Newspaper clippings and bumper stickers formerly included in a package have given way to paperback books and cassette tapes of selected speeches by the candidate. Envelopes are often designed to resemble Western Union telegrams, income tax information, or other official government communiqués; sometimes a statement on the envelope directs the recipient to open the letter immediately. Senator Bob Dole's 1988 presidential campaign sent thousands of letters in an envelope marked Document ##00-952774, with the admonition, "Please verify receipt." On the outside of the document was the legend: "Officially sealed." Mock election ballots are still popular direct mail tools among PACs and the national parties, as are plastic membership cards and the traditional family snapshot of the candidate, spouse, their children, and the inevitable family pet. More recently, the emphasis is on larger, more striking, more sophisticated packaging and enclosures that will dispose the prospective contributor to send a donation. One of the most lucrative direct mail packages for Bruce Eberle in the 1986 election cycle was also one of his more expensive, at a cost of 55 cents apiece. According to Eberle, "Given the proliferation and competitive nature of the direct mail field, it will make it necessary to start doing things that are very special to get attention."

In the past, an attempt was made to have letters appear as though on the candidate's personal or business stationery. But the low grade paper that was used and the fuzzy print made them look more like photocopies than individually typewritten pieces. Now, however, it is possible, by using high quality paper and print, to make each piece appear as though individually produced. A machine similar in technology and speed to a laser printer produces an apparently handwritten piece, and is now being used by direct mail firms, though at considerable cost. The ink dots used in the laser process to simulate the typewritten word are, in this machine, bled together to form scripted words, so that the results are hardly distinguishable from an original, handwritten note by the candidate. Observed Bob Odell, "Laser printing is the biggest recent change in direct mail. Not only is it fast, but it increases the number of variables in the package." Even the signature has become more authentic looking, with the invention of the "auto-pen" machine that can "hand sign" each letter in ink, individually. Thus, letter personalization is now within the financial range of even a modestly funded congressional candidate.

It is not uncommon to find direct mail combined with several other modern campaign techniques, especially in those election contests where personal voter contact with the candidate is limited. An often used and effective direct mail piece, generally sent to new contributors, highlights favorable survey results from the candidate's latest poll, along with a "confidential" commentary by the pollster. Although this type of direct mail is particularly well suited to a challenger who is gaining ground on the incumbent, it can also be used by incumbents to heighten voter interest and raise additional funds. The letter is computerized, using a software package that "personalizes" each piece (particularly important in the case of those who have previously received the usual standardized letter), and addresses the recipient by name throughout the piece.

Computer technology has become a partner to direct mail technology in other ways. As stated earlier, an effective direct mail piece is one that has a specific message or goal and is accurately targeted to those individuals who will respond as desired, with their support or money. Computerization speeds the production of the mail piece, lowers the cost, and therefore increases the potential number of people who can thus be reached. Said Bruce Eberle, "Because issues are quite volatile, it is very important to compress, as much as possible, the time frame between the original test of a direct mail letter and the subsequent rollout. Through computerization, it is possible to substantially upgrade the size of the average contribution received through house mailings. We simply could not be as fast or effective without our computers." Many firms now subscribe to NEXIS, a computer-assisted information service that provides instant access to many of the world's most important newspapers, magazines, news wires, and reference works. This allows a firm to update continuously the research and documentation for its direct mail packages, increasing the speed of production and the timeliness of every direct mail letter.

The Eberle firm has also developed a sophisticated three-tiered computerized system that can reduce the number of duplicate mailings to the same individual to less than 1 percent of the total mailing, a reduction that saves the client hundreds, if not thousands, of dollars. Eberle's computers first match each name in the house file against every other for similarities. The next step is to match all the names in all prospecting lists, where the vast majority of duplicates are found. Finally, the house contributor file is used as a kill tape against all prospecting files to insure that no current contributor will also receive the more generalized prospective mailing. Other leading direct mail firms have developed similar software programs to weed out duplicates.

Performance analysis of direct mail effectiveness also depends now on computer technology. Computerized daily tabulations of donor replies to test packages allow the direct mail firm to determine, instantly, which letters are bringing in the most net dollars for the client. Providing both daily and weekly figures, the tabulation program itemizes and analyzes the income (contributions) and the outflow (expenses), and is an important tool in the effort to maximize the former and minimize the latter.

Computerization, along with the very recent advent of intricate targeting techniques, has also made it possible to separate a constituency into hundreds of different categories, based on income, employment status, race, religion, age, sex, housing, or any combination of these and other census characteristics. An increasing number of consulting firms are converting the details contained in US census data (which breaks down each state geographically into thousands of census "tracks") to a computer software package or service which allows a candidate to target voters demographically on a neighborhood-by-neighborhood basis. In what must be considered a remarkable advance in electioneering, campaigns now have the capacity to determine which neighborhoods have the most children, the greatest percentage of elderly residents, the highest income, the largest number of owned (as compared with rented) houses, and about thirty-five other potentially important variables that may influence the way someone votes. It is now technologically possible to target a specific message directly to a distinct demographic group located in a particular neighborhood. The state of the art is such that a candidate can target a letter to single, white female Democrats aged twenty-five to thirty, stressing support of legalized abortion. Jewish voters can be sent letters that talk solely about Israel, and Cuban Americans can receive letters written in Spanish.

Although computerization has been used with targeted direct mail for several years, only recently have candidates begun to use the technology to its full advantage. In part, this exploitation has relieved the pressure on time and money. Since the computer can produce thousands of similar letters, each one slightly different from all the others, a computerized direct mail effort can, rapidly and inexpensively, incorporate pertinent facts about an individual and a neighborhood. By making use of accurate polling data as well, the result is a properly targeted, effective direct mail piece with a high likelihood of success. An outstanding example of the use of targeted direct mail is the 1980 West

Virginia Senate race, where Democratic millionaire Jay Rockefeller sent as many as ten different direct mail pieces to a single family, each letter containing a specific message that had appeal for a particular audience. It was an expensive but highly successful effort.

The combination of polling data, demographics, computerization, and direct mail reached a new level of electoral sophistication in the 1982 California gubernatorial campaign of George Deukmejian. His staff compiled a target list of registered Republicans likely to support his candidacy, fed those names into the computer, and then used the list to mail out millions of absentee ballots along with the standard fundraising letters. The absentee ballot effort gave Deukmejian his margin of victory in the election, and added yet another innovation to direct mail technology.

The 1986 Colorado Senate campaign of Ken Kramer, by using President Reagan's visit to the state for a fundraising effort, broke new ground in the effectiveness of direct mail. In only one September afternoon, the Kramer campaign raised nearly one million dollars, and an estimated 40 percent of the donors had never before contributed to a political campaign.[9] The names of potential donors were gleaned from more than 200 lists, many of them purchased for the occasion. But of the 400,000 people on the lists, only 10,000 received invitations for the $500-a-plate fundraising event. Computers cross-checked each list against the others, selecting only those individuals whose name appeared on several key lists. According to the event director, Brad O'Leary, computerized cross-checking saved the Kramer campaign $230,000. As had been anticipated, the response rate was high, with 1,760 guests in all. The total cost for the event was about $125,000, leaving Kramer with a net balance of almost $800,000, attributable to direct mail technology.

Challengers concerned with cutting costs have historically opted for fewer of the technically modern fundraising techniques. Said Bob Odell, "You may have laser printing. You may have personalization. But when you talk to the guy running for Congress in Kansas, he's just trying to get stamps and envelopes." However, with the growth of new, albeit expensive, electoral services now being offered to any candidate with sufficient funds, challengers have been able to expand their fundraising capabilities through direct mail. For challengers, the technology provides vital pseudo-personal access to a large number of people in a short period of time, necessary for raising adequate funds in the early, lean stages of the campaign, while leaving the candidate personally free to complete other tasks, among them raising additional funds to pay for all the various important campaign services. It is frequently the only way for first-time candidates who have limited name recognition and public support, and for candidates without personal wealth, to acquire sufficient grassroots financial backing.[10]

Another feature of direct mail is its ability to tap into funds from "outside" sources. Republican Congressman Robert Dornan narrowly defeated an entrenched incumbent in a Democratic-leaning district by raising a significant amount of his money from out-of-state sources, in a way made possible only through direct mail. "Though these people lived outside my district and beyond the borders of California, they nevertheless contributed heavily because they liked what I stood for." Dornan had a member of his staff compose and organize the various direct mail solicitations, while he himself combed the district in search of votes. Since it took only a few minutes to read and approve each piece, the candidate was able to increase his campaign coffers subtantially with minimum effort and time, particularly important in the vital early stages of the contest.

Of course, most challengers lack Bob Dornan's initial advantages of high name recognition early in the campaign, a defined and well known ideology, and a proven financial base. For those with little name recognition and no defined constituency, direct mail may not yield the same immediate reward. "It's tough for challengers to compete financially," claimed Bob Odell. "The money for challengers just doesn't add up very quickly. Challengers should not rely on a financial base that is created solely through direct mail." Said Roger Craver, "Few congressional campaign staffs have the necessary national audience, the necessary management skills and patience to turn the direct mail process to their advantage." Even popular Florida Governor Robert Graham was advised by his consultants not to depend on direct mail because "Nobody outside Florida knows who Bob Graham is," and "you can spend an awful lot of money before it starts paying off."[11]

Although direct mail is still used primarily to raise money, it also provides candidates with a valuable opportunity to augment, and sometimes replace, television and other advertising – literally "bringing home the message" to voters in an expanded format. All financial solicitations contain a pitch for voter support, but there also exists an entirely different form of direct mail, often overlooked by social scientists studying American elections, that is primarily designed not to raise money but to move voters. As escalating costs have put television, radio, and newspaper advertising beyond the means of some campaigns, direct mail advertising, randomly referred to as "candidate advocacy," "voter persuasion" or "voter contact" direct mail, has become a popular alternative method of communicating with the electorate. In fact, voter persuasion mail, not radio or television, is now the the dominant advertising technique of congressional candidates in California and in other urban areas of America. "Television may make you real," summarized David Welch, consultant and former director of direct mail communications at the National Republican Congressional

Committee, "but direct mail is the quiet medium, and it works."

According to veteran consultant Walter Devries, "Voter persuasion mail is highly effective, because it represents personal contact from the candidate, and that is still the most important way to contact voters – personal contact." Voter persuasion mail uses a distinctly different approach and style from that of direct mail fundraising: it can employ subtleties that are rarely seen in fundraising packages. "The best way to raise money from someone is to scare the hell out of them," says political consultant Roger Stone. "But if I want to win their vote, then a little more persuasion is in order." Added Welch, "attacking an opponent with humor is a lot more effective than the meat-axe approach."

As with direct mail fundraising, important advances have taken place in the consultant's ability to target voter persuasion mail. From conception to delivery, it is now possible to flood a constituency with a highly effective voter persuasion piece within just thirty-six hours. Unlike television, radio, and newspaper advertising, voter persuasion mail can literally be targeted down to a street-by-street level – choosing those issues, themes or graphics that the consultant believes will have the greatest impact on the particular recipients. Moreover, Congressional candidates from New York, Los Angeles, and other major metropolitan centers generally cannot afford to buy television or significant radio air time. Such major market advertising is clearly not as cost effective as voter persuasion mail, because it is so expensive and reaches an audience that, for the most part, is not in the candidate's congressional district. Radio, though easier to target, still reaches too great an audience. In congressional races, radio and television advertising have proven to be most cost effective when used only as a reinforcement to voter persuasion mail rather than serving as the primary message delivery system themselves.

Voter persuasion specialists have also become considerably more creative in package design, using strategy and techniques previously reserved for other forms of advertising. Some consultants will even hire professional models and shoot their photographs on location in the constituency to reinforce a particular message. Former Deputy White House Political Director Bill Lacy now considers well-executed direct mail to be another form of political commercial: "It is not that different from television advertising. With numerous pictures and light graphics, it is almost like a 30-second TV spot by mail." Like television advertising in the more generously financed or sophisticated contest, a campaign may even request the direct mail firm or an independent pollster to test the "persuasive ability" and "recall" of a particular candidate advocacy package or series of mailings, at critical periods during the election. To Richard Viguerie, all direct mail, whether voter persuasion or fundraising, is basically a form of advertising, regardless of its stated purpose. "It's a way of mobilizing our people, it's a way of communicating with our people, it identifies our people, and it marshals our people."[12]

One of the great believers in voter persuasion mailings is Congressman Cooper Evans, who was seeking election to an Iowan congressional seat being vacated by popular incumbent Charles Grassley in 1980. Throughout the race, Evans sought to identify himself closely with Grassley, both in advertising and direct mail, in an effort to ride into office on the former congressman's coat-tails. "Almost every letter we mailed had Grassley's name mentioned throughout," Evans said later, "and I think this was an important factor in my victory. Television alone probably would not have done the trick." Despite its many advantages, the majority of consultants interviewed by this author find it difficult to convince their clients to use voter persuasion technology. Veteran consultant Matt Reece explained the major reason why: "It's very easy to convince candidates to use television. They love to see themselves up there. Candidates are less willing to spend money on voter persuasion mail because there's less of that star quality." Added Welch, "A candidate would never think of doing their own television commercials, hiring the camera crew, editing the spots. But with direct mail, they feel that they can save money. They'll use their wife or family or next-door-neighbor to write the copy and produce the graphics. Then they wonder why it looks no better than junk mail."

Aside from the importance of direct mail to challengers and to candidates competing for open seats, its greatest benefits have more recently been reserved for those individuals that used to suffer the most from its use – incumbent candidates. Several factors, namely the recent computerization of nearly all congressional offices, the increase in franking privileges, and the increased availability of key census data, have combined to make voter persuasion direct mail a useful campaign tool 365 days a year. Although congressmen and senators are forbidden to raise funds or electioneer from their Capitol Hill offices, nevertheless, much of the outgoing mail from the offices of those up for re-election has the look of high quality, scientifically targeted voter persuasion packages.

Direct mail fundraising and voter persuasion firms have an abundance of evidence to prove (as they are often called upon to do) the necessity and usefulness of their craft. In a survey conducted by *Public Opinion* magazine, 63 percent of those questioned said they looked forward to collecting their mail more than any other daily activity that was listed – more than watching television, sleeping, eating lunch or dinner, or any of seventeen other activities.[13] According to a *Campaign Insights* report, during the early days of the direct mail boom, over three-fourths of the direct mail recipients actually read the piece.[14] In a poll of candidates, conducted by Roger Craver following the 1982 elections, 42 percent said direct mail was very important in their campaign, compared with only 13 percent who said it was not. In particular, direct mail has continued to provide candidates with a steady stream of small contributions which, when added together, can total many thousands of dollars. Statistics released by the Democratic Study Group in 1985 show that from 1974 to 1984 there was a considerable increase in $100 or smaller contributions to federal candidates, a clear indication of the added usefulness of direct mail. (See table 5.1.)

**Table 5.1**   *Trends in small contributions to congressional candidates (donations of $100 or less)*[1]

|  | 1974 ($ m) | 1976 ($ m) | 1987 ($ m) | 1980 ($ m) | 1982 ($ m) | 1984 ($ m) |
|---|---|---|---|---|---|---|
| House | 20.8 | 23.7 | 35.4 | 37.8 | 41.8 | 39.8 |
| Senate | 10.6 | 11.1 | 29.2 | 20.7 | 22.9 | 36.0 |
| % House gain 1974–84 |  | 91% |  |  |  |  |
| % Senate gain 1974–84 |  | 240% |  |  |  |  |

[1] General election candidates only.

*Source*: Democratic Study Group Report No. 99–22, October 22, 1985, pp. 31, 35

Furthermore, there are still some areas of America where, because of changing demographics, direct mail has not even begun to reach a peak in effectiveness. Direct mail has proven to be a particularly effective method of both fundraising and vote-getting among the growing number of retirement communities. "I'd love to have a gubernatorial candidate in Florida," remarked Robert Odell. "We could do a great job through mail. Why? They're all old, and old people read their mail." It is therefore no surprise that Florida Senator Paula Hawkins had one of the most successful direct mail campaigns of the 1986 elections.

Paralleling the empirical evidence in support of direct mail is the growing number of candidates who publicly attest to its influence on election results. Said Oklahoma Senator David Boren, one of three senators who refuse all PAC contributions: "I raised over 90 percent of my contributions from my home state, all from individuals. . . . I had not only raised enough to finance my campaign, but I had also helped rebuild my political organization at the grass roots. And I would suggest that is the way the system ought to be working."[15]

New Hampshire Senator Gordon Humphrey is another direct mail advocate. Because his name appeared on a Viguerie mailing list, he was invited to a gathering that opposed the Panama Canal Treaty. At the meeting Humphrey volunteered to serve as chairman for a forthcoming "Keep our Canal" rally. Although only nine people had showed up for the initial meeting, nearly 500 came to the rally, forming the nucleus for the 1500-strong New Hampshire Conservative Caucus. The Caucus, and Viguerie, provided the unknown candidate with a powerful network that enabled him to defeat his opponents in the Republican primary for US Senate. Turning again to his extensive direct mail lists, Viguerie raised enough money for Humphrey to hire a leading national political consultant as well as to purchase advertising on the expensive, but crucial, Boston television market. Direct mail thus helped Humphrey defeat a popular sixteen-year Democratic incumbent in one of the major upsets of 1978. In Humphrey's own words, "I wouldn't have won without the new technology. I wouldn't have won without direct mail."

Even well-known members of congress have benefited from direct mail. Arizona Representative Morris Udall raised $400,000 in direct mail solicitations in 1982, more than some Senate candidates that year. "I have been fortunate in that the direct mail has been very good to me," said Udall, whose direct mail efforts raised nearly one-half of his total campaign expenditures.[16]

It was through PAC solicitations that modern-day direct mail specialists developed direct mail "scare tactics," effectively combining pure emotion along with the inflammatory issues and controversial personalities of the day into a financially successful package that had only limited risk for the client. It is a common belief among fundraisers that negative reactions are easier to tap than positive ones. The most effective way to bring in the dollars is to focus on the negative, creating a specific "evil" that must be defeated, whether it be a person, a cause or an issue. According to the late Terry Dolan, former National Conservative Political Action Committee director, "People are only motivated to give when they feel threatened. They have to believe that their contribution will go to some candidate who *has* to be elected or the country will be in deep trouble." In fact, most direct mail specialists will not argue when the term "scare tactics" is used to describe their strategy. "Sometimes scare tactics are necessary," claimed Robert Odell, "because sometimes the opponent is a scary person, and what that person advocates is scary. If it comes out scary, so be it."

The examples of scare tactics used against controversial politicians are numerous. Dolan apparently enjoyed the public outcry at what was perhaps his most controversial direct mail letter and also one of NCPAC's most successful. Signed by Senator Jesse Helms, it read: "Your tax dollars are being used to pay for grade school classes that teach our children that CANNIBALISM, WIFE-SWAPPING, and the MURDER of infants and the elderly are acceptable behavior." Many direct mail practitioners openly acknowledge and defend the deliberate use of fear in their trade. "When you are a 62-year-old and I tell you your Social Security is about to be cut off by a cold-hearted Ronald Reagan, that is a scare tactic," said Craver. "It is also the truth, and there is nothing wrong with the truth."

According to author and political scientist Larry Sabato, "Former Secretary of the Interior James Watt was a gold mine for environmentalist PACs; prominent mention of his name in a direct mail piece would usually increase the group's profit. Senator Edward Kennedy performs the same function for the right-wing."[17] Following President Reagan's nomination of Judge Robert Bork to the Supreme Court, anti-Bork forces turned to direct mail to get their message out – and to raise millions of dollars. Read one particularly aggressive letter (a reprint of a speech given by Senator Edward Kennedy): "Robert Bork's America is a land in which women would be forced into back-alley abortions, blacks would sit at segregated lunch counters, rogue police could break down citizens' doors in midnight raids . . . and the doors of the federal courts would be shut on millions of citizens." Explained Roger Craver, who had five different anti-Bork clients, "This is the equivalent of Jim Watt wanting to flood the Grand Canyon."

Yet direct mail, like every other election tool, eventually reaches a saturation point where even the most emotional letter about a much disliked politician will yield decreasing results. Conservatives, in particular, are only now learning this fact. Donors, no longer threatened by a liberal establishment, are not pulling out their checkbooks as they read their mail. Said Eberle, a conservative, "We have beaten up so much on Kennedy that the issue has pretty much worn itself out. I'm sure we'll be able to come up with other hot issues."

Fundraisers in general and direct mail specialists in particular are significantly more ideological than other specialist consultants. A candidate's ideology is often a significant factor in the decision of the fundraiser to accept the individual as a client. Many direct mail specialists dislike moderate candidates and will refuse to sign them on as clients. Since fundraisers are measured by their monetary and not electoral successes, they are considerably more likely to work for extreme (and less electable) candidates than media professionals, pollsters, and general consultants. It is therefore understandable that none of the seven fundraisers interviewed by this author believed their won–lost record was important to the success of their consulting firm (as compared with 70 percent among other consultants. (See survey 5.1.)

Explanations vary for fundraiser concern with ideology, though the consensus among consultants is that raising money for middle-of-the-

**Survey 5.1**  *Is your won-lost record very important to you and your firm?*

| Total | Yes (%) | No (%) |
| --- | --- | --- |
| Total | 59 | 41 |
| Media consultants | 78 | 22 |
| Pollsters | 62 | 38 |
| General consultants | 50 | 50 |
| Fundraisers | 0 | 100 |

road candidates is too difficult when the technique that is used depends primarily on intensifying emotions. "Intensely moderate people cannot raise money on intensely moderate issues," claims veteran Democratic consultant William Hamilton. Walter Devries concurred: "In order for direct mail to work, it has to be extremist in some form." Roger Craver, who will not work for moderates, claimed that in direct mail, ". . . you work in the polar positions of an issue. The issues we mail on are so polar that they bring out the passion. I tell these middle-of-the-roaders, 'No one buys a Buick because General Motors needs the money.'"

But there are exceptions. According to Robert Odell, "I don't believe any more that it is more difficult to raise money for moderate candidates. There are those who catergorized George Bush as a moderate, though we raised a ton of money for him in 1980, and the things we are doing for him now are very successful." Few politically astute individuals consider New York Senator Alfonse D'Amato to be highly ideological, yet he raised $1.2 million in "special emergency contributions" of $10 each in a non-ideological direct mail.[18]

Many of the leading direct mail practitioners prefer raising money for political action committees and challengers rather than for incumbents and moderates, because of the comparative ease in creating an emotional, negative, and anti-incumbent theme. "In most cases in conservative direct mail, the strategy must be a negative one directed at the incumbent," remarked a leading direct mail specialist, adding, "We like to go after challengers. . . . With challengers you can really take out after an incumbent."[19] According to Richard Viguerie, " It's seldom that you will find older, established [incumbent] candidates that will be interested in using direct mail. Things you don't understand you don't feel comfortable with."[20] Since the criterion for judging a direct mail consultant's success is the amount of funding raised, not the eventual victory or defeat of the client, most major direct mail firms are just as willing to associate themselves with long-shots as with entrenched incumbents.

The Viguerie Company, the most famous of the political direct mail firms, now insists that clients, at the outset, must prove their ability to raise significant funds on their own – partly because of the huge initial costs involved in a direct mail program. And Bob Odell acknowledged that not all candidates necessarily benefit financially from direct mail: "A guy who is struggling probably shouldn't be using direct mail as his primary source for raising money. If a campaign isn't going to be big enough and successful enough, we really can't afford to get involved because we will be a hindrance to them, taking too much of their hardest earned cash they will raise." When pressed further, Odell conceded that in the short term, direct mail is the costliest method of fundraising; but not all direct mail consultants are as candid with potential clients as Robert Odell. Some novice candidates have become embittered as they watched their campaign dollars dwindle and disappear because of the exceedingly high fees and unforeseen additional charges levied by the direct mail firms. In some documented cases, Viguerie has actually kept for himself more than 75 percent of the money he raised for the client.[21]

Many candidates and organizations really do not need the constant mailings that some direct mail consultants push on their clients. The National Conservative Political Action Committee, one of Viguerie's oldest and largest continuous clients, had run up nearly $4 million in debts; more than half that debt was attributed to Viguerie's constant mailings.[22] In the disastrous 1980 presidential campaign of Illinois Congressman Phil Crane, Viguerie insisted on continuous prospecting for new contributors despite Crane's expressed desire to resolicit those already on his house list. Viguerie and Crane parted company acrimoniously, amid threatened law suits, but not before Viguerie had raised more than $3 million for Crane. Yet much of the money was kept by Viguerie himself. The net yield for the Crane campaign was barely $300,000. Thus, despite the many success stories, there are still circumstances where direct mail can be both unprofitable and unnecessary.

There also remains some question among candidates about direct mail's effectiveness and reliability, and about the honesty of some direct mail consultants. Granted, concepts are often "borrowed" and re-used, but there are a number of documented cases where direct mail specialists are stealing entire phrases from each other, word for word. Paragraphs in a letter written for Congressman Robert Edgar in his 1986 Pennsylvania senatorial campaign became the centerpiece of a mailing for a Republican congressional hopeful only one month later.[23] Fundraiser Robert Odell, in an off-the-record comment, even accused a well-known Republican competitor of "copy theft."

Odell also blames the unreasonably high expectations of many candidates for much of their criticisms. "Candidates are upset when they don't make money through prospecting, because they have a higher expectation factor. They're all optimists, and they have a false belief that if you mail a lot, you get a lot of money. It's just not true." Some of this problem stems from the varying methods direct mail consultants use to charge clients for their services. Some specialists charge a flat fee per program, some request a monthly retainer, and others (the majority) charge a percentage of what they raise. Candidates generally prefer to pay on a percentage basis, yet this leads to bitter recriminations when the bills finally come due. Roger Craver also believes direct mail venders are somewhat responsible for candidate disappointment:

Direct mail continues to be employed by an awful lot of people who don't know what they are doing, and more and more people write it, and therefore it appears more and more ineffective. You have a lot of homemade efforts that aren't very productive. . . . We were better off in the early days when relatively few candidates were using direct mail but they were using professionals to do it.

An acknowledged problem in the direct mail community is the rising number of errors in the overall process. The rapid expansion in the number of prospective donors (that is, those who have contributed to like-minded candidates or PACs) being placed on a computerized fundraising mailing list has increased the problem of letter duplication, wherein an individual receives multiple copies of the same direct mail package. Recent advances in computer software have reduced this problem, but less technically proficient direct mail firms and campaigns, dealing with the large numbers of potential contributors, often fail to prevent mass duplicate mailings. Duplication not only wastes the candidate's money but may also engender an annoyed and unsupportive voter.

Another problem, that of mistargeted mail, is not new to the field. One famous presidential campaign blunder was the accidental mailing of a 1972 Nixon re-election letter to his opponent, Hubert Humphrey. More recently, Texas Governor Mark White, a Democrat, received a 1986 fundraising letter from President Reagan, inviting him to become a GOP financial supporter. Ironically, White's campaign accidentally sent a fundraising letter to the wife of his opponent, former Governor William Clements, asking her to serve as a hostess at his $1,000-a-plate dinner. Unfortunately for the candidates, mistargeting occurs too frequently. A Republican congressman from New Jersey sent out a carefully crafted and targeted letter to specific Democrats asking for their support. It was good strategy, but then the congressman, against the advice of his consultant, committed a cardinal error in direct mail. The response was so affirmative that he mistakenly ordered the letter to be sent to all Democrats indiscriminately, forgetting the fundamental rule that what appeals to one voter may alienate another. Preparing the proper message and then sending it to the wrong voters was a waste of the candidate's limited resources, though the consultant honored the congressman's request, since it put a few extra thousand dollars in the consultant's pocket.

On the other hand, there are cases in which the wrong message was sent to the right people, again at the insistence of the candidate. In 1986, North Carolina Congressman Bill Cobey sent out a voter persuasion letter to 2,500 of his constituents regarding his efforts in Congress "as an Ambassador for Christ." The letter began "Dear Christian Friend," and asked for help "so our voice will not be silenced and then replaced by someone who is not willing to take a strong stand for the principles outlined in the Word of God." Cobey was condemned for the letter by many of its recipients, even though most were born again Christians, and by the press, who had little difficulty obtaining a copy. As a result, he was one of only five incumbent Republicans defeated in the November elections. Former Congressman Mark Siljander was the only Republican defeated in a 1986 primary contest after he sent a direct mail package (which featured his message on cassette tape) to local ministers, urging them to "break the back of Satan" by helping him win. "That was it, no question," Siljander said, explaining his defeat. "There's no question the major bomb was the tape."[24]

In many campaigns, the candidate and direct mail consultant never again meet or even speak once the contract has been signed, a practice that can lead to unnecessary misunderstanding and mistrust. The direct mail firm that initially handled the 1986 Colorado Senate race of Kenneth Kramer had to institute legal action to collect from him on overdue bills. "I don't think Ken knew anything about it until the day the suit was filed," said consultant Robert Odell. Odell blamed the campaign manager for the dispute, although he did suggest that Kramer's propensity to avoid making difficult campaign decisions contributed to the problems.

A frequent source of bitterness and conflict between the candidate and the direct mail consultant is the question of who has legal ownership of the house mailing list. Direct mail firms often require their clients to sign an agreement allowing the firm to retain co-ownership of a list once the fundraising program is completed. Frequently, the clause is buried deep in the contract and the candidate does not realize its significance. Fundraisers Richard Viguerie and Bruce Eberle allow no exceptions. Said Eberle, "We believe that to do so would be a disservice to our clients and would be shortsighted and counterproductive in the long run." By maintaining co-ownership, fundraisers can legally solicit the names previously accrued in a direct mail effort for one campaign, on behalf of another campaign. The problems generally arise when a candidate does not desire to share his contributors with another campaign but is ignored by the direct mail firm. If the candidate then decides to dismiss the firm and seek another direct mail outfit, the resulting difficulties can be even more complex. For their part, direct mail firms have often been justly accused of secretly using a client's list before their fundraising program for the client is terminated, a major breach of both the contract and political ethics. In October 1986, Citizens for Reagan, a leading conservative PAC, launched a $5 million lawsuit against a direct mail firm, contending that the firm used its private donor lists to raise money for other groups.[25]

Too often, candidates have no idea what is being produced on their letterhead, and have not read the piece being sent out in their name. According to Robert Odell, "Candidates often delegate the wrong things – like direct mail copy. They don't like to be involved in it. It is a laborious process, so they'd rather delegate it to someone else." Gerald Ford's 1976 presidential campaign was an example. However, although Ford was quite unfamiliar with the direct mail created by his campaign staff, it was one of the most successful aspects of his campaign for the Republican presidential nomination. Likewise, in the Florida campaign of Paula Hawkins, neither the handwriting (several letters only appeared to be written by her to add a personal touch) nor the wording of the letters ever came from the candidate, yet the direct mail was the most successful aspect of her campaign.

Other candidates go to the extreme of involving themselves in every minor detail of their direct mail program. "Jimmy Carter used to inspect every tiny detail," claimed Democratic fundraiser Peter Kelly, "and it would drive us crazy. The letter would go through nine different drafts, and the issue would be gone by the time we finished it." Voicing the opinion of other direct mail specialists, Bob Odell spoke harshly about the annoying perfectionism of some of his clients. "We don't like candidates nit-picking. We'll craft the letter that hopefully will get the job done. We have candidates that nickel and dime, and all they are doing is killing themselves timewise."

Many direct mail consultants actually do want their clients involved in the process, but not overly involved. "I like to sit with my candidates," says Robert Odell, "because they really do help write the letter. We need some of his emotion, some of his passion. The candidate is usually better than the messages contrived around him." But when candidates do choose to involve themselves in the process, they are frequently disappointed, upset or even angry about what is being produced by the direct mail firm. Not surprisingly, most of the criticisms are directed at the text of the direct mail piece. Complained Democratic fundraiser Craver: "Most political candidates can read, and some can write. The difficulty is that they think that because this direct mail stuff is on paper, it's easy. Well, it isn't. They don't realize what makes it work. The words may not be subtle, but the techniques behind them are. Candidates don't understand the whole process." Conservatives also have some difficulty. "A lot of my clients don't like the copy," admitted Richard Viguerie, "because they say it sounds too cornball, too controversial. It's not dignified. But people respond to emotionalism."[26] Other consultants echoed Viguerie's rejection of these candidate criticisms. "Few of my candidates really enjoy or appreciate the importance of the negative aspects of their campaign, particularly the direct mail effort," remarked Roger Stone, adding emphatically, "yet it is all a part of the political world. It can't be avoided."

Similarly, direct mail practitioner Robert Smith advised campaigns contemplating a direct mail program to "Find your candidate a nasty enemy. Tell the people they're threatened in some way. . . . It's a cheap trick but the simplest."[27] Unfortunately, once the enemy is chosen by the campaign, the decision is not always passed on to, let alone approved by, the candidate. Commented Smith's partner, Roger Craver, "With most experienced politicians, it is quite hard to get them to sign a hard-hitting letter."

The less negative elements of direct mail apparently do not attract candidate attention. To quote from a direct mail proposal by Bruce Eberle's firm: "The fundraising appeals created will be submitted to the Client's representative for approval." It is only deep within the proposal that the firm even mentions "candidate approval," a telling indication of anticipated candidate non-involvement. Even the simple detail of choosing the direct mail signatory is often ignored by the candidate. According to Eberle, "It is simply not that difficult to obtain a good letter signer. But all too frequently, that extra effort is not made by the client and the net result is that the direct mail fundraising program suffers." As Craver concluded, "Candidates can no longer turn their direct mail over to volunteers who write, fold, and stuff the direct mail piece and drop it off at the post office."

To protect the influence and authority of the direct mail firm when there is sharp disagreement with the client, many consultants have a clause such as the following in their proposals:

The Client acknowledges the Agency's expertise in direct mail fundraising, and thus agrees to limit modifications in packages prepared to matters of fact, law and policy. In order to achieve success on behalf of the Client, the Agency shall make decisions regarding graphics, techniques, lists and copy without stylistic changes by the Client.

Eberle even adds the following:

In order to be successful on behalf of the client, the Agency must be given license to create copy and techniques. . . . Any interference in this area by the

Client immediately negates projections and estimates . . . and will ultimately result in the severance of the Agreement between the parties.

Yet contracts aside, fundraising consultants in general, and direct mail specialists in particular, have grown accustomed to uncooperative and unappreciative candidate-clients.

Candidate lack of interest in the project, and the confusion and outright skepticism regarding direct mail are not hard to understand. Candidates usually do not comprehend the process and often disapprove of the tactics. Since the direct mail firm works mainly with the staff, the candidate is isolated from the operations, which contributes to the feelings described by mail guru Robert Odell: "Win, lose or draw, we're not perceived to be the ones who made the difference."[28] But although the candidate may have little involvement in the direct mail process, he nevertheless remains an important factor in its success. As Roger Craver aptly concluded, "No technology, no matter how sophisticated, can replace ideas, issues, and bold candidates. That is the stuff of successful direct mail fundraising."

# 6

# The bad boys of politics:
# PACs and independent expenditures

Is there anyone naive enough to believe that there is not an indirect relationship between the skyrocketing costs of campaigns and the tens of millions of new money being pumped into campaign financing by special interest groups?

Senator David Boren[1]

Gathering these hundreds of thousands of dollars of campaign cash is a cinch. You don't have to go to PACs. PACs come to you. They come with their tongue hanging out and their wallets wide open. It is like sitting under an apple tree, loaded with apples in a windstorm. It's almost an embarrassment. . . .

Senator William Proxmire[2]

Since PACs are growing in terms of how much money they can give, independent expenditures not only will continue, but they will increase. PACs are raising more money than they are able to give, and they are going to want to do other things to impact races – particularly independent expenditures.

Victor Kamber, political consultant

In what some consider the greatest miscalculation in American election legislation history, reforms intended to restrict the influence of wealthy individuals and organizations in electioneering have resulted, instead, in the creation of public electoral committees representing business, labor, and other special interest groups, and with financial power never dreamed of by the congressional reformers of the early 1970s. The Federal Election Campaign Act of 1971 (FECA) and the FECA amendments in 1974 paved the way for the legal creation of political action committees (PACs) which could represent almost anything, from a single issue group, a corporation, or a particular labor organization up to an entire industry or a nationwide special interest group. These newly created PACs were legally empowered to spend as much as $10,0000 in any election cycle ($5,000 total for either the convention or primary, or both, and $5,000 for the general election). By raising money on a voluntary basis from those they represented, such as union members, corporation employees, or those sympathetic to a particular issue or special interest, PACs have been able to influence election results with contributions to candidates that far exceed the legal limits for individual contributors. PACs have forced candidates to rethink electoral strategy and adapt to "new rules" in the raising of funds. And they have, singlehandedly, developed tactics and policies that have drastically altered the technical aspects of electioneering.

The proliferation of PACs has continued unabated since the mid-1970s; they have increased in numbers in every two-year election cycle since the Federal Election Commission (FEC) began keeping statistics in 1974. (See table 6.1.) Following the 1974 elections, there were about 600 PACs in existence, a slow start that some attributed to the Watergate era. Corporate executives, in particular, may have been afraid that by creating a PAC, they might be put in the position of being forced by politicians into making undesired, and occasionally illegal, contributions. The number of PACs, particularly in the corporate and non-connected sector, including trade, membership, and ideological

Table 6.1  *Growth of political action committees (1974–1986)*

| Year[1] | Total | Corporate | Labor | Trade/member-ship/health | Non-connected[2] | Other[3] |
|---|---|---|---|---|---|---|
| 1974 | 608 | 89 | 201 | 318* | * | * |
| 1976 | 1,146 | 433 | 224 | 489* | * | * |
| 1978 | 1,653 | 785 | 217 | 453 | 162 | 36 |
| 1980 | 2,551 | 1,206 | 297 | 576 | 374 | 98 |
| 1982 | 3,371 | 1,469 | 380 | 649 | 723 | 150 |
| 1984 | 4,009 | 1,682 | 394 | 698 | 1,503 | 182 |
| 1986 | 4,157 | 1,744 | 384 | 745 | 1,077 | 207 |

% increase in total PACs 1974–86:  584%
% increase in total PACs 1980–6:  63%

* For the years 1974–6, the specific numbers of non-connected and other PACs are unavailable. The FEC included them in the Trade/membership/health category through December 1977.

[1] As of 31 December of each year.
[2] Ideological and single issue PACs.
[3] Cooperative and corporation without stock.

*Source*: Compiled from FEC Press Release, 12 January 1987

PACs, eventually began to explode in the late 1970s, doubling to 1,200 in 1977 and yet again to 2,400 by the 1980 elections. The rate of growth has slowed somewhat since 1982, though more than 3,500 PACs had registered with the FEC by early 1984, rising to slightly over 4,100 as recorded in the December 1986 FEC report on PACs.

Although the number of PACs is still on the rise, the growth has not been evenly distributed within FEC defined PAC categories. (See table 6.2.) Corporate PACs, initially slow to organize, continue to outnumber PACs from the other FEC categories, though the percentage of corporate PACs in relation to all PACs has fallen from 47 percent in 1980 to 42 percent in 1986. The greatest rise has been in the non-connected category, dominated by ideological and single issue organizations, which have grown from 10 percent of all PACs in 1978 to 26 percent in 1986. In fact, from 1975 to 1982, the period of greatest growth in PACs, ideological PACs have grown in overall numbers by an average of 47 percent per year as compared with 21 percent for corporate PACs, 12 percent for labor and only 8 percent for trade, membership, and health association PACs.

The growth in overall PAC spending since 1972 has been astronomical. (See table 6.3.) In actual amounts donated to congressional candidates, the numbers have been dramatic. In just their first decade, direct

Table 6.2  *Percentage of PACs in FEC categories (1974–1986)*

| Date[1] | Corporate (%) | Labor (%) | Trade/ member- ship/health (%) | Non- connected[2] (%) | Other (%)[3] |
|---|---|---|---|---|---|
| 1974 | 15 | 33 | 52* | * | * |
| 1976 | 38 | 20 | 42* | * | * |
| 1978 | 47 | 13 | 27 | 10 | 3 |
| 1980 | 47 | 12 | 23 | 15 | 3 |
| 1982 | 44 | 11 | 19 | 21 | 5 |
| 1984 | 42 | 10 | 17 | 26 | 5 |
| 1986 | 42 | 9 | 18 | 26 | 5 |
| % increase 1974–86 | 1860% | 91% | * | * | |
| % increase 1980–6 | 45% | | 29% | 188% | |

* For the years 1974–6, the specific numbers and percentages of non-connected and other PACs are unavailable. All non-corporate and non-labor PACs were included under the heading Trade/membership/health.

[1] As of 31 December of each year.
[2] Ideological and single issue PACs.
[3] Corporation without stock (1986: 4%); Cooperative (1986: 1%).

*Source*: Compiled from FEC Press Release: "FEC Releases New PAC Count," 12 January 1987

Table 6.3    *PAC contributions in each election cycle**

| Cycle[1] | Total No. of PACs[2] | Total No. of contributions[3] | All Federal elections ($ m) | House elections ($ m) | Senate elections ($ m) |
|---|---|---|---|---|---|
| 77–8 | 1,949 | 1,474 | 35.2 | 25.0 | 10.1 |
| 79–80 | 2,785 | 2,155 | 60.2 | 39.2 | 19.2 |
| 81–2 | 3,722 | 2,665 | 87.6 | 62.4 | 25.1 |
| 83–4 | 4,347 | 3,046 | 113.0 | 77.4 | 34.1 |
| 85–6 | 4,568 | 3,152 | 139.5 | 89.5 | 49.9 |

* Includes donations to candidates up for election in other election cycles.

[1] Election cycles begin on 1 January of each odd-numbered year and continue through the first Tuesday after the first Monday in November of each even-numbered year.
[2] Total number of PACs that were registered at any time during the election cycle.
[3] Total number of PACs that contributed to presidential, House, and Senate candidates at any time during the election cycle.
[4] This figure includes contributions to presidential candidates as well as House and Senate candidates, regardless of whether they were up for election in that particular cycle.

*Source*: FEC Press Releases, 24 April 1980, 21 February 1982, 29 November 1983, 1 December 1985

contributions from PACs to federal candidates increased from $12 million (in 1974) to nearly $112 million (in 1984), more than an 800 percent gain.[3] It should be noted, however, that in the 1981–2 election cycle, more than a thousand PACs registered with the FEC did not make a single campaign contribution. By 1985–6, only 69 percent of all PACs actually made campaign donations, leaving more than fourteen hundred who sat out the election. Examining PAC contributions more carefully, only 369 of the 4,347 PACs registered in 1984 gave the maximum general election contribution of $5,000 to at least one Senate candidate. Still fewer, 117 in total, donated the maximum primary and general election contribution of $10,000 to at least one Senate candidate. But of the $34 million contributed by PACs to Senate candidates in 1984, more than 10 percent – $4.6 million – was contributed in $10,000 amounts.

The rapidly expanding use of technology by the political action committees has also been impressive. Conservative and business PACs were the first to use modern campaign technology effectively, particularly in the 1978 and 1980 elections. Recently, however, it has been the pro-liberal, pro-Democratic PACs who have instituted more state-of-the-art techniques in electioneering. This change, which has largely gone unnoticed, has been experienced particularly since 1982. According to Larry Sabato, left-wing PACs have "showed much greater savvy in targeting marginal races and in using the money at their disposal, and they have also begun to offer some of the same auxiliary services that corporate and independent conservative groups offer."[4] The Sierra Club, an aggressive pro-environment group, computerized its invaluable anti-James Watt petition lists and then supplied them to individually chosen pro-environment candidates to be used for direct mail purposes. The National Association of Realtors PAC (RPAC) formed and operated a phone bank operation and get-out-the-vote drive, which helped the 1982 re-election campaign of Montana Senator John Melcher at exactly the right time with exactly the right resources to insure his election.

The AFL-CIO PAC (COPE) dedicated many hours and dollars to a massive voter registration drive in 1984 that added a reported 3 million new voters. They also used targeted, personal direct mail appeals to names in their computer files, and greatly improved their phone bank operations. A COPE contribution of $5,000 in campaign assistance and resources was thus worth far more than the money alone would have been. As of October 1987, the Teamsters' political action committee had dispensed campaign donations to 114 House and Senate candidates. With 18 percent of the Teamster membership already participating in a voluntary checkoff agreement (automatic payroll deductions), the largest of any union, the potential for the Teamster PAC growth is enormous.

One of the fastest growing innovations, important because it enables candidates to opt out of the vicious election-year battle for PAC funds, is the candidate-centered PAC. These PACs are formed by presidential and congressional candidates for the explicit purpose of providing campaign money not only to themselves but to other like-minded candidates for Congress as well. In most cases, contributors are led to believe they are donating to a particular candidate, not realizing the funds may also be funneled out to other candidates and causes. The first and foremost practitioner of this, Senator Jesse Helms, created the Congressional Club PAC in the late 1970s as a vehicle for continuous, year-round solicitations, thus allowing him to amass a vast war chest that he could turn to every six years. The Congressional Club has spared Helms from PAC appeals and cash shortages that otherwise might have hampered his political career. But although vast sums pour in for Senator Helms each year, the Congressional Club also uses its financial power to influence North Carolina congressional races and other southern elections as well. According to an influential political consultant attached to the Congressional Club, several of his candidates have "been encouraged to become ideological friends of Jesse Helms – even if they hate his guts."

Congressional PACs handed out more than $9 million to congressional candidates in 1984.[5] Although this practice is dominated by Republican candidates, Democrats have not been excluded from it.

California Congressman Henry Waxman operates in a similar vein to that of former House Speaker Thomas P. O'Neill, handing out contributions to duly approved liberal candidates. Likewise, Democratic leader Daniel Rostenkowski contributed more than $140,000 to other House candidates in the 1984 election cycle, though he has more recently called for an end to this practice. This notwithstanding, the FEC estimates there were at least twenty-three formally organized congressional PACs as of March 1986.[6]

Candidates not fortunate enough to have a private political action committee find PAC financial support has become crucial if they are involved in a contested race. According to Senate Majority Leader Robert Byrd, "Given the high and increasing costs of running for public office in this age of television, many candidates conclude that they have no choice but to accept PAC contributions."[7] Senator Proxmire concurred. "Worst of all," he said, "it becomes politically stupid, in most cases, not to take this subtle, sophisticated, invisible, and legalized big money payoff."[8]

Only now are many of the young political hopefuls beginning to realize what professionals like Byrd and Proxmire have known for some time – that the millions of dollars in overall PAC spending have obscured the important electoral fact that PAC contributions, as a percentage of overall candidate contributions are increasing with every election cycle. (See table 6.4.) In 1974, PAC contributions made up 11 percent of total Senate contributions, increasing to 17 percent in just one decade – a figure even more impressive when one considers that the average winning candidate spent $2.9 million in 1984 and just $600,000 in 1976.[9] Put another way, while individual campaign contributions to Senate candidates, as a percentage of total receipts, fell from 38 percent to 28 percent in the decade from 1974 to 1984, PAC contributions rose from 11 to 17 percent, and again to 21 percent in 1986.[10] In 1984 alone, twenty-three successful Senate candidates raised more than $500,000 each from PACs, averaging 27.8 percent of their campaign contributions.[11] By 1986, thirty-one of the thirty-four Senate candidates elected had raised more than $500,000 each from PACs.[12]

House candidates received, on average, just 14 percent of their contributions in 1972 from political action committees, though this increased sharply to 21 percent in 1978, and again to 34 percent in the 1984 elections. More importantly, in the Congress elected in 1984, the winners received an average of 41 percent of their campaign funds from PACs, as compared to just 26 percent in 1974, and 163 Congressmen (that is, 37 percent of the House) received at least half of their funding from PACs.[13] As can be seen, with each succeeding election, PAC contributions have become ever more crucial in the raising of sufficient funds to wage a proper campaign.

Many of the larger political action committees have also adopted the

**Table 6.4**  *PAC contributions as a percentage of total campaign contributions*

| Cycle | Total | | Senate | | House | |
|---|---|---|---|---|---|---|
| | ($ m) | (%) | ($ m) | (%) | ($ m) | (%) |
| 77–8 | 34.1 | 17 | 9.7 | 11 | 24.4 | 21 |
| 79–80 | 55.2 | 22 | 17.3 | 17 | 37.9 | 26 |
| 81–2 | 83.6 | 24 | 22.5 | 16 | 61.1 | 29 |
| 83–4 | 105.4 | 26 | 29.7 | 17 | 75.7 | 34 |
| 85–6 | 132.2 | 28 | 45.0 | 21 | 87.2 | 34 |

*Source*: FEC Press Releases, "FEC Releases Final Report on 1984 Congressional Elections," 8 December 1985, 10 May 1987

practice of "bundling" contributions (discussed in detail in chapter 1), another successful effort to avoid the legal contribution limits. PACs are legally allowed to solicit individual contributions in the name of the candidate. Funds thus raised are then bundled together and passed directly to the candidate. The PAC gets the "credit" for the contribution, and no law has been breached. The candidate not only benefits from the money provided, but is also spared the high costs that accompany individual solicitations. The bundling procedure is thus extremely profitable for the candidate. The insurance agency PAC (Alignpac) provided one lucky candidate with over $200,000 in bundled contributions.[14] Defense-related PACs have also exploited the bundling loophole on behalf of those members of Congress whom they deem pro-defense and consider vital to their interests. In fact, to avoid alienating any candidate, there is a growing practice whereby a PAC donates to competing candidates in the same race, known as "double-giving."

There are, roughly, two dozen congressmen and five senators who have publicly announced their policy of refusing all, or most, PAC contributions.[15] Most of them, however, come from "safe seats," where even credible opponents with well financed campaigns would be expected to receive only 30 to 40 percent of the vote in any election.

The others, according to Senator Robert Byrd, "do not have to depend on PACs. They have vast wealth, and they are able to resort to the spending of their own moneys."[16] Senator William Proxmire, the leading PAC adversary in Congress, refuses to accept any contributions whatsoever. He is independently wealthy, and has never received under 64 percent of the vote in the past two decades. Massachusetts Senator John Kerry and his opponents agreed not to accept any PAC dollars in 1984, making that Senate race the very first PAC-free race; but it also left Kerry with a massive half-million dollar deficit. Former Congresswoman Millicent Fenwick (New Jersey) had little difficulty raising sufficient funding in her successful congressional elections despite her refusal to accept PAC contributions. But a decision to maintain that pledge in 1982 probably cost her the election. Faced with a candidate who spent more than $5 million of his own money, Fenwick's refusal to accept PAC support left her campaign continually short of cash at crucial moments. Not many office holders can survive without the thousands of dollars poured into campaigns by political action committees.

Fenwick's loss underscored the fact that successful politicians are often those that put electoral pragmatism ahead of political idealism. According to Congressman John Bryant of Texas, "I'm a realist and I play by the rules of the day. Right now, I am pursuing campaign contributions in any way I can, and I'll continue to play by those rules until they are changed."[17] On the other hand, the attitude of former Congressman Mark Marks, who was clearly uncomfortable with growing PAC power, was representative of the majority opinion of members of Congress as expressed in the Congressional Record. "It's truly difficult on a candidate," he said, "because if we don't accept their contributions, someone else will, and the PACs really do have a lot of money to spend."

There has been a disparity perceived in PAC contributions, based on an unfounded belief that Republicans have been favored over Democratic candidates. But Democrats have raised more PAC money than Republicans in every election cycle since 1978, even with the more rapid growth of pro-Republican corporate PACs over their pro-Democratic labor counterparts. (See table 6.5.)

In actuality, the average PAC donation to Democratic congressional candidates in 1982 was $891 as compared with $736 for Republicans.[18] More recently, of the top twenty-five congressional recipients of 1986 PAC contributions, nineteen were Democrats and only six were

Table 6.5   *PAC contributions by party affiliation*

| Cycle | Republican | | Democrat | |
|-------|------------|------|----------|------|
|       | ($ m) | (%) | ($ m) | (%) |
| 77–8  | 15.3 | 43 | 19.9 | 57 |
| 79–80 | 28.7 | 48 | 31.4 | 52 |
| 81–2  | 40.2 | 46 | 47.3 | 54 |
| 83–4  | 48.9 | 43 | 64.0 | 57 |
| 85–6  | 60.7 | 44 | 78.7 | 56 |

*Source*: FEC Press Releases, 24 April 1980, 21 February 1982, 29 November 1983, 1 December 1985, 21 May 1987

Republicans.[19] It has been suggested that such statistics are misleading because Democrats have more incumbents and are therefore, naturally, more likely to receive PAC contributions. However, in the 1986 election cycle, among House challengers, four of the top five and eight of the top ten PAC recipients were Democrats.[20] In addition, PAC contributions to Democratic incumbents make up a higher percentage of the campaign receipts than do PAC contributions to Republican incumbents. In 1984, PAC contributions to Republican Senate incumbents represented 21.4 percent of their total receipts. But Democratic Senate incumbents received 28.9 of their total receipts from PACs.[21] Two years later, eighteen of the top twenty-five (that is, top candidates in the percentage of their campaign money raised from PACs) were Democrats, while only seven were Republicans.

Although debate continues over which party's candidates are the beneficiaries of more late PAC money, its impact on the eventual outcome of close races is in no doubt – particularly if the donation arrives at a crucial moment during the election. According to political scientist Michael Malbin: "Late money [is] crucial in a close race. . . . Without late money, underdogs cannot buy advertising for the final push against a front-runner. The underdog cannot hoard money, because the underdog has to work hard to reach the point where late spending might even make a difference."[22]

Incumbents are known, on occasion (usually in tight re-election races), to reverse their anti-PAC stance and agree to accept PAC donations – and are often well rewarded for their change of heart. Successful Massachusetts Senate candidate John Kerry, however, could not be enticed into taking PAC contributions, though the offer was tempting. "I cannot tell you how many lobbyists have come to me in Washington and said, 'If you only took PAC money, we could wipe your debt out in a week or with one event. . . .' It means it would be easier for me not to have a debt if I took PAC money."[23]

Incumbent Iowa Congressman Cooper Evans was narrowly elected in 1980 despite having outspent his opponent by more than two to one. Facing the same strong opponent in 1982, Evans reversed his position and encouraged PAC contributions, allowing him again to outspend his opponent and successfully win re-election. But although PAC funding eventually represented 40 percent of Evans's total contributions, his successful solicitations came slowly at first, as PAC managers demonstrated their displeasure with his earlier anti-PAC stand. "Sure, I changed sides," Evans candidly remarked in a 1985 interview, "and I am still wary of PAC influence. But they are a fact of life, they are not going anywhere, and as a candidate up for re-election, I cannot help but accept that fact." PACs even continued to donate to the campaign of Congressman Thomas Railsback in his unsuccessful 1982 re-election bid, despite his nearly successful attempt at pushing through congressional legislation, introduced in 1979, that would have put stricter limits on the amount PACs could donate and candidates could accept in any particular campaign.

In actuality, it is not unusual for many of the strongest congressional supporters of campaign election reform to continue to accept PAC contributions. Even those who publicly attack PACs for having too much influence may really be indirectly soliciting their support. By announcing a critical view of PAC donations, the candidate is also acknowledging the responsibility placed on the person who accepts such funds. Texas Congressman John Bryant told the *Washington Post*, in 1983, that "Any time someone, whether a person or a PAC, gives you a large sum of money, you can't help but feel the need to give them extra attention, whether it is access to your time or, subconsciously, the obligation to vote with them."[24] New York Congressman Richard Ottinger concurred: "I take money from labor, and I have to think twice in voting against their interests."[25] Successful 1982 Democratic House challenger Robert Torricelli of New Jersey, a leading electoral reformer, attempted to gain political mileage in 1982 from his request that congressional candidates limit PAC gifts to a third of their treasuries. Torricelli actually outspent his opponent but stayed just below 33 percent on PAC contributions. But despite such pronouncements and pledges, few candidates have shown a willingness to return all those substantial PAC contributions. As Congressman Torricelli acknowledged in a subsequent interview, the benefits of accepting PAC money far outweigh possible voter scorn. According to pollster Linda DiVall, "In about six years on that issue, I haven't seen anybody win. . . . It just doesn't seem to have much of an impact."[26] As Senator Robert Byrd concluded: "It is a case of survival. Self survival is one of the first laws of nature."[27]

Challengers rarely experience moral qualms about PAC donations, because historically they are faced with a difficult, uphill battle to obtain PAC funding. By their own admission, PACs, in general, are less likely to support challengers than incumbents. (See table 6.6.) On still closer examination, PAC support for incumbent candidates is staggering. According to Philip Stern, founder and co-chairman of Citizens Against PACs, in three states (Alabama, Arizona, and Kentucky) PACs did not give a single contribution to any House challenger.[28] In several larger states, including Florida, New Jersey, and Illinois, House incumbents received 97 percent of all PAC contributions.[29] Of the thirty top House candidates in PAC receipts in 1986, a staggering twenty-nine were incumbents.[30] Every 1982 Senate incumbent but two (who had refused all PAC contributions) raised more PAC money than their opponents.[31] In 1986, thirteen of the top fifteen PAC recipients as of 30 June, receiving crucial early dollars, were Senate incumbents.[32]

In the last six elections, only once did donations to challengers make

**Table 6.6**  *PAC contributions by candidate status*

| Cycle | Total | Incumbent | | Challenger | | Open seat[1] | |
|---|---|---|---|---|---|---|---|
| | ($ m) | ($ m) | (%) | ($ m) | (%) | ($ m) | (%) |
| 77–8 | 35.2 | 20.0 | 57 | 7.8 | 22 | 7.4 | 21 |
| 79–80 | 60.2 | 36.8 | 61 | 16.2 | 27 | 7.2 | 12 |
| 81–2 | 87.6 | 58.4 | 67 | 16.7 | 19 | 12.5 | 14 |
| 83–4 | 113.0 | 81.2 | 72 | 19.1 | 17 | 12.7 | 11 |
| 85–6 | 139.5 | 96.1 | 69 | 19.8 | 14 | 23.5 | 17 |

[1] Open seat races are those in which the incumbent did not seek re-election.

*Source*: Compiled from FEC Press Releases: 24 April 1980, 21 February 1982, 29 November 1983, 1 December 1985, 10 May 1987

up more than a quarter of all PAC contributions.[33] In 1982 alone, PACs spent more than three times as much money on incumbents as they did on challengers, and in no election since 1972 has the margin been less than two to one.[34] Among corporate and trade PACs in 1982, incumbents were favored by an overwhelming eleven to two margin.[35]

After election day, PACs quite openly seek to exert influence, and so as to assure access, obviously want to be aligned with the winner. "It's obvious they [PACs] think I've got a better change of winning this time," explained congressional hopeful William Wachob one month before his second electoral defeat, though he raised more money from PACs than any House challenger in 1986.[36] According to Senator Rudy Boschwitz, "Very frankly, sometimes the only philosophy PACs have is something like a horsetrader; they want to bet on a winner. . . . They want to go back to the members of their PAC and say, 'Look at the 80 or 90 percent of the dollars we expended; see how well we did.'"[37] Democratic Senatorial Campaign Committee finance director Keith Abbott concurred: "Washington money, by and large, is smart money. Most PACs are not a bit interested in supporting people who they don't think will win."[38] Incumbents, particularly those with seniority and major committee assignments, have the greatest likelihood of being returned to office, a factor that has proven decisive in determining which candidates will receive PAC support.

It is only a few select challengers who are successful in obtaining PAC funding, though those that do have a two-fold advantage. First, when PAC contributions in 1982 were finally awarded, the average contribution from a PAC to a challenger exceeded that for an incumbent, $1,025 for the challenger compared with $745 for the incumbent.[39] This is because incumbent money tends to be distributed more equally by PACs, while challenger contributions are concentrated on close races.[40] Second, PAC contributions generally make up a higher percentage (almost double) of overall incumbent fundraising compared with challengers'. Since challengers generally aim to keep the ratio of incumbent to challenger dollars as close as possible, a challenger that is successful in raising PAC dollars is thereby reducing the marginal value of the incumbent's PAC drive. For example, three of the seven House incumbents defeated in November 1986 faced challengers who ranked among the top ten in challenger PAC fundraising. It should be noted, however, that according to Michael Malbin, a well-financed challenger will in all likelihood spark his opponent into redoubling his PAC fundraising efforts: ". . . challengers have to spend increasing amounts of money in order to win. In protective reaction, incumbents raise more to preserve their safety. The result is that incumbents . . . devote more time and effort to raising early money. The need to raise funds in turn means that members spend more of their personal time at fund raisers."[41]

The two ways most commonly used by challengers to overcome multiple obstacles and obtain PAC support are to produce and submit a "PAC kit," and to solicit PAC aid personally, both in their local communities and in Washington, DC. PAC kits have varied considerably, from candidate to candidate and election to election. Until 1980, most PAC kits contained only a short biography of the candidate, a family photograph, the electoral history of the state or district, a brief voting record of the opponent, and a few favorable press clippings. As PACs grew in number and power, campaigns then tended to produce more sophisticated kits which, in addition to the basic items, also contained a detailed campaign strategy and budget plan, the latest demographic statistics, information about the general staff, including their background and responsibilities, and, in particular, any polling data (by a reputable firm) that demonstrates the incumbent is vulnerable, even if it does not show the challenger is ahead or roughly on a par with the incumbent. If the incumbent's share of the vote is below 50 percent, PAC directors will regard him as beatable. Conversely, if only 40 percent (or less) of the population suggest that the incumbent deserves re-election, regardless of the challenger, then the challenger is considered to have some prospect for success.

Recently, with the growing number and increased recognition of career consultants having given them considerable importance (to the disdain of some candidates), the use of campaign consultants is prominently highlighted in any candidate–PAC correspondence. Although more concerned with content than production, some campaigns now have their PAC kit produced on high quality paper, professionally bound, and mailed in attention-grabbing packaging – in an effort to attract the attention of PAC directors swamped with funding requests.

An important aspect of the PAC kit is the candidate's written appeal for support. And of course a personal letter is considerably more effective than a form letter. (Direct mail to PACs is not dissimilar in this respect to voter direct mail.) Only the poorest funded or least experienced candidate still uses the stereotyped "Dear PAC" direct mail. As Terry Cooper, former administrator of Motorola's PAC, advised candidates in a recent PAC solicitation manual, "Be literate: Would you want to entrust the making of our laws to someone who can't write or speak the language? Use some three-dollar words. Be graphic and memorable."[42] The goal of all PAC solicitations is, according to professional PAC fundraiser Michael Petro, "to personalize your appeal, to make people in Washington feel like full partners in a campaign taking place [somewhere else.]"[43]

Once candidates have assembled tangible evidence of their viability, such as the demonstration of fundraising ability, and support from other PACs and the local news media, they are ready to plead their cases before the national PAC representatives. Candidate excursions to Washington, DC, to seek PAC support personally, seldom yield an immediate harvest; yet they are crucial in preparing the ground for later contributions. "PACs expect to be worked personally by a candidate," said Brad O'Leary, a major Republican fundraiser. Since PACs frequently work in groups, all waiting for the others to pass judgment before deciding on their own allocations, a candidate's visit to Washington which is successful in persuading one PAC to support him may find other PACs quickly following suit. Being placed on the Chamber of Commerce "opportunity race" target list, for example, indicates to the business PAC community that support for that candidate is desirable; and that can mean tens of thousands of dollars in eventual PAC donations. Since PACs tend to contribute early to incumbents but wait for challengers to prove their viability, it becomes even more critical for the challenger to secure early PAC funding. For example, according to FEC election studies, slightly more than half of all donations were given by 30 June for the November 1982 elections, while PACs had donated only 42 percent of their eventual total. Challengers, however, had received barely a fifth of their eventual PAC funding, demonstrating that PACs like to give first to incumbents and only later to challengers.[44]

Although some national PACs (particularly organized labor) leave the eventual decision to contribute up to their state and local branches, support from the national PAC organization will generally depend on a decision made in Washington. The National Assocation of Realtors, political action committee (RPAC) was the 1984 leader in direct contributions to congressional candidates, and typifies the PAC financial decision making process. Representing the 700,000 member National Assocation of Realtors, RPAC is governed by a twenty-one-member Board of Trustees that is responsible for determining the recipients of RPAC contributions. The specific criteria used by the Board include: 1) formal, written requests from local and state boards of realtors for contributions to specific candidates; 2) a review of the potential recipient's voting record on housing and real estate issues; and 3) analysis of the viability of the proposed candidate's campaign, based on such factors as polling data, local media response, and the campaign plan.[45] According to Realtors' President Clark Wallace, RPAC Trustees have supported the requests from the local realtors more than 87 percent of the time. Nevertheless, the final decision was still made in Washington.[46] Candidates are thus forced to make the Capital rounds, sometimes two or three times, in search of support from Washington PAC officials. According to political scientist Larry Sabato, "It is not uncommon now for candidates to spend more time in the PAC suites than on the campaign trail in the pre-Labor Day period, and a trip to see the PAC managers in Washington . . . is almost obligatory."[47]

Not all PACs render their decisions primarily on the personal meeting with the candidate. Many use a detailed questionnaire asking candidate opinions on a wide variety of subjects, including issues other than those of direct concern to the particular PAC. Polling data supplied to the PAC from the national party organizations can be crucial in swinging support behind a candidate, as can favorable press coverage in the home district or state. The factors in candidate selection and support differ from PAC to PAC, even among organizations closely aligned; there is no sure formula for a candidate that will guarantee PAC funding, and the number of variables seems to grow with each election.

Rarely are congressional incumbents themselves immersed in PAC solicitations. Because of the fear of charges of influence peddling (selling their vote for a campaign contribution), most incumbent senators and congressmen leave a substantial portion of the PAC fundraising chores to their administrative assistants or high level campaign staff members, although the occasional personal phone call or meeting to apply additional pressure is not uncommon. The Capitol Hill fundraiser gathering, which, it is hoped, will be attended by numerous PAC directors or representatives, has become the most convenient, least expensive, and most often used means to obtain PAC funding. According to *Congressional Quarterly*, "Almost every available source agrees that there are more Washington fundraisers, that ticket prices have soared, and that they are scheduled earlier in each campaign cycle."[48] For incumbents, the overall appeal for contributions has not changed significantly in the past decade despite the proliferation of PACs. "They always say they're in trouble," said Ben Albert of COPE, commenting on the most common incumbent plea for funds.[49]

Another approach, considerably more direct though used somewhat less frequently, is to remind the particular PAC of the candidate's "crucial position" on some committee or of a previous "tie-breaking" vote he cast for or against a weighty piece of legislation. Incumbents use this carrot and stick technique to suggest it may be disastrous if the incumbent is not returned to Congress, although the larger PACs are well aware of the candidate's past voting record and effectiveness – or lack of it – in getting desired legislation passed. In 1984, 80 percent of the 248 members who had voted in accordance with the National Rifle Association (NRA) on a key piece of legislation received financial support from them, while 80 percent of the members who had voted "incorrectly" received nothing.[50] Most PACs are well aware of what the candidate thinks, perhaps more so than the candidate might expect.

From the candidate's viewpoint, perhaps the greatest change in PAC solicitation is the growing importance of specialist PAC consultants. Responsible for everything from the design and construction of the PAC kit to all follow-up newsletters and telephone or person-to-person fundraising appeals with PAC directors and committees, as well as appointments and preparation for all PAC-candidate meetings, the PAC coordinator has become a crucial cog in high budget campaigns. According to DSCC finance director Keith Abbott, his 1986 candidates had at least one, and as many as four, professional PAC fundraisers on their campaign staffs.[51] These new consultants do not come cheap; most of them charge a percentage of what they raise, in addition to a set monthly consulting fee. However, the fact that a growing number of candidates is willing to pay these costs is clearly an indication that the PAC consultant is considered a worthy addition to the electioneering process.

Candidates who employ PAC consultants have found that although their direct communication with the various PACs is tightly controlled, the financial return measured against the time spent is much higher now than in the late 1970s, when these specialists did not exist. No longer are candidates successfully able to demand PAC funding without presenting a hand-tailored winning image, obtained through the assistance of a PAC consultant. No longer are candidates so willing to complete the all-important PAC questionnaire without professional guidance. In fact, they are even known to plead with the PAC director to provide them with the "correct answers," as perceived by the particular PAC. According to 1976 and 1980 US Senate candidate James Buckley, "I personally used up more time in 1976 dealing with PACs because they had easy access. It certainly was much easier in 1980, and we raised just as much money in a much more professional manner. I left my PAC fundraising in good hands ... to a professional." Political consultant Roger Stone concluded, "If the candidate isn't absolutely needed, why should he waste his time? If we can get the PAC director on our time, our turf and our conditions, so much the better for our candidate. That's the role of the PAC specialist."

A growing number of PACs are going beyond the requests of PAC consultants, and even of the candidates, in their involvement in campaigns that they support. No longer content with just a straightforward contribution, PACs are increasingly demanding a say in the way their money is spent, thus maximizing the value of their contributions. By offering "in-kind" services (polls, phone banks, mailings, and other tangible campaign services) that are organized, paid for, and supplied by the PAC directly to the campaign, the PAC gains more influence and control over the candidate and the campaign. In this vein, some PACs have a favorite pollster, media consultant, or fundraising expert whom they strongly recommend to friendly candidates. The American Security Council (ASC) concentrates almost exclusively on fundraising, and arranges high level meetings where like-minded PACs can meet and contribute to friendly candidates. These meetings may only cost about $200 each to set up and conduct, but they usually raise from $30,000 to $100,000 for the candidate. As Gary South, independent expenditure supervisor for the Realtors' PAC, concluded, "Our philosophy in making a contribution to a candidate is not simply that we are handing out a lollipop. . . . It's because we want to be involved in a race so that we can make a difference in the outcome."[52]

The PAC most involved in providing in-kind contributions and campaign services is the liberal, ideological National Committee for an Effective Congress (NCEC). By having numerous consultants on retainer in almost every aspect of electioneering, NCEC saves friendly candidates thousands of dollars, while providing excellent advice. In 1982 alone, NCEC funded thirty polls, ten direct mail programs, fifty research projects, and thirty-five on-site visits by consultants.[53] Citizens in Politics, an innovative program that arranges appearances by famous Hollywood stars for politically like-minded candidates, was organized by NCEC to aid those candidates in marginal districts. NCEC also produces a detailed targeting report, compiled through its in-house computers and designed to provide individually tailored information to the candidates they support. Now that PACs like NCEC have entered the strategy game, it enables the candidates they support to reduce their paid staff and their dependence on privately hired consultants, as well as on the national and state party organizations.

A further example of PAC power, which ultimately derives from the enormous quantities of money they raise and spend, can be traced back to a momentous decision by the Supreme Court. In 1976, in *Buckley* v. *Valeo*, the Supreme Court created a loophole in previously enacted federal campaign laws by upholding unlimited political spending in a

**Table 6.7** *Independent expenditure by PAC categories*

| Cycle | Total[1] | Corporate ($ m) | (%) | Labor ($ m) | (%) | Non-affiliated ($ m) | (%) | Trade/membership/health ($ m) | (%) | Other ($ m) | (%) |
|---|---|---|---|---|---|---|---|---|---|---|---|
| 79–80 | 14.2 | 0.02 | 0 | 0.08 | 1 | 13.1 | 92 | 1.0 | 7 | 0.0 | 0 |
| 81–2 | 5.7 | 0.02 | 0 | 0.01 | 0 | 4.9 | 86 | 0.8 | 14 | 0.0 | 0 |
| 83–4 | 22.2 | 0.03 | 0 | 0.30 | 1 | 19.1 | 86 | 1.9 | 9 | 0.8 | 4 |
| 85–6 | 9.5 | 0.01 | 0 | 0.04 | 0 | 5.1 | 54 | 4.1 | 43 | 0.3 | 3 |

[1] Includes presidential, senatorial, and congressional campaigns.

*Source:* FEC Press Releases, 21 February 1982, 29 November 1983, 1 December 1985, 21 May 1987

particular race, by individuals or committees, provided the expenditure was without the knowledge or consent of the candidate or his campaign. The Federal Election Commission defined an "independent expenditure" as:

expenditure by a person expressly advocating the election or defeat of a clearly identified candidate which is made without cooperation or consultation with any candidate, or any authorized agency of such candidate, and which is not made in concert with, or at the request or suggestion of, any such candidate.[54]

Such "independent expenditure" campaigns, overturning one of the 1974 FECA Amendments, were deemed fully legal as long as the money was spent for communication purposes, such as television, radio, or newspaper advertising or the purchase of billboards, bumper stickers, or buttons. Although the Supreme Court ruling was directed more to individuals than organizations, it is, in fact, political organizations that have exploited the legal loophole to the greatest degree. The most likely participants in independent expenditure efforts are the PACs, and the strategy they frequently use in congressional races (often to the embarrassment of the candidates they purport to help) is the negative campaign. Spawned in the modern age of electioneering, they are aptly described by the Twentieth Century Fund task force on PACs as "the creatures of modern campaign technology, their funds raised with the help of high speed computers and spent on electronic media."[55]

Inasmuch as candidates can lose support by attacking their opposition too often, it is frequently to their benefit if some outside party, particularly if perceived by the voting public as an independent force, makes the case against their opponent. The frequently quoted remark by Terry Dolan, made when he was director of the National Conservative Political Action Committee (NCPAC), is telling. "A group like ours could lie through its teeth, and the candidate it helps stays clean."[56]

The modern history of independent expenditure campaigns began when a pro-environment organization targeted twelve members of Congress in 1972, the "Dirty Dozen," for their anti-conservationist voting records. However, even after the *Buckley* v. *Valeo* decision supported the legality of independent expenditure, it was at first rarely exploited, and in that year only $2 million was spent in such a manner, almost exclusively on the presidential race. Yet the potential of such an obvious loophole was not overlooked for long, and in 1978, several incumbent senators were defeated as an indirect result of independently waged campaigns. In 1980, the amount of money spent on independent expenditures exceeded $14 million, well over half of it in the presidential contest. (See table 6.7.)

The National Conservative Political Action Committee (NCPAC), the foremost exponent of independent expenditures in the 1980s, was itself involved in less ambitious independent campaign efforts before its highly publicized success in 1980. A grassroots conservative organization, NCPAC purchased in 1978 a small amount of television air time to target three Senate incumbents for their support of the Panama Canal Treaty. This action contributed in part to the defeat of two, Senator Dick Clark of Iowa and Senator William McIntyre of New Hampshire, both of whom had been representing constituencies considerably more conservative than their voting record. It was only after extensive post-election analysis of the 1978 results that the then NCPAC director Terry Dolan decided that a well-financed independent expenditure campaign could have a far greater impact on the outcome of Senate and House races than was imagined at that time. "It was an experiment that was more important in what it told us about the future than its immediate success. So in that sense, 1980 and our involvement in it could not have happened without 1978 and the lessons it taught." While other conservative organizations were targeting President Carter for defeat in 1980, NCPAC waged an extremely successful independent expenditure campaign against six liberal incumbent senators. Prompted by a belief that the free press did not report the voting records of these incumbents properly — if at all — NCPAC spent $1.2 million in their highly visible negative advertising effort. Four of the six NCPAC-targeted senators were defeated.

Having observed the success of NCPAC in 1978 and 1980, liberal organizations decided themselves to enter into independent expenditure campaigning for the first time, in 1982. Overall independent campaigning that year nearly topped the $6 million mark in total spending (the previous comparable election, 1978, saw just $300,000 spent in a similar fashion). New Mexico Senator Harrison Schmitt became the first conservative target — and fatality — of the liberal attack, defeated by PROPAC, the largest liberal independent expenditure organization at that time. Maryland Senator Paul Sarbanes entered the political record books as the first individual in Congress to have two highly funded independent expenditure campaigns waged in his election — one in support and the other in opposition — prompting one consultant to label the race "PAC Wars." But NCPAC and Jesse Helms's Congressional Club, by far the two largest independent PACs, did not live up to their 1980 reputation, winning only a small fraction of their targeted races in 1982.

Senator Robert Byrd, an easy survivor from NCPAC's 1982 efforts, remarked after his re-election that NCPAC was "on its way out, and I hope its kind of activity will disappear from the political landscape."[57] Even the *Washington Post*, respectful yet resentful of past independent expenditure success, wrote of the 1982 exercise: "[It was] the most futile since John Connally spent $11 million for one presidential delegate in 1980."[58] But Senator Byrd and the *Washington Post* aside, careful scrutiny of polling data provided by NCPAC as well as by independent pollsters indicates that many of the independent expenditure campaigns still had a favorable impact on the voters they wished to reach. Even in the Sarbanes election, NCPAC's involvement significantly raised the incumbent's negative ratings, despite the candidate's eventual landslide victory. For example, in the 1982 Maryland Senate race, prior to NCPAC's entry, Senator Paul Sarbanes had a 43 percent favorable rating and a 12 percent unfavorable rating. After running its negative campaign, NCPAC follow-up surveys had the incumbent at just 24 percent favorable and 25 percent unfavorable, a remarkable although quite temporary shift of opinion. According to Terry Dolan: "We have never seen a liberal backlash against a candidate we are supporting. The attitude of the public toward NCPAC simply does not affect whether they vote for our candidate or not. The more controversial we are, the more effective we are. We have the survey data to prove it."

As might be expected, in the 1984 and 1986 elections, the independent expenditure campaign reached new levels of financing and sophistication. According to Gary South, director of independent expenditures for the Realtors' PAC (RPAC), their 1982 direct mail campaign was "utterly ineffective."[59] This prompted an abrupt change in tactics, so that there was more emphasis on television advertising and a virtual elimination of direct mail in subsequent elections. The shift in strategy helped elect at least one House challenger in 1984, Helen Bentley. Despite having run short of funds, Bentley narrowly defeated an entrenched incumbent due to RPAC's independently produced and financed television advertising in the closing weeks of the campaign.

In 1986, the extensive use of independent campaigns – but by non-ideological PACs – somewhat shocked the political world. RPAC spent nearly $500,000 on behalf of Oklahoma Senate candidate James Jones, while the American Medical Association PAC (AMPAC) spent $315,000 in their attempt to defeat Congressman Andrew Jacobs, record campaign expenditures by both organizations.[60] RPAC also established a record of sorts when it spent more money in a 1986 Louisiana congressional race than either candidate.[61] An association of imported car dealers initiated independent expenditure efforts for the first time in 1986 when it spent more than $1 million on behalf of seven Senate candidates; and the National Rifle Association raised so much money that it was able to fund seventeen independent expenditure campaigns, even after providing direct contributions to all its selected candidates.[62] Since federal law continues to prohibit PACs from giving more than $5,000 per election in direct contributions, a sizeable number of PACs with excess dollars have launched independent expenditure efforts in 1988.

Advertising, including television, radio, and direct mail, maintains its dominant role in independent campaigns, but some organizations are adding polling, phone banks, and get-out-the-vote services to their efforts. A few organizations, such as the Moral Majority, still focus solely on grassroots campaigning, has initiated positive themes in the expert in negative campaigning, has initiated positive themes in favor of candidates it supports, although its switch in strategy was primarily due to the refusal of television stations in three states to carry its controversial negative advertisements out of the fear that the material in the commercials, if proven false, could possibly lead to a libel suit against the station.

Unlike most PACs, political consulting firms, and to some extent political parties, that prosper or fail depending on their won–lost record, organizations waging independent expenditure campaigns do not have the chance of success or failure uppermost when certain senators are targeted for defeat. Most independent expenditure campaigns are waged by ideological political action committees and are prompted by ideological concerns and not by a realistic assessment of the candidate's chances. (See table 6.7.)

Corporate, labor, and most trade and membership PACs have remained wary of independent expenditure campaigns since the consequences of a failed campaign would exceed the benefits of a successful effort. These PACs must lobby for votes in Congress after the election, and may find themselves penalized if a candidate they opposed wins. Independent expenditure campaigns involve far more funding than the maximum $5,000 contribution allowed to PACs under federal election law, and a business or labor PAC is not likely to be forgiven by a candidate it failed to defeat. Time and again, congressional opponents of a particular lobby or organization have proved that they can do more damage to that group's interests than its proponents can repair. Thus, independent campaigns create many more enemies than friends. The 1986 election cycle was the first in which a significant number of trade and membership PACs ignored the risks inherent in an independent expenditure effort. As RPAC's independent expenditure director explained, "Instead of trying to pick a race and jump on the caboose of the winner and then pat ourselves on the back because we gave them a little money, we decided [in 1986] to make a stand."[63]

In contrast, the role of an ideological PAC-sponsored independent expenditure campaign ends on election day. Ideological PACs need not worry about alienating those individuals they oppose, and consequently have a freedom denied to other PACs. This accounts for NCPAC's willingness to spend hundreds of thousands of dollars against Massachusetts Senator Ted Kennedy's re-election bid, a race they knew they could not win. Dolan described the most important elements in selecting which candidates to oppose:

Their political vulnerability is important, probably more so than the availability of effective challengers. But most important is their liberal ideology and whether it is or is not out of touch with the electorate. It is less important for us to elect conservatives than it is to defeat dangerous liberals, and this fits in well with the general strategy behind independent expenditures.

A typical independent expenditure campaign run by a PAC can begin as much as two years before election day. Since funding is so important for such efforts, PACs will frequently attempt to build up a large war chest before commencing the campaign. Extensive survey research and close monitoring of all potentially targeted races are also undertaken at an early stage in the election cycle. Once the targets are chosen and the strategy determined (positive – for the candidate; negative – against the opponent), the first series of advertisements are then created to match survey data in the district or state. Soon after the effort has begun, surveys are again taken (polling is particularly important with regard to independent expenditure efforts) to determine the effectiveness of the campaign, while new strategy is mapped out. Negative independent expenditure campaigns strive for a political "blitzkrieg" – shattering the public image of the targeted individuals and destabilizing their campaigns early in the contest and as quickly as possible. Negative campaigns usually end several months before the election, to avoid a backlash of sympathy for the candidate they are opposing, although a positive campaign in support of a particular candidate can start much later and may run right up to election day. The whole independent expenditure process can last from several weeks to an entire year.

NCPAC was widely regarded as the most professional of the independent expenditure organizations, though their tactics were often criticized and their success rate challenged. Although it is no longer feared by its potential targets, and there are rumors in the political community that its final demise is imminent, a look at NCPAC in its heyday and what went on behind closed doors helps explain the workings of large, ideological political action committees and their involvement in independent expenditures.

In the past, NCPAC's public strategy was first to invite previous contributors to submit a list of the senators and congressmen they most wanted to defeat. This would be accompanied by yet another contribution request – no letter ever left the office of NCPAC without a request for funds. Apparently using this public response to add or eliminate various individuals on their "hit list," NCPAC then generally presented the press and the public with the names of approximately fifteen members of Congress who were targeted for defeat, although in fact a much smaller number of major campaigns were planned. The decision about whom to target was made by Dolan and several key financial advisors, not by NCPAC contributors. A few potential targets, like Senator Ted Kennedy and House Speaker Tip O'Neill, were chosen not for their vulnerability, since their re-election was assured, but for their fundraising appeal to conservative contributors. Anti-Kennedy direct mail has raised NCPAC literally hundreds of thousands of dollars, which has then been redirected to other independent expenditure races. NCPAC thus distributed its money where it was most needed and not necessarily where the contributor wished it to go.

Internally, NCPAC did not take a step in an independent expenditure effort without consulting two sources: its polling statistics and its financial advisors. NCPAC's electoral strategy is determined by polling data down to the smallest detail. Every television commercial or radio spot is designed with the polling data in mind. Following the initial airing, further tracking polls are conducted to assess effectiveness as quickly as possible. In 1980, both NCPAC's polls and the polls of their opponents showed the negative impact the independent expenditure campaigns were having on targeted liberal Democrats. "Sure, I watched my numbers drop," George McGovern, a 1980 high priority NCPAC target, said later. "I talked to Frank [Church] and the others about it, and the same thing was happening to them. There was nothing we could do about it but watch. We tried to fight back, but it didn't work." Survey statistics were so important that a NCPAC staffer who inadvertently released private polling data at a press conference on the 1982 Maryland Senate race, following NCPAC's first wave of activity, was fired for his indiscretion.

The financial aspect of NCPAC's campaigns are similarly important to their overall strategy. No campaign or project is initiated without a prior financial analysis and careful scrutiny of the organization's budget. As stated above, NCPAC had no expectation of toppling either Senator Edward Kennedy or House Speaker Tip O'Neill, although polls were commissioned to explore the possibility. Yet, despite the negative poll results, NCPAC went ahead with its efforts (publicly extensive but privately limited) only because they would raise additional dollars for other NCPAC projects. It was strategy like this that enabled NCPAC to grow from 80,000 contributors in 1978 to to 250,000 in 1980 and to maintain that level in 1982 and 1984.[64]

According to former NCPAC employee Cheryl Altmire, the decision in 1984 to suspend independent expenditure efforts against liberal senators and congressmen and to concentrate instead on the presidential race was as much financial as political. Since NCPAC was already heavily in debt, the opinion was that it would be easier on the budget to run a massive independent expenditure on behalf of President Reagan than to engage in a series of smaller congressional campaigns. And as regular contributors were more concerned with re-electing the president than with defeating a handful of lesser known liberals, this new strategy perfectly matched NCPAC's fundraising capabilities. Independent expenditure efforts depend on proper financing, without which they cannot opperate effectively. NCPAC's first concern, understandably, has always been to maintain its list of financial contributors.

Debate still rages among political observers as to whether the independent expenditure efforts of controversial organizations – like NCPAC – are helpful or harmful to the candidates they support. George McGovern is widely considered to have been a victim of NCPAC in 1980, but the Republican State Chairman in South Dakota is skeptical. "I don't think you can defeat George McGovern by standing up cussing him."[65] McGovern's Republican opponent, James Abdnor, went so far as to file a complaint with the Federal Election Commission to force NCPAC out of the race, claiming unauthorized use of his name in their advertising. A fact not widely known is that, initially, a NCPAC representative met with Abdnor in an attempt to convince him to run. After conducting a poll that indicated that McGovern could be beaten, pollster Arthur Finkelstein spoke on several occasions to their skeptical candidate, who eventually agreed to enter the race. In a 1986 interview, Dolan said, "Sure we encouraged him to run. He knows it and we know it. But I'm not going to admit that to the FEC. No way." Said Abdnor, "Yea, they got me interested. But I didn't want them around. No way. They were so negative, they would have cost me every vote I earned." Abdnor took a similar public view of the 1986 independent expenditure campaign on his behalf by RPAC, though not before the association had helped him defeat a popular primary opponent.[66] Another successful Senate Republican candidate concluded that NCPAC made no difference in the electoral outcome, despite NCPAC'S extensive paid advertising budget. An aide to Republican candidate Steve Symms, who defeated Idaho Senator Frank Church, the target of NCPAC's most extensive media blitz in 1980, claimed NCPAC's strategy and tactics actually backfired, thus hindering the campaign against Church.[67] And Democratic media consultant Frank Greer suggested that appearing on a "NCPAC hit list" was actually a plus. "There are a lot of candidates who can't wait to be targeted by NCPAC because it will do wonders for their fundraising efforts."

But despite the ongoing debate over its help or harm, few deny the potential effectiveness of the independent expenditure effort. An influential McGovern staffer admitted that the South Dakota Senator's favorable rating dropped 20 percent during NCPAC's pre-primary activities, an obvious sign of NCPAC's success.[68] NCPAC's own post election polls indicated that while their organization was highly unpopular in the various targeted races, it was still instrumental in destroying their opponents' favorable ratings and weakening their candidacies. A staff member on Birch Bayh's unsuccessful re-election drive expressed no doubts about the impact of NCPAC's independent expenditure efforts:

From the time NCPAC put us on their list, I don't think there was one story I read in an Indiana paper that didn't start off, or have parenthetically in one of the first three paragraphs, "Birch Bayh, one of the five most liberal senators targeted by conservative groups." It began to dominate the news. Wherever Bayh went, instead of the things being covered the way we wanted it, the story was these groups picketing him.[69]

Common Cause President Fred Wertheimer concurred: "They are damaging, particularly early in the race, in undermining public confidence in a candidate. For that reason alone, they have a major impact, and particularly on television. Television is the most dangerous place for independent expenditures."

Not all PACs, however, follow a practice of waging negative campaigns. In fact, candidates have witnessed a strong trend toward positive independent expenditure efforts in the two most recent elections. (See table 6.8.)

The American Medical Association Political Action Committee (AMPAC) has led all trade and association PACs in the numbers and scope of their independent expenditure efforts, and each one has been conducted in a positive fashion. Fred Rainey, Chairman of AMPAC's Board of Directors, told the Senate Rules and Administration Committee: "AMPAC's activities are directed entirely toward candidate support. AMPAC has never, by the use of independent expenditure or otherwise, advocated the defeat of or directed criticism against a specific candidate."[70]

AMPAC operates differently from its counterparts in other ways as well. Whereas RPAC's independent expenditure committee operates wholly outside the organization's PAC, to the extent that there are totally separate staffs and that the RPAC Trustees have no involvement in deciding where to launch independent expenditure campaigns, AMPAC's decisions on contributions and on independent expenditures are made by the same four-member committee. Recommendations for candidate support commence with local area physicians, and are passed on to be studied by the state AMPAC committee. Recommendations from the state committee are in turn passed on to the national board, the Congressional Review Committee, which consists of four members from AMPAC's Board of Directors. Unlike the case with some of the largest trade and association PACs, no candidate will receive AMPAC assistance without the support of the local and state AMPAC committees. And unlike the case with NCPAC supported candidates, AMPAC reported its customers were very satisfied. Said Rainey, "All of the candidates involved felt that this [independent expenditure effort] was an extremely valuable program."[71]

Individuals can also wage independent expenditure campaigns, although in most cases such efforts involve paid political advertising and little else. The largest individual independent expenditure campaign on behalf of a presidential candidate occurred in 1980, when a Texas

Table 6.8    *Independent expenditures for/against House and Senate*
*candidates*

| Cycle | Total ($ m) | On behalf of ($ m) | On behalf of (%) | Against ($ m) | Against (%) |
|---|---|---|---|---|---|
| 79–80 | 2.2 | 0.9 | 41 | 1.3 | 59 |
| 81–2 | 5.7 | 1.2 | 21 | 4.5 | 79 |
| 83–4 | 4.9 | 3.4 | 69 | 1.5 | 31 |
| 85–6 | 8.5 | 7.4 | 87 | 1.1 | 13 |

*Source*: FEC Press Release: 21 February 1982, 7 March 1982, 29 November 1983, 1 December 1985, 21 May 1987

industrialist spent more than $400,000 on behalf of Ronald Reagan, mainly for newspaper advertising. Two other individuals spent about $100,000 each in support of independent presidential candidate John Anderson. One of them, General Motors heir Stewart Mott, had spent hundreds of thousands of dollars for liberal candidates in previous elections, both in direct contributions and in more private efforts. But the largest single independent expenditure campaign by an individual was waged against Illinois Senator Charles Percy in 1984. Michael Goland, a Jewish activist from California, spent one million dollars in the primary and election campaigns in a successful effort to defeat the high ranking Republican, who had voted against Israeli interests on several occasions in the US Senate.[72] Nonetheless, it is currently still rare for wealthy individuals to engage in independent expenditure campaigns. As long as there remain extensive reporting requirements and much publicity for those individuals who advance large sums, it is highly unlikely that the number of independent expenditure campaigns by individuals will increase greatly in the future. There are few people, no matter how dedicated to a political cause, who care to risk a charge of collusion. Nevertheless, according to media consultant Charles Guggenheim, "Independent expenditures will continue as long as you have people who are obsessed."

No one doubts that the creation of the independent expenditure has made life considerably more difficult for the candidates involved. Independent expenditure campaigns, said Texas Senator Lloyd Bentsen, "distort an election by doubling the voices against a candidate and forcing that candidate to spend his funds not on election issues but in reply to an outside group."[73] Former White House political advisor Lyn Nofziger criticized the practice from the candidate's point of view: "You cannot tell me," he complained, "that I cannot speak to some guy who's out there running ads, allegedly on my behalf, even though he may be messing up everything I'm trying to do!"

Such a situation manifested itself in the 1986 Maryland Senate race, when an obscure independent organziation, the Anti-Terrorism American Committee, announced they would spend $250,000 on behalf of Republican candidate Linda Chavez. Her press secretary was not pleased: "If they think they are being helpful, they are mistaken. We have some issues we are trying to focus on, and it's difficult when there are distractions coming in all directions."[74] Nofziger also noted that if a candidate were to ask an independent expenditure campaign, directly, to change its strategy, that candidate would be in breach of federal election law, a position no candidate wants to be in. Republican Senate candidate Kenneth Kramer faced this particular dilemma in the highly contested 1986 Colorado election. NCPAC had been asked to leave Colorado by the Republican state chairman, and Kramer aides had told the press that NCPAC's assistance "has not been sought, wanted or needed," and that Kramer "prefers they leave."[75] But Kramer himself never asked NCPAC to depart, either publicly or privately.

Candidates themselves are somewhat wary of having an independent expenditure waged against their opponents. Most prefer to feel in total control of their campaign efforts, even if this control is more perception than reality. Outside forces, no matter how well intentioned, tend to upset a candidate's delicate balance over issues and strategy. As an example, NCPAC had hoped to persuade popular Congresswoman Marjorie Holt to challenge incumbent Senator Paul Sarbanes in the 1982 Maryland Senate race. They ran extensive advertisements with the slogan "Paul Sarbanes is too liberal for Maryland," temporarily weakening his position in the polls. The strategy backfired, however, when Sarbanes made NCPAC, not his voting record, the central issue in his re-election fight. Soon after the Sarbanes counterattack, Holt announced she would not stand against him, having no desire to participate in a "NCPAC race."

Sarbanes, an effective but reluctant campaigner, was wisely prodded to hit the streets early in the 1982 election, immediately following the first NCPAC attack, and this was a key factor in his ultimate victory. His eventual opponent, Larry Hogan, went from passive ambivalence to outright hostility over NCPAC's activity, exclaiming "I hereby denounce NCPAC" during a televised debate toward the later stages of the campaign.[76] NCPAC had failed to set the issues agenda, and thereby condemned Hogan, the eventual opponent who had replaced Holt, to a hostile and defensive electoral environment he had no responsibility for creating. Senior Maryland Senator Charles Mathias concluded, while presiding over hearings on the effect of independent expenditures, that the race was over before it even began: "[Sarbanes's] opponent, who might have had a chance otherwise, was really ruled out of the race without a chance to campaign because, by the time the campaign began, NCPAC had pulled out the shield of invulnerability over its target."[77]

The re-election campaign of New York Senator Daniel Patrick Moynihan was an exemplary demonstration of a vulnerable candidate turning a potentially dangerous electoral situation into a major tactical victory. Moynihan's campaign manager skillfully managed to coerce television stations in his state to refuse to run NCPAC advertising, warning them that although the ads were paid for by NCPAC, the television stations themselves were not immune from libel action for any misrepresentations or factual errors. A year earlier, in a 31 May 1981 front-page article in the *New York Times*, it was reported that NCPAC had made several major errors in its television advertisements against several US Senators. Among the errors reported were the inaccurate claim that Missouri Senator Tom Eagleton had supported aid to the "repressive communist dictatorship" in Nicaragua (Eagleton did not vote for or support the measure); and the erroneous charge that Arizona Senator Dennis DeConcini supported abortion (he does not).

According to Frank Greer, a leading anti-independent expenditure strategist:

Under the fairness doctrine of the Federal Communications Code, you are not required to sell time to independent parties in a federal election. If you do sell time, and you are a station manager, you may create a fairness obligation to provide response time free to the candidate who is being attacked. If I say that to a television station before the negative campaign begins, most stations will say, "I want no part of this".

As a consequence, not a single television spot from NCPAC was ever broadcast in New York. But Moynihan's real success was in turning NCPAC's attack *on him* into an effective direct mail pitch *for him*, which brought in thousands of dollars in anti-NCPAC funding while uniting undecided Democratic opponents (including the Liberal Party, who had once refused their endorsement) behind his candidacy. There is no doubt that candidates like Moynihan have become better prepared to answer the charges levelled by the ideological PACs; moreover, those who are attacked have often found themselves attracting a significant sympathy vote from the electorate.

Charles Grassley, one of a crop of successful Senate candidates in 1980, adopted a unique approach that allowed his campaign to receive all the benefits of an independent expenditure campaign against his opponents without much of the backlash or the problem of conflicting strategies. The independent expenditure campaigns would "leak" their plan of attack to the press who, as might have been expected, were eager to publish every detail. Then Grassley himself would criticize the parts he did not like or want, blaming them on NCPAC or whoever seemed appropriate. By communicating through the press this way,

Grassley was able to control the independent campaign strategy without breaking any federal election laws.

Some candidates, however, are not as successful in their independent expenditure strategy. Many believe that Illinois Senator Charles Percy, a victim of a 1984 independent expenditure campaign, could have survived the contest if he had raised the funds necessary to fight back. Percy chose instead to ignore his attackers. As Common Cause President Fred Wertheimer noted, "We shouldn't leave a candidate vulnerable to being murdered. If Senator Percy had been given one million dollars in response to the million that had been spent against him, he would have been able to answer and neutralize the charges." "If there was a NCPAC attacking me, I would respond," remarked Connecticut Congressman John Rowland, himself the target of a small independent campaign by a liberal organization. "I would attack them back. You have to." Candidates have been forced to recognize that well-financed independent expenditures cannot go ignored; those that act on this premise are generally successful, but those that do not have experienced considerable difficulty. Direct mail consultant Bob Odell concurred: "If I were under attack by an independent expenditure, I would stand up and say, 'See, they're ganging up on me. I didn't give these people special favors so what are they doing, these rich guys? They're coming into our district. They are not your friends.'"

Terry Dolan acknowledged in 1982 that independent expenditures alone do not decide election outcomes. "Our experience . . . simply demonstrates that NCPAC cannot defeat Democratic senators in strongly Democratic states without the help of other factors." DCCC Chairman Tony Coelho claimed that the failures of many independent efforts in the 1986 elections "send a message to other incumbents that you need not worry if your record is solid."[78] Even the best planned and financed independent expenditure strategy can fail, as surely every practitioner will admit. Yet regardless of their ethics, tactics and controversial nature, independent expenditures are legitimate and have rapidly become an accepted part of modern electioneering, having taken on the appearance of full-fledged campaigns by themselves. Barring some change in the election laws, and as long as their fundraising efforts succeed, independent expenditure campaigns will continue to grow in number and scope over the coming elections.

In addition to the independent expenditure campaigns, some PACs now offer candidate training schools to equip challengers with the necessary skills to fight the opposition. NCPAC, in particular, has set up highly intensified three-day and five-day courses taught by national political experts in polling, scheduling, media, fundraising, etc., and also dealing with personal topics, such as handling the candidate's spouse and dressing for press conferences. To the mutual satisfaction of PACs, candidates, and consultants, it is not uncommon for an enrollee to hire one or more of his instructors upon completion of the course. Added Cheryl Altmire, an aide to former NCPAC director Terry Dolan, "Candidates who attend our schools also have a greater chance of picking up financial contributions among those PACs favorable to conservative candidates."

In every election cycle, NCPAC, through its research and educational arm, the National Conservative Foundation, hosts numerous campaign management schools and fundraising seminars, training over 300 potential election workers annually in modern campaign technology. A record of all course participants is retained in NCPAC's files, to be supplied to favored candidates seeking trained staff people – yet another in-kind service.

Some national PACs are also taking an active role in candidate recruitment, one of the most controversial new trends in PAC electoral involvement. Confined mainly to ideological PACs, such as NCPAC, the Committee for the Survival of a Free Congress (CSFC), the Congressional Club, and organized labor PACs – these organizations all place great emphasis on recruiting like-minded individuals to run against candidates of the opposite philosophical persuasion. No longer constrained by a limited field of candidates, these PACs have become increasingly willing to expend resources to find those individuals who most closely fit their specifications. Recruitment drives by conservative PACs have resulted, albeit infrequently, in the election of several statewide candidates, such as New Hampshire Governor John Sununu (NCPAC), Senator Jeremiah Denton (CSFC), and Senator John East (Congressional Club). More importantly, candidate recruitment has transformed a PAC's role in elections from that of a keen observer to an active participant.

But a number of the more controversial ideological and single issue PACs are finding their contributions not welcomed by those candidates they wish to support – even given the typical candidate's insatiable appetite for money. The Human Rights Campaign Fund (HRCF), a gay political action committee, has had numerous contributions returned because of its controversial nature. Most candidates, at one time or another, face the difficult decision of whether a particular donation or expression of support is worth the probable backlash. But with the number of PACs, and their contributions, growing rapidly, and with the exorbitant sums needed by candidates, it is increasingly difficult for most candidates to be selective about the source of their financial support.

In short, the tactics used by political action committees to influence elections can range widely, from a mere endorsement or small financial contribution, to the donation of valuable campaign service, and even to a full-fledged independent expenditure effort worth thousands of dollars. For the most part, PACs have proven themselves useful to the candidates they support, and a serious threat to those whom they oppose. As political scientist and election expert Richard Scammon summarized it in 1986: "The idea that the PACs go out and buy somebody is pretty far fetched. What they do is find where their friends are and finance them."[79] Furthermore, unlike many hidebound candidates, the political action committees have shown themselves to be adaptive to new strategies and new campaign technologies. Innovations in PAC electoral activities promise to keep them at the forefront of American politics for years to come.

# 7

# Modern campaign technology
# in the 1990s

Consultants . . . recognize that running the best and most commercials
won't do the job any more. Figuring out new winning ways is unnerving.
The stakes are about as high as they get.

Patricia Sellers, journalist[1]

Of course, no one can predict the future with certainty. The modern
campaign technology of 1988 may seem primitive in four years, just as
what was innovative in 1984 is commonplace today. That said, it is
already possible to detect several trends in American electoral politics as
well as certain techniques which, although currently in their earliest
stages of development, may have the potential to revolutionize the
campaign process in the next decade. The first step in looking for
electoral innovations is to examine those areas where new methods in
campaigning are most often created. Since presidential campaigns
generate significantly more press attention and scholarly research than
statewide or congressional races, what appear to be innovative
campaign techniques are, from time to time, first observed at the
presidential level and heralded by political observers as a new
breakthrough in electioneering. Closer examination, however, may
reveal that many of these supposedly new techniques and strategies
have already been used successfully in earlier, non-presidential elections.
Thus, while it may appear that many technical innovations begin at the
presidential level and then filter down to statewide and congressional
races, the truth, according to America's leading political consultants, is
otherwise. Of those questioned, nearly 80 percent said most technological innovations in electioneering start at the statewide and congressional
level. (See survey 7.1.)

Although several developing technologies that will be described here
were first tested on the presidential level, for the most part, new ideas in

campaigning are usually tried out in lower level races before being used on a national level. Statewide races clearly offer the greatest opportunity for experimentation, particularly in well-funded challenger races. According to pollster Harrison Hickman: "If a challenger has enough money and similar views to the incumbent, but less name recognition and standing among the voters, he's got to figure out ways to beat the incumbent. Need generates innovation, and challengers find themselves more often in needy situations."

**Survey 7.1**　*Do technological innovations in electioneering generally start at the presidential level and filter down, or do they start at the statewide and congressional level and filter up?*

|  | % |
| --- | --- |
| Filter up from state and congressional level | 75 |
| Filter down from presidential level | 6 |
| Filter equally up and down (volunteered) | 19 |

Many of the latest campaign innovations are actually an integration of formerly separate areas of campaign technology. As campaigns have grown more technically complicated, candidates have been forced to turn to a wider variety of specialist consultants, not only to obtain expert advice on a particular technology, but also to integrate and systematize the different products necessary for running an effective race. It was inevitable that these specialists would find themselves not only working in their own area but also working cooperatively, in the interest of the campaign, to resolve problems affecting campaign functions other than their own. Certain recent advances in campaign technology have also followed this trend, and straddle the demarcation lines of what were once separate and distinct spheres of campaigning – areas such as polling, direct mail, and political advertising.

Also coming to the fore is the emphasis on demographic decentraliza-tion. As campaign costs continue to spiral upwards, the necessity to target the right voters accurately and send them the right message at the lowest possible cost has become crucial. As a result, there is a trend in political campaigning toward dividing and subdividing the electorate into smaller, more narrowly defined subsections. New techniques are currently being developed and tested for this specific purpose, and many of the recent advances in electioneering have taken place because of great advancements in computer technology.

The development of campaign software has become one of the fastest growing specialties in political consulting. Designed to be usable even by computer illiterates, software created for the 1986 and 1988 election cycles eclipsed all first generation software (1982–4) in its flexibility in accessing data and its ability to computerize major elements of a political campaign. The charts and graphs that now accompany most political survey reports were made possible because of the current availability and practicality of appropriate computer software Candidates and campaign managers are no longer forced to spend hours pouring over complicated computer printouts to retrieve relatively simple information.

**Sample list of campaign tasks conducted by computer**

*Candidate/Voter/Volunteer Management*
  Voter registration drives
  Absentee ballot distribution and
    collection
  Phone bank operations

  Election day voter turnout
  Candidate scheduling
  General issue research

*Demographic Targeting*
  List segmentation to include:
    age, sex, income, occupation,
    education, ethnicity, ancestry,
    family status, housing type and
    value, neighborhood growth
    and mobility, and other census
    data

*Financial Management*
  FEC filing reports

  Solicitation/collection of pledges
  PAC solicitations
  Maintenance of house
    contributor file
  Payroll reports

*Voter List Maintenance*
  Conversion of voter tapes to
    allow downloading or
    uploading of all voter lists

The continued drop in price, and increase in density, of hard disks will allow more statewide candidates to utilize in-house computers for maintaining their computer lists of voters, donors, and demographic information, eliminating the need to rely on service bureaus. The newest personal computers can now support "multitasking" (the capability to run two programs at once and switch between them easily) along with the usual word processing functions. This development provides a campaign with the convenience of having information stored and readily available in the campaign headquarters. According to John Paul Phaup, vice-president of the Brady Group, a leading software company that had eleven Senate candidates as clients in 1986, the financial barriers to campaign computerization are being eliminated. "With a small computer, the sophistication once reserved for the big guys is now within the grasp of the little guys with just a few thousand dollars to spend."[2] As of June 1986, about a dozen companies specialized in political software, with product names like "Politech" and "The Election Machine." Costs for the various software packages currently range from $595 to about $2,000, depending on the sophistication and applicability to a political campaign.

Microcomputers have already been used for small group targeting in several 1986 races, and will enable an increasing number of campaigns to complete in-house geodemographic targeting plans in upcoming election cycles. Geodemographics, combining the information of census data, survey research, election data, and voter lists, is significantly advancing the ability of candidates to reach specific voters with a specific message. In a state-of-the-art geodemographic direct mail targeting plan, past election data is gathered by the campaign by precincts (chosen because they are the smallest unit for which election results are tabulated), dividing the constituency into core Republican, core Democratic, and ticket-splitting areas, as well as likely voter turnout percentages. The microcomputer overlaps this information with specific neighborhood demographic data provided by the US Census Bureau, such as sex, age, race, income, occupation, home ownership, etc. The mainframe computer then uses the constituency voter list to add a name and address (and phone number if the individual is to be contacted by a phone bank), thus filtering out unregistered voters.

In perhaps the most important step, the newly matched lists are merged once more, to create the text of a unique, personalized letter. An unlimited number of phrases, sentences, and paragraphs on various themes and issues are arbitrarily assigned a code and entered into a computer database. Survey research results tell the campaign the issues and phrases that are most important, and which ones to avoid, when contacting individuals of the various demographic groups and partisan affiliations. Automatically, the computer selects from the database those coded paragraphs and phrases most likely to influence the recipient favorably. Thus, a fifty-year-old Democratic businessman who lives in a wealthy neighborhood will receive a letter entirely different than a twenty-year-old male Democratic student who lives on a college campus. Even though they are both Democratic men, younger and older Democratic men are not necessarily concerned about the same issues.

Lastly, the now uniquely designed letter is sent back to the mainframe for high volume printing. Voters will thus receive a letter addressed to them personally which contains specific information that is likely to appeal to their particular demographic and voter background.

In addition, a number of newly formed companies have begun to offer special election services to campaigns with a computer terminal and modem. For an annual subscription, *Washington On-Line*, through its "Campaign Contribution Tracking System," allows campaigns to examine and print out Federal Election Commission reports on any campaign, political action committee (PAC), or political party organization. In addition, *Washington On-Line* also has a bill tracking system and a bill text service, which provide full information and text on all congressional legislation. Two other commercial data-base systems, "Legi-Slate," owned by the *Washington Post*, and *Congressional Quarterly*'s "Washington Alert Service," offer profiles of members of Congress and their districts, including valuable biographical, political, and demographic material essential to a campaign's opposition research department. All three systems have analytical capabilities that allow the user to perform sophisticated research that was once arduously performed by hand. Another computer information service, the *Presidential Campaign Hotline*, provides presidential candidates and the news media with the latest political information, analysis, polls, and gossip for a fee of $150 to $350 a month. Inaugurated in September 1987, the *Hotline* allows subscribers to "down-load" a daily fifteen- to thirty-page report that features exclusive material issued by the presidential campaigns, and an insider's summary of important political events.

The rapidly increasing political capacity of computers comes at a time when computerization of voter registration lists for nearly every state, city, and town in the country is approaching completion. This means that by the end of 1988, campaigns will be able to target specific constituents in any voting district they may select. Since this project is led by the national party organizations, the effort should further strengthen their role in the election process, adding yet another service they can provide for their candidates, at little or no cost. The Republican National Committee (RNC) has gone a step further, having developed its own (minicomputer) campaign software package for use by state party organizations. Moreover, as census data becomes even more sophisticated, it too will be increasingly computerized by political campaigns.

In short, the use of computers in electioneering, while no longer a rarity, is still in its infancy. As it grows, with each election cycle, it will continue to transform electoral politics. Said John Brady, president of the Brady Group, in a 1986 interview: "The things being done now [with microcomputers] are so elementary compared to what is possible."[3]

Because of this development in computer technology, political survey research has become more sophisticated, accurate, informative, precise, and timely — all for substantially less money. And the outlook is for these trends to increase in the future. Polling methodology, both the measurement and the analytical techniques, has undergone considerable refinement in the past decade alone. Since the 1970s, pollsters have been able to predict election outcomes with a high degree of accuracy. Today, pollsters also routinely measure voter perceptions of a candidate's personality and character, in addition to attitudes on issues and partisan attachment.

Nearly every major political polling firm is currently engaged in specialized research into new areas of voter behavior, targeted to probe voters' underlying attitudes about a candidate. For example, the Democratic polling firm Hickman–Maslin Research has made an in-depth study of candidate stereotyping with regard to physical, personality, and character traits, to find which stereotypes will favor their candidate and which will lessen his appeal to the electorate. In the first (benchmark) survey, the polling firm considers the basic information that voters will first learn about their candidate (sex, party, age, incumbency, home) and determines what various stereotypes are attached to those characteristics. The candidate is then "introduced" to the public, reshaped to address the negative correlations while maintaining the positive ones. Hamilton, Frederick and Schneiders, whose presidential campaign client list includes Jimmy Carter and Walter Mondale, are developing a "life-cycle segmentation system" in an effort to design a demographic database that cuts across geographic boundaries, and can provide comparative information to assist in media buying, direct mail, and phone campaigning. Market Opinion Research president Bob Teeter, an advisor to Vice-President George Bush, has broken new ground in geodemographic targeting, the combination of census data and survey research.

Most of the larger survey firms are in the process of installing a computer aided telephone interviewing system (CATI) which plugs voter responses immediately into a computerized cross-tabulation program. In past years, telephone survey interviews were conducted by individuals who read from long, complicated scripts. The interviewers were entirely responsible for screening questions (that is, asking specific questions of specific respondents, and not of the entire survey sample; respondents with an opinion of a particular politician are often asked additional questions about that politician which are not asked of other interviewees). Each response was recorded on paper by the interviewer, and the results then turned over to a key-punch operator before being analyzed by the pollster.

With CATI, the key-punch process is eliminated, since voter responses are typed directly into the computer (open-ended questions, by their nature, still require manual, written answers). This system gives the pollster completed survey results almost instantaneously, sharply reducing turnaround time and thereby enabling a campaign to react quickly and accurately to the changing political climate. Equally important, the interviewers are no longer burdened by complicated survey questionnaires and difficult screening procedures. With CATI, each interviewer sits behind a computer terminal and is only required to read the question displayed on the monitor and type in the voter's reponse. The computer automatically dials the phone number, completes the screening procedure, and selects the proper questions, thus allowing interviewers to think more about developing rapport with the respondent on the other end of the phone and less about which page to turn to next. More importantly, pollsters are now able to design surveys containing finely detailed screening questions which capture more information about the respondent and thus yield more precise results. As the explosion in public opinion polling and telemarketing (selling via the phone) continues, and the refusal rate (the number of those contacted who do not wish to be polled) increases, it will become even more crucial for pollsters to use the new computer technology to speed turnaround.

Currently, however, few polling firms have switched their entire operation to CATI because of the expensive start-up costs. Roughly $4,000 is required to computerize each polling station (that is, each phone), and a firm would need to install computers in at least thirty stations, at a total of $120,000, before CATI could become fully operational and yield maximum benefits to the pollster. The 1989–90 election cycle will probably be the first in which a majority of polling operations will be completely on a CATI system.

Changes already on the threshold in political advertising are actually adaptations of innovations in commercial advertising. Historically, political electioneering has borrowed – often directly and heavily – many of its techniques from the business community. For many years, sophisticated methods have been used by commercial advertisers to evaluate customer reactions to new products and to test alternative advertising appeals. But according to political consultant David Keene, campaigns tend to be somewhat behind the business sector in the use of marketing and new technology. "About 80 percent of what is theoretically possible in politics is thrown out by the candidates because they have neither the time nor the resources to do it." Media advisor Ken Swope, formerly a commercial advertiser, made the additional point that "Political advertising is really very primitive by comparison. The techniques used in commercial advertising, tapping into people's psyches, trying to affect people's emotions, are not currently done in political advertising."

Author Gary Mauser wrote in 1983: "Techniques such as concept testing, multidimensional scaling, audience measurement, and computer simulation are routinely used in new product development. As yet, these techniques are not widely used in campaign politics."[4] The reason why few, if any, statewide or regional campaigns were using such tactics, Mauser explained, was due to the excessive cost in time and money that such market research would entail. Another contributing factor was the persistent and vocal opposition of most media consultants, who felt that such testing would limit their creativity. Since then, however, most media consultants have come to realize that commercial testing can serve as a "disaster check" to pick out flawed advertisements that inadvertently might have undermined the candidate they were created to help.

Not unexpectedly, commercial testing techniques have found their way into a growing number of recent campaigns. Three formats, pre-testing, on-air testing, and post-testing, are all in various stages of development and use. The easiest, cheapest, and most commonly used of the three is the pre-testing technique.

Here, persons with low political awareness are gathered together in clusters of fifteen to twenty-five at a time (each gathering is referred to as a "focus group") while a pollster continuously measures the individual attitudes and opinions of those in each group as they view the candidate's latest campaign commercials. Often, the same individuals will also be shown the opposition's commercials, again to determine voter attitudes and opinions. The focus groups are meant to serve as an early warning system, alerting the pollster and media consultant to a commercial that might not generate the desired response from the voting public. Although several media advisors warned about the limits of focus group testing (Roger Ailes spoke harshly of a candidate's wife who began to conduct unauthorized, unsolicited, and unscientific testing, to the despair of the campaign organization), it is now a widely used and accepted technique in the pre-testing of political ads. According to pollster Robert Teeter, more than 50 percent of his statewide clients used some form of pre-testing in 1986, a significant increase over 1984 levels.

In on-air testing, a campaign's new commercials are aired in a selected small media market. Individuals are contacted (and paid) in advance, and asked to watch television on a particular channel for a two-hour period. They are told they will be called the next day to answer questions about the programs, but are not informed that the political commercials will be the primary focus. Like pre-testing, on-air testing measures attitudes and opinions of the viewers toward the new spots, and towards the candidates after viewing the spots. The primary advantage of on-air testing over pre-testing is that it allows the consultants to determine whether a candidate's political advertising is strong enough to stand out against the clutter of commercial advertisements. However, on-air testing is too costly and time consuming for most statewide campaigns, and is generally reserved for presidential candidates and for the earliest wave of television spots in statewide races.

The third and least utilized method of analyzing the quality of a candidate's campaign commercials is post-testing, examining the impact of a political commercial after it has aired. The problem here is the difficulty of isolating the political commercials from other sources of political information in the voter's mind, which limits this technique's usefulness during, and even more importantly after, a campaign. Only a small number of wealthy candidates have engaged in post-testing. As John Deardourff noted: "After election day, the losers are too financially strapped, and the winners don't care. If they won, they won, and they couldn't care less why."

The Reagan–Bush re-election campaign in 1984 was one of the first to utilize fully a number of commercial techniques to test, analyze, and target its political advertising. Ample time and funding allowed Reagan's pollster and media consultants (the latter included individuals responsible for the Gallo Wine and Pepsi advertising) to break new ground in political market testing, when they borrowed many of the procedures used by business consultants and adapted them to the "selling" of their political product. Reagan pollster Richard Wirthlin was instrumental in pioneering a new technique, Values in Strategic Assessment (VISTA), a multi-stage process that explores the path from issues to consequences to values in a very successful effort at measuring voter behavior and response to the Reagan media campaign. In fact, according to author Nicholas Lemann, "The makers of the [Reagan] ads quite openly modeled them on successful campaigns for companies such as Pepsi Cola and McDonald's," because commercial testing methods indicated that voters would respond best to this style of advertising.[5]

In general, however, the application of commercial techniques to political campaigns (outside the national party organizations) is still at a primitive stage. Said Edward Mahe: "We've never had the money to do in-depth market research to determine what works and what doesn't on TV, so we tended to follow the commercial marketplace and then tried to figure out how to wrap our message into the format they have already set." Added Deardourff, "It is very difficult for the candidates to justify in their own minds this expenditure. They have no qualms about spending \$400,000 to put the advertising on the air, but they are usually unwilling to spend \$20,000 to test it." Further experimentation and development of pre-testing, on-air testing, and post-testing will certainly continue, but it will be another election cycle before the use of these techniques is widespread.

Another growing political phenomenon, though primarily reserved for presidential candidates, is the use of instant audience measurement systems to gauge immediate voter perceptions of candidates appearing in debates or similar televised forums. This technique was originally developed in the 1930s for the business world, and its introduction into politics did not occur for several decades. Gauging public responses to campaign debates began in 1960, when pollster Louis Harris sampled viewers' opinions of the Nixon–Kennedy debates to help determine campaign strategy. More recently, it was not uncommon for the wealthier Senate and gubernatorial campaigns to gather focus groups of ten to twenty-five people who were questioned about their attitudes towards the candidates before and after viewing a debate.

Today, however, after-the-fact telephone interviews and focus group sessions no longer yield maximum information in the shortest amount of time. Some campaigns are turning to continuous response technology and instant computer analysis of debates and other public appearances to determine the strengths and weaknesses of their candidate. Such methods allow a campaign to analyze more precisely what voters like about a candidate and why.

Although the firms marketing this technology have different names for their product, including the "Perception Analyzer," "Tell-Back," and "Ballot Box," the technology and process itself are essentially the same. Groups of 50 to 100 people, usually paid for their time, are each provided with a portable, hand-held, computer-linked device that has a circular, numbered dial. The participants are asked to turn the numbered dial lower if they get a negative impression of what they hear and see, or higher if their impression is favorable. The dial turning provides a continuous response from each individual that is fed into the main computer every three seconds. Average scores, the distribution of positive and negative opinions, and various subgroup ratings are plotted in spreadsheet and graphic form and superimposed on the television screen as each candidate speaks. These synchronized readings enable consultants to monitor an audience's responses to candidates and learn the areas in which a candidate communicates well, and also where the help of a professional media advisor is needed.

The 1988 presidential campaigns of Democrat Paul Simon and Republican George Bush, the first in their respective parties to use this technology, both gained invaluable data from the process, which was immediately incorporated into their campaign messages. At a cost of about $10,000 per application, the use of instant audience response technology can be expected to spread rapidly through the political world.

The 1984 Mondale presidential campaign was also an "electioneering laboratory," and became the source of a major technological breakthrough destined to transform statewide campaigning in future election cycles. It is interesting that two of the most recent technological breakthroughs took place in a presidential race. According to fundraiser Roger Craver, who has handled more presidential contests than any other direct mail firm, "National politicians are generally not risk takers, so they will inevitably be the last to convert to unconventional technologies, and least likely to experiment. The only exceptions were Barry Goldwater and George McGovern, and they were the biggest losers in the last two decades." Mondale was the first candidate to test and use satellite technology to reach the voters. Frank Greer, a member of the Mondale team and currently one of the most successful Democratic media consultants, developed the new technology, and described its first major application and success:

While we were campaigning in Atlanta, Georgia, before the Super Tuesday primaries, Mondale sat down and did six television interviews, via satellite, in one hour, and three interviews were with Miami stations. That evening, Walter Mondale was the lead item on all three. [Opponent] John Glenn flew personally to Miami, but was only covered by two stations, and one of them buried him deep in the program. We had never set foot in Florida, only by satellite, but we got better press coverage than our opponent. The satellite technology was there, it was relatively inexpensive, and we were the only ones using it.

Following the 1984 elections, only half of the nation's television stations had satellites. By November 1986, the percentage had increased to over 90 percent.[6] Profiting from the experience gained in the Mondale race, Greer then went on to exploit satellite technology in the 1986 Georgia US Senate race. Wyche Fowler, Greer's client, participated in twelve television interviews in one hour, thereby blanketing the state and dominating that night's news coverage without his ever leaving a TV studio in Atlanta. Fowler's use of satellite television contributed significantly to his primary and general election victories.

In an early 1987 interview, Greer said he expected the satellite technology to "explode" in future elections "because it has been tried, tested, and it works, and it is easy on the candidate." But no one could have forseen the advances that took place in less than eighteen months. The spread of mobile satellite trucks and the increased availability of transmission frequencies have made the technology accessible to almost any candidate. In fact, every 1988 presidential hopeful used a satellite feed at least once during the campaign. During a brief swing through Iowa, Illinois Senator Paul Simon, in a matter of minutes, completed six out-of-state "live" interviews conducted from a rented satellite truck (an expenditure of less than $3,000). The process was so quick that aides had to provide Simon with cue-cards so he would not mix up the first names of the six anchormen. At a cost of nine thousand dollars, Massachusetts gubernatorial candidate Mike Dukakis created his own instant television network when he addressed 2,500 college students live by satellite on 56 campuses around the country. Future elections are likely to see a massive expansion of satellite press releases, with news-conscious incumbents now able to beam home to their local stations timely coverage of national issues and same-day coverage of committee hearings, where there is particular constituent interest. As long as the Senate (the House is somewhat behind in the technology) continues to maintain its recording studio, and as long as local television stations maintain their willingness to use the satellite feeds, the future for satellite campaigning appears bright indeed.

By 1990, there will be several new broadcasting outlets reaching enough viewers to attract the interest of media consultants and their clients. Cable television, teletext services, video text two-way transmissions, subscription television, low power television, and electronic mail are all in various stages of development, and all offer varying potential for political use in the next decade.

Cable television has already attracted some attention from candidates and their advisors. According to *Congressional Quarterly*, "The advent of cable television has given political candidates the ability to offer well-tailored political messages to viewers — generally at much lower advertising rates than on regular TV stations."[7] The number of households with a cable system hookup is increasing rapidly, from 29 percent in 1982 to 38 percent in 1983 and more than 50 percent in 1986.[8] Along with the increase in cable TV subscribers and video cassette recorder (VCR) ownerships, now estimated at over 50 percent, has come a corresponding fall-off in the network television audience. Gradually, the network affiliates are losing their position of dominance in the television market place.

At the present time, there are four types of cable broadcasting: 1) the retransmission of imported signals (by the superstations, such as WTBS and WOR); 2) original satellite programming (Cable News Network–CNN, Public Affairs Network – CSPAN, Entertainment and Sports Network – ESPN); 3) "must carry" stations (local network affiliated and independent television stations); and 4) local cable originated programming.

The advantage that cable offers candidates is similar to that of radio: highly targeted audiences, and at less cost than regular network advertising. According to communications law attorney Richard N. Neustadt: "The new TV will mean longer messages for smaller audiences. When we watch the narrowcasting [cable] networks, we may see campaign ads and news programs showing candidates advocating bilingual education on Spanish channels, defending Social Security on channels aimed at the elderly, or playing football on sports channels."[9] Cable television can also be used in place of direct mail, probably at a saving to the campaign. In 1982, Mike Dukakis contacted one set of voters by mail and another set with cable, asking them to call a certain telephone number to register for a political caucus. Dukakis's campaign said the response to cable was higher than the response to mail, and cheaper — $11 per caller, as opposed to $16 per caller for mail.[10] Concluded Richard Viguerie: "Cable television could be to the politics of the 1990s what direct mail was to the 1970s."

Of the other emerging broadcast outlets, video text appears to have the greatest potential for political use. Already available on some cable systems, video text is a two-way medium that permits subscribers to respond directly to messages provided textually and graphically. Although most commonly used for banking and shopping at home, video text systems can also employ that same technology to solicit and tabulate public opinion, a practice already tested on an Ohio cable system. Television stations received authorization in March 1983 to engage in teletext services. These allow stations to broadcast, on the vertical blanking interval (VBI), textual and graphic matter which then appears on the television screens of their subscribers. A number of teletext systems were put into limited operation across the country in 1984, and most have become affiliated with various cable systems that distribute the teletext stations and signals as a part of their overall cable service.

Looking ahead to the 1990s and beyond, low power television (LPTV) may become useful to candidates in rural and suburban areas. Using weak signals (a maximum of 1,000 watts, compared to 5 million for standard broadcast stations in major cities) to broadcast over a small area, usually no greater than fifteen miles, these TV stations operate much like local radio stations, except that they provide a picture to go with the sound. The Federal Communications Commission, after receiving thousands of applications for LPTV licenses, began granting them in 1983 to stations in rural areas. The potential for LPTV stations may lie in targeting particular ethnic or racial communities, or possibly suburban areas now served only by metropolitan-wide stations.

Computer mail, with the capability of precise message delivery, may also become a vehicle for electioneering in the mid-1990s. As the number of home computers continues to rise, it will soon be feasible to reach mass numbers of voters through their home computers, using telephone or cable lines. Electronic mail is already being used by the national party organizations to communicate with their staff in the field and with candidates in their districts. Said Roger Craver, "Ten years from now, the thing that will eclipse television will be the home computer. The sheer amount of information that they can give quickly will spell the difference."

Home video may soon be another source of electioneering, particularly in relation to direct mail and personal appearances. Walter Mondale used video cassettes to bolster his fundraising during his 1984 campaign. In 1986, the National Republican Senatorial Committee produced a home video for its major contributors, highlighting Republican candidates for the US Senate. According to media consultant Frank Greer, "Since two-thirds of the people in this country now have a home video unit, candidates may get to the point where they are sending out tapes instead of direct mail pieces."

Presidential candidates are also beginning to use video tapes in place of personal campaigning. Of the thirteen major party candidates for the presidency in 1988, eleven produced home videos, ranging in length from eight minutes (Jack Kemp) to fifty-four minutes (Pat Robertson). Although the technology is similar, style and substance vary from candidate to candidate. The presidential campaign of former NATO commander Al Haig produced a fourteen minute video to be played at American Legion and Veterans of Foreign Wars halls in an effort to drum up support among retired military personnel; whereas the Mike Dukakis media team produced two different videos to allow the campaign to target its audience. In New Hampshire alone, literally thousands of "video parties" were held in preparation for their presidential primary.

At a cost of from $10,000 to $40,000 dollars, home videos are relatively inexpensive to prepare, and can also save the campaign money by using video footage for their television advertising, or vice versa. These cassettes allow the candidate to appear "in person" at five or even fifty places at once, and are designed to give voters a personal sense of the candidate, not just a recitation of proposals or issues. In fact, it was reported that the highly acclaimed campaign video for Bob Dole, written, directed, and produced by the political advertising firm of Murphy and Castellanos, was so effective in detailing the numerous personal obstacles overcome by the Kansas Senator that some voters left the showing in tears. Said John Buckley, press secretary to Kemp, "It's the political equivalent of cloning."[11]

One 1988 presidential candidate has used VCR technology to an even greater degree. In addition to mailing 450 home videos to a target group of 450 uncommitted Democratic activists in New Hampshire, Bruce Babbitt greatly improved his television image by carrying with him a videocassette camera recorder as he campaigned and continually reviewing tapes of his appearances. "You don't need a lot of coaching," he told the *New York Times*. "What you have to do is talk, film, and then watch it as it's played back. You can see what you're doing wrong."[12] The campaign of another 1988 presidential hopeful, Mike Dukakis, prepared a video tape that showed a speech by former candidate Joseph Biden and an earlier speech by British Labour Party leader Neil Kinnock. The tape, which illustrated remarkable similarities in the speeches, was sent to news organizations and was dubbed the first "attack video" in political history by the Des Moines Register. Biden left the presidential race only days later, though Dukakis also lost support because of this (thus far) unique video incident.

The political ads themselves will have a new look in future campaigns because of the rapid improvements in video equipment that have occurred since 1980. Since 1968, a major topic of debate among media consultants has been the choice of format – film or video – for shooting commercials. The major difference between the two is image clarity. A filmed image has more depth and can be made softer and given a dream-like quality, as seen in motion pictures. Film has a higher resolution than video and is significantly more sensitive to light. There is also a greater variety of lenses for film cameras than for video cameras. Video footage has a less professional appearance, because it does not capture shadows or details as well as film. In a video production the picture seems alive and the action appears to be happening right before your eyes, like a newscast.

Despite the quality advantage of film, a growing number of political commercials will undoubtedly be shot with video tape instead of film for two reasons: money and turnaround time. The escalating costs of television air time, coupled with the increasing number of different commercials required to run an effective race, will soon force all but the most affluent campaigns to turn to video instead of film. Moreover, video tape allows the media consultant to shoot, edit, and produce a commercial within twenty-four hours, significantly less than it takes to process, transfer, and edit a film spot. As many of the leading media consultants recognize, the perceptual differences between film and tape are seldom fully understood by their clients. But money and media turnaround are factors that even the most inexperienced candidate can appreciate.

There will be other important changes in the appearance of future campaign commercials as well. Political advertising is just entering the age of computer-generated video graphics, where electronic methods are used to twist, turn, flip, augment, and color an image or a scene, and produce other unusual effects. Computer-generated graphics can help create logos, negative spots or multiple images, and will provide media producers and directors with a technology that encourages creativity in ways previously unimagined. Image manipulation tools have been in existence for some years. However, only since 1984 has the political world had access to true state-of-the-art graphic generators, with creative limits yet unknown. A highly regarded production house in New York even retains a staff programmer whose sole responsibility is to explore new techniques in computer graphics. Used correctly, image creation and manipulation will help campaigns break through the clutter of commercial advertising and, it is hoped, implant their message into the public's consciousness.

Direct mail specialists, pollsters, and many party officials have themselves been experimenting with new campaign techniques, though with somewhat less success than the media gurus. Tests are continuing on automated dialing devices – tape recorded messages and interactive response systems that solicit opinions and funds. By using a campaign database of donors or prospective voters, these "computer telephones," with minimum human involvement, can make thousands of calls a day. Increased sophistication has enabled the recorded messages to pause at the sound of a human voice, as well as interact with the database to choose the "right" message from an extensive collection of prerecorded sermonettes, thus personalizing each call. Since a large number of people can be reached this way in a short period of time, it is also possible to use a computer phone system to conduct survey research, and several state and national party organizations have integrated these systems into their get-out-the-vote efforts. According to an advertisement for Cybertronix's "Power Phone," one of the largest computerized phone services: "[Their] recording, unlike a human interviewer, presents your message exactly the same every time, unaffected by attitudes or fatigue."[13]

Nevertheless, voters who generally respond favorably to personal contact with a candidate tend to respond negatively to this form of communication. And although it was once heralded by Larry Sabato, an academic expert in modern campaign technology, as a "grand new telephonic scheme," the great expectations once held for it have so far failed to materialize.[14] Currently, as far as can be determined, hardly a direct mail consultant or a pollster, if any, has had significant success with the automated dialing device. Nor do any of the consultants interviewed for this book anticipate using automated phoning systems to any great degree in future campaigns. "Their effectiveness in fundraising is questionable," said Roger Craver, "and our testing of totally automated calling has not proven cost effective for campaigns." Concluded pollster Bill Hamilton, "Voters want human contact. Even if they like the person on the tape, they won't pay much attention to the message if it isn't live."

Even direct mail, subject to ongoing experimentation, is currently yielding only limited benefits. The days of easy money, when virtually anyone could send out a direct mail piece and expect a reasonable return, are now gone. Results of the 1986 election cycle have suggested to political observers that direct mail, as a means of fundraising, has reached a plateau, if not its peak. Various explanations of this leveling-out have recently been offered, for the first time, by direct mail specialists and other consultants who feel the need to defend what has been an important fundraising tool.

Of the fundraisers interviewed for this book, only Brad O'Leary and Roger Craver claimed to have had greater success with direct mail in 1986 than in the past. Said O'Leary, "The key is innovation and experimentation. They [other direct mail specialists] do the same thing year after year. We don't. That's the difference." According to Paul Manafort, "While direct mail is less effective today than it used to be when used at the beginning of a campaign, it is still effective at the end of the campaign, when people are paying attention to the election." Terry Dolan, in a mid-1986 interview, suggested that the targets for attack are not as effective for fundraising as they once were. "It was much easier when liberals like McGovern, Church, and Bayh sat in the Senate. Most of the liberals are gone now, and as a result, people don't feel as threatened." Bob Odell believes that direct mail has only reached the first of many successively higher peaks, but added,

One of the great dangers we've had forever is that at some point people would learn to say no. For a long time it was very difficult for people to read those personalized letters and come to the point of saying no. They'd say, "I can't let down President Reagan." Now they say, "I got a letter from him last week, this week, and I'll probably get a letter from him tomorrow. I can't answer them all so I'll pick just one."

Fundraiser Bruce Eberle blames over-solicitation during the presidential election cycle for the problems faced by direct mailers since November 1984. "When one of your guys is running, politics gets very intense and there is a certain amount of burnout once it is over. People also tend to give more money than they normally would, so there is some financial burnout as well."

Discouraging reports on the future of direct mail fundraising also emanate from the relatively unbiased national party organizations. "Direct mail has been off industry wide," claimed DNC spokesman Terry Michael. "It has just hit the saturation point."[15] Explained RNC spokesman Robert Schmermund, "We don't have the quantum leaps in technology that we had five or six years ago."[16] Even if this trend should continue through the next election, direct mail will still be a widely used tool for campaign fundraising into the 1990s. Some political analysts see the advances in electronic direct mail, using the Western Union-style mailgram format, as a powerful force that may revitalize the industry. This virtually untapped technology allows a campaign to get a specific letter to a specific voter or group overnight. However, it is clear that the luster of direct mail fundraising – so bright in the early 1980s – has been tarnished somewhat in most recent elections, and already a search has begun for the next "miracle" fundraising technique.

Unlike direct mail fundraising, voter persuasion direct mail has a promising future as a popular method of campaign communication. As the increasing cost of television (and relative inability to differentiate a campaign message) puts the medium beyond the reach of a growing number of candidates, candidate advocacy direct mail is increasingly being looked on as an excellent, and much less expensive, alternative. California, where few congressional candidates can afford the high price of television, is currently the only state where campaigns regularly produce high quality, sophisticated, appeal oriented direct mail, though a number of consultants, including several media specialists, expect this strategy to spread rapidly in the next few election cycles.

One may wonder how all these innovations affect the campaign consultants. According to veteran consultant Joseph Cerrell, past president of the American Academy of Political Consultants, "Generalist consultants may have been the rule in the past, but the industry is turning to specialists because the work has become more sophisticated."[17] Pollsters, in particular, have begun to assume the strategic role once held by the general consultant. Of the hundreds of new consultants who have entered the political field in the past five years, many have come to realize that there is insufficient business to support all the general practitioners. Consequently, many are attempting to make a niche for themselves by specializing in a single aspect of electioneering. Paul Manafort maintains that even specialization has already reached its peak, and the future will see yet another trend. "We are now moving into the stage of conglomeration. In the last few years, several of the major consulting firms have all started to take on individuals with specific skills and bring them together under one roof."

The trend toward conglomeration has furthered the closer working relationship beginning to develop among consultants, and this will continue as coming innovations integrate the various campaign specialties. Certain pollsters and media consultants have already found themselves working more cooperatively than in the past – and have deemed it mutually beneficial. According to media specialist Bob Squier, in campaigns of the near future computerization will enhance this relationship even further:

Pollsters are a little behind the curve, but you will soon see a situation where before I go to bed at night, I can just walk into my study and call up on my computer the various places where we are polling and read the numbers that have been done that night. We have the computer, we have the system, we are tied to a file system in a central bank. We are ready to do it. We are just waiting for a polling firm that is willing to flip the switch on its side.

The necessity for pollsters and media consultants to be able to interact is crucial. As campaign technology, both hardware and software, becomes more advanced (and complicated), the winners will be those candidates and campaigns that are the quickest to detect and respond, correctly, to changes in the electoral environment. Said media consultant John Deardourff, "For most people, the electoral process is a 72-hour phenomenon. It puts too high a premium on the work of people like me." Ray Strother noted in his private memo to Gary Hart, "Campaign strategies now often change between a Saturday night cocktail and a Monday morning shower. . . . The chess game has become a boxing match of short counter punches."

Despite the many innovative developments, a sizeable number of political consultants do not foresee any major breakthroughs in campaign technology; rather they expect significant refinement in existing techniques. "Technological advances usually came when there was a vacuum," said Lance Tarrance, "and that was in the 1960s and 1970s. But once the vacuum was filled, it has become a case of who is leaner and meaner in the utilization of technological advances." Tarrance believes the next major breakthrough will not occur "until candidates come to a cash ceiling, where something will have to give."

It is on the future costs of electioneering that consultants most closely agree, more so than on any other issue. (See survey 7.2.) According to Peter Kelly, "Polling costs, media costs, fundraising costs, staff costs have all blown campaign expenses out of the water, and it's not going to change. In fact, it is only going to get worse." Noted Lyn Nofziger, "The costs of campaign will continue to spiral upward, since the expanding technology means that you have to spend more money for its usage." As long as the demand for the latest (and often most expensive) techniques in electioneering continues, there is little doubt that the financial cost of running for office will continue to rise.

**Survey 7.2**  *Do you see the costs of political campaigns continuing to spiral upward in the upcoming election cycles?*

|  | % |
|---|---|
| Yes | 88 |
| No | 12 |

   The failure of many candidates to retire debts incurred during their campaign is also responsible for changes in electioneering. More and more consultants are "front loading" their bills, forcing candidates to pay most, or all, consulting fees up front. Many merchants have put their clients on notice that, from now on, their business is still wanted but their credit is no good. This injection of business-like practices into politics has raised some protest among candidates, and forced less wealthy contestants to forgo some instruments of modern campaign technology. It is a trend likely to continue. As Harrison Hickman concluded, "If firms want to stay in business very long, they have to act like businesses."

   It is unlikely that many candidates will be able to take the time required to master the intricacies of the newly evolving campaign techniques – especially the computer and other increasingly sophisticated tools of electioneering. Many will not even care to. Undoubtedly expressing the sentiments shared by more than a few House veterans, the late Stewart McKinney said in a 1986 interview with this author, "We've gotten as modern as I want to get. I want to keep it homey. You can't change this old dog." As advancing campaign technology becomes more complex, the gap already present between the technology experts and the uncomprehending candidate will continue to grow, so that in campaigns of the future the candidate will be increasingly, and unavoidably, dependent upon the professional handlers. The candidate's primary task will be fundraising. And even for that, he will look to the professionals for direction.

# 8

## Candidates, consultants, and the American democratic process

> Under the current system, few candidates relish the task of getting elected. There is increasing awareness that modern campaign technologies have fostered a remoteness from the voters. ... The expertise of campaign professionals – political consultants, media advisors, pollsters, direct mail specialists – lies in the techniques of mass marketing, not in fostering personal contact between candidates and the voters.
>
> Former US Senator Charles Mathias[1]

> I do not think there is anything more fundamental to preserving our system of free government than to secure the integrity of the election process. ... It is the proliferation of pollsters, direct mailers, and professional consultants, with their packaging and marketing of candidates, who are changing the character of campaigns and driving the quality down.
>
> Former US Senator Barry Goldwater[2]

> Technology is like fire. It can do wonderful things, or it can destroy. It can be used to bring information to people, or it can be used to mislead them.
>
> Richard Viguerie, fundraiser

The purpose of this book has been to describe the latest methods of electioneering by focusing on the candidates, the professional advisors, and the methods used to win election. Yet in one sense, this has been little more than a description of how a product (the candidate) is sold to the buyer (the electorate), using the ancient skill of marketing. The use of marketing in politics is not new. Every successful presidential candidate from Dwight Eisenhower to Ronald Reagan was packaged to some degree by image makers of the period. Modern campaign technology has developed and is increasingly utilized because it appears, at present, to be the best means for influencing mass behavior so as to obtain the desired political reward – victory at the polls. Political marketing is often reviled, though it is not inherently evil. It is disliked and distrusted, probably because some exponents have dared to discuss openly the marketing strategies and tactics which less candid politicians and professional advisors prefer to discuss in private. Although the voter is subjected on all sides to marketing in one form or another, there seems to be particular resentment, justified or not, toward the marketing of those aspiring to public office.

Critics of the current system have, from time to time, complained about the negative impact of certain election legislation and the resultant new techniques in electioneering, both of which have been examined in these pages. There seems little doubt that the conventional wisdom, as reflected in newspapers, magazines, and television editorials, considers the style and strategy employed by candidates seeking elective office today to be at best uninspiring, and at worst a threat to the very institutions they seek membership in. On the surface, many of the criticisms contain some validity, but this author believes that the majority of electoral innovations since the mid-1970s have, in fact, had a positive impact on the American democratic process.

No issue in electoral politics has attracted as much attention and debate as the role of money in electing candidates. Ironically, the problem of money in political campaigns is actually an outgrowth of the federal election laws that were designed to contain it. As examined earlier, political action committees were insignificant, and independent expenditures nonexistent, until Congress decided to regulate the way in which candidates ran for office. The unpredictability of human behavior led to the failure of well-intentioned election laws to work as planned. The Supreme Court added to the political plight when it struck down certain campaign laws while upholding others. In all fairness, the candidates of today are merely trying to use the current legal restrictions to their own best interest. Basically, it is not the rise of modern campaign technology but the campaign legislation of the 1970s that is the root of the problem.

No aspect of the election law is more criticized than the clause creating the political action committee. Even among political consultants, who are generally paid, in part, from the PAC contributions received by their clients (not to mention those consultants who are on PAC payrolls), the opinion of the role of political action committees in American electoral politics is somewhat more unfavorable than favorable, though party affiliation is clearly a vital factor in their attitude toward PACs. (See survey 8.1.)

In every presidential election cycle since PACs rose to the forefront in 1976, pronouncements of righteous indignation have been issued by PAC critics, and the attacks appear to be growing in numbers and

Survey 8.1  *In general, does the political action committee play a positive or negative role in American politics?*

|  | Total (%) | Republican consultants (%) | Democratic consultants (%) |
|---|---|---|---|
| Positive | 44 | 65 | 14 |
| Negative | 47 | 30 | 72 |
| Neutral (response volunteered) | 9 | 5 | 14 |

scope. Some of the harshest criticisms of PAC power have come from former presidential candidates, due in large measure to the importance of PAC involvement (direct and indirect) in the presidential nomination and general election process. Though often ignored by the news media and overlooked by the academic community, the continuing debate on new measures to limit PAC contributions has aroused a barrage of counterattacks, accusing many of the anti-PAC candidate-crusaders of electoral hypocrisy for accepting contributions from the very PACs they seek to eliminate.

Leading the current anti-PAC crusade in the House of Representatives is Arizona Congressman Morris Udall, who ran unsuccessfully for the presidency in 1976. "The role of the PACs in our system of campaign finance has become nothing short of scandalous," Udall declared in a 1983 fundraising letter. "I'm talking about the dangerous and corrupting influence of the outrageous sums of money – campaign contributions – which have become a paralyzing obscenity." Exempted from Udall's attack was Independent Action, Inc., a political action committee that raised over one million dollars in the 1981–2 election cycle. While outwardly and outspokenly anti-PAC, Udall was, in fact, Independent Action's leader, and served as the signatory for many of its fundraising letters. The Arizona Congressman had also criticized independent expenditure campaigns waged by PACs, yet his own Independent Action ranked ninth on the list of PACs that spent the most money independently in the 1982 elections.[3]

Walter Mondale faced similar charges of hypocrisy in his 1984 presidential bid, because of his numerous anti-PAC speeches. At the outset of his campaign, he even pledged not to accept any PAC money. Yet Mondale's "Committee for the Future of America" PAC had raised over $2 million in the 1981–2 electoral period alone, and independent committees formed by his supporters collected about $300,000 on his behalf from PAC donations.[4] Mondale's opponents, led by Senator Gary Hart, repeatedly condemned Mondale's private willingness to solicit financial support from the very same organizations (PACs) whose influence he publicly denounced.

Certainly, many criticisms of PACs are fully justified. If a truly democratic election means that both candidates would have access to relatively equal resources, then PACs must be considered a negative influence, at least in electoral terms. Because the basic purpose of many PACs that make contributions is to influence congressional decisions, most of their money goes to incumbents. If PACs continue to play a growing role in financing elections, challengers will be faced with increasing difficulty in maintaining reasonable financial viability.

Moreover, if PAC contributions to candidates were limited by new legislation, the PACs would simply find other, possibly less accountable, ways to spend their money. In 1986, PACs representing numerous diverse interests, such as realtors, physicians, and imported car dealers, easily evaded the intended legislative spending limits by pouring hundreds of thousands of dollars into independent expenditure campaigns on behalf of candidates they supported. Whether right or wrong, Congress chose to impose certain contribution limits, which all individuals and organizations alike should be required to follow. However, by exploiting the independent expenditure vehicle, PACs and certain wealthy individuals have legally circumvented the intent of Congress when it imposed such funding limits. As a result, they can, and do, spend substantial sums, far in excess of the statutory contribution limits, to support or attack candidates.

Proponents of the independent expenditure campaign suggest that its primary function is to encourage political participation, educate the voters on selected issues, and make elected officials more accountable to the people who elected them. In some circumstances independent expenditures can be beneficial to the political process. They can help underfinanced challengers take on a powerful incumbent; and they often heighten debate and discussion about more sensitive issues in the elections in which these campaigns participate. Yet independent spenders are themselves dangerously unaccountable. Unlike elected office holders, independent spenders are not held answerable at election time, nor need they fear political fallout should they misrepresent any facts (except for the possible adverse effect on future fundraising appeals). They are freed from many of the constraints faced by candidates seeking office, and, directly at least, cannot be punished by voters for any real or perceived distortions perpetrated in their support of, or opposition to, their targets. In addition, independent spenders can seriously unbalance the competition between candidates just by allocating thousands of dollars to attack a candidate's opponent, when no similar amount has been provided for the opponent's response.

It should also be pointed out that some recent independent expenditure efforts, particularly by the ideological PACs, have backfired, reflecting poorly on the candidate they purported to help, and forcing the hapless candidate to defend an organization which he was powerless to control. Thus, as long as the independent expenditure loophole remains, further legal restraint on PAC contributions can only be counterproductive, since it will lead to more independent expenditures and reduced candidate accountability – unless PACs are eliminated altogether.

The availability of PAC money is but one factor contributing to the extreme dependence on money for electoral success, considered by many to be the single greatest threat to the continued operation of fair and open elections. Senator Charles Mathias, former Chairman of the Senate Rules and Administration Committee, said during a hearing regarding changes in campaign finance laws: "Many talented men and women choose not to enter the political arena because they simply cannot face, will not face, the need to raise hundreds of thousands, or even millions, of dollars to run a campaign."[5] While such an assertion is difficult to prove overall, it is known that, in 1986, four incumbent senators (Barry Goldwater, Thomas Eagleton, Charles Mathias, and Russell Long) chose retirement rather than having to raise millions of dollars for their re-election. The distaste for long and costly campaigning was also a factor in the retirement of Washington Senator Daniel Evans prior to the 1988 elections.

There is no question that too much of the valuable time of members of Congress is devoted to fundraising, and that this demand on their time comes, as it must, at the expense of their legislative duties and personal contact with their constituents. Challengers, also, must spend a disproportionate amount of time dealing with the financial aspects of campaigning, if they are to mount a serious challenge. The age of shoe-string campaign budgets and shoe-leather campaigning is dead. Said political columnist Tom Wicker: "Raising these necessary sums can be so time- and energy-consuming that a candidate has little of either for anything else. . . . Fundraising leaves little opportunity for live contact with the voting public."[6]

Of late, there is a growing feeling among some candidates and campaign consultants that a high percentage of expenditures is actually unnecessary and wasteful. Each year, election observers can point to an increasing number of candidates who are spending far more money than necessary on their campaigns. There is significant support in Congress for placing limits on campaign expenditures alongside the current contribution limits. Unfortunately, the end result would be to restrict the candidates' efforts to communicate their message to the voters. Furthermore, taking into account the inflationary spiral and the increased costs of postage and television air time, a $1,000 contribution today, the maximum individual contribution currently allowed by law, is roughly equivalent to $250 in 1974. Refusal to raise the ceiling set in

1974 on political contributions has in itself been somewhat of a deterrent to massive increases in spending in real monetary terms, though expenditures do continue to rise.

Candidates can limit their expenditures voluntarily, if they care to, and some have done so. The effect, however, is difficult to assess, since the stress and the constraints on time that campaigns generate are impediments to testing the efficiency of campaign expenditures. In fact, during the latter stages of the campaign, often the only financial discipline displayed is an attempt to keep expenditures even with receipts, which is overwhelmingly motivated by the candidate's fear of going deep into debt. The general attitude of most candidates is to get as much money as they can – and then spend it – since more ways to spend money can always be found as long as the money itself is available.

Nevertheless, studies conducted by several consultants show that money spent beyond a certain threshold level did not correlate to a higher percentage of the vote. The law of diminishing returns is as applicable to politics as elsewhere, although few candidates willingly apply it, particularly in tight races. Yet money does not guarantee winning, and there are limitations on what it can do. This was clearly exemplified when six of the top twelve Senate fundraisers in 1986 lost their election bids.[7] As a national party official noted, "There are only so many 30-second spots you can buy, only so many balloons you can inflate."

A candidate need not match an opponent's financial resources as long as he has enough money to get a message across to the voters – provided, of course, it is a message the voters want to support. The indication is that the candidates, not the technology, are out of control. If candidates' distaste for wasting money was as great as their distaste for raising it, election expenditures could be reduced dramatically. "I went into debt and quit my job," said Connecticut Congressman John Rowland. "It was the stupidest thing to do financially. But it was something I wanted to do." Added Congressman Peter Viscloski, after his 1984 victory left him in debt, "I was only hurting myself, not forcing it on anyone else."[8]

The current situation, in which a candidate can outspend an opponent by margins of three or four to one, is indeed alarming, particularly when that money comes from the candidate's own deep pockets. It means that wealthy candidates start with a significant advantage because they are freed from the chore of raising hundreds of individual contributions in amounts under $1,000. Said Congressman John Rowland, "You cannot run for the Senate unless you are a millionaire. Period. To run for Congress, you have to be rich or crazy." Although some consultants counsel their clients against putting their own money into their campaign, there are still a number of senators, governors, and congressmen who were elected because they could afford to do so – and did. Among the notable candidates whose personal money probably provided the margin of victory were John Danforth (Missouri 1982 re-election campaign), Frank Lautenberg (New Jersey 1982 open seat), Jeff Bingaman (New Mexico challenger), and John D. Rockefeller IV (West Virginia 1984 open seat).

In simpler times, candidates of substance could use their money to overwhelm their opponents merely with extra political buttons, bumper stickers, billboards, lawn signs, and similar modes of communication. All the financially deprived candidates could fight back with was a grassroots campaign. Yet the two could be equally effective. As noted in chapter 1, certain millionaire candidates were recently defeated (mostly in primaries) by aggressive challengers who convinced voters that campaign funds were not a substitute for campaign ideas. For the most part, however, in today's political environment, a massive media campaign (particularly in congressional races where there is less free media coverage) can blot out the message of a candidate's opponent, even where he has a strong grassroots organization. The medium may be different but the effect is the same. The rich have always had an advantage in American elections; and now, with the strict legal limits on how much individuals other than the candidate can contribute to his campaign, the advantage of having personal money can be even greater than ever. So long as the Supreme Court maintains the judgment in *Buckley* v. *Valeo* (see chapter 2), that limiting a candidate's use of personal money in his campaign represents an infringement on his freedom of speech, money will continue to talk. Clearly, the problem of money in politics is due as much to the election laws as to modern campaign technology.

Moreover, the corrosive effect of money in politics may persist well after election day. There is evidence that some new members of Congress, particularly those less well off, purposely seek specific committee assignments solely because they will provide good fundraising opportunities in the future. In addition, many incumbent congressmen, and a few senators, anxious to build up a sizeable war chest, continue to raise money regardless of how distant their next election may be. It is currently estimated that senators who took office in January 1987 will have to spend an average of $9 million to be re-elected in 1992.[9] This means they will each have to raise an average of $125,000 a month over the next six years. Campaigns are likely to begin even earlier, primarily to raise money, and some will be forced to employ a permanent fundraising staff. Thus, a good fundraising base from a heavily lobbied committee has its allure for candidates anxious to clear campaign debts or desirous of PAC financial support. In a properly (or ideally) functioning system, committee assignments would be sought because of their relevance to the state, district, or a particular interest of the elected official, and not because of the fundraising potential.

But denouncing money for its importance in the current electioneering process can be misleading, inasmuch as the role of money is not an absolute negative. In fact, a persuasive argument could be made that it has had some positive impact on the democratic character of American elections. The ability of one candidate to raise more money than another is, like having more volunteers, a legitimate demonstration of public support. Before the FECA laws went into effect, all a candidate had to do to prove financial support was to attract a few large donations from wealthy individuals. Today, with strict ceilings on the size of contributions, candidates have to demonstrate an ability to draw numerous small donations from many less affluent contributors. Candidates and consultants generally believe that if a candidate lacks the ideology, intelligence, drive, charisma, or whatever is required to attract financial support or supporters under the current system, even if on a limited scale, then he was probably a weak candidate initially. There seems to be a correlation between the inability of candidates to persuade potential constituents to contribute to their campaign and their difficulty in persuading these same consituents to support their candidacy.

Direct mail, the technology employed to raise money and broaden campaign support, is a significant improvement on the old system of appealing to a few millionaires for large contributions. Direct mail is a more democratic process, because it reaches a greater number of people than the old fundraising techniques, and with a larger number of people participating in and financing a campaign, the less influence any single self-interest is likely to have. In addition, direct mail, being information intensive, brings issues to the forefront and thereby lessens the influence of personality and image. Through direct mail the candidate explains his philosophy or contrasts his vision of government with that of the opponent. Issues, therefore, are of crucial importance in direct mail fundraising.

The constantly increasing expenditures in electoral politics might suggest to some political observers that the consultants have taken over and driven up the price of politics, while cheapening the product and demeaning the salesmen – the candidates. Generally, however, the evidence seems to refute this. In Florida, media advisor Bob Squier received a $60,000 fee plus a 15 percent placement commission from the Senate campaign of Bob Graham, to produce and schedule his television commercials. The $60,000 represented about 1 percent of Graham's total expenditures on the race. The 15 percent placement commission is standard in both political and commercial advertising, and has not changed in years. In fact, the only costs "driven up" in the Graham campaign were the prices charged by the television stations for air time.

Political consultants do not establish postal rates; political consultants do not fix the rates for radio and television time or for advertising space in newspapers. They recommend how much television and radio advertising to purchase and how many letters to mail, but it is the candidate, not the consultant, who signs the checks.

Some have suggested that the expertise of campaign professionals lies in the techniques of mass marketing, not in fostering personal contact between candidates and the voters. It can be easily argued, however, that direct mail specialists, pollsters, and media consultants have actually enhanced and sharpened the dialogue between candidate and voter. In the 1960s and early 1970s, the most popular political TV ads were devoid of any issue content. However, as voters became more sophisticated and demanded more from their candidates, pollsters found that imagery spots were growing less effective in swinging undecided voters. They so advised the media gurus, who then turned to producing more issue-oriented commercials. In the late 1970s, pollsters began to find that the voters were tiring of these as well, and now were demanding to know how and why one candidate was better than another. Although negative – or comparative – political advertising (depending on whether you are the attacker or the attacked) has been widely criticized, it does tend to give the voters a better sense of who the candidates are and what they stand for.

An even more direct communication between voter and candidate is possible through candidate advocacy mailings. With modern campaign technology, direct mail specialists enable candidates to reach the desired audience with an appropriate message. Long gone are the days when candidates could limit the issue content of their appeal to mere general philosophy or party affiliation. Currently, the most effective candidate advocacy mail contrasts the opposing candidates' approach to the major issues and legislation of the day, and is scientifically targeted to provide specific information sought after by specific voters. Using the technological skills of the direct mail specialist, the campaign (through mail) informs families with children about the candidate's position on education, the elderly about congressional votes on Social Security, and the unemployed about the jobs program advocated by the candidate compared with that of the opponent. The electoral process has benefited substantially from the technological advancements.

Although today's voters may have less personal communication with the candidate than in the past, they do have considerable contact with at least one of the candidate's hired representatives, namely the pollster. Pollsters garner information from the voters, which is then used by the media consultants to assist the candidate in responding to voter concerns. Pollsters and media consultants, working together, have become a positive force in campaigns, enabling their clients to be better heard and understood by the voters they seek to reach. If, for instance, a candidate's constituency is primarily interested in one or two issues, then it is crucial that the candidate know and address those particular issues. This two-way feedback between candidates and their constituents, even if conducted through a third party, contributes to maintaining a representative, democratic system. Prior to the age of polling, office holders voting on legislation had little or no knowledge of constituent opinion. Today, nearly all elected officials have the ability to ascertain public opinion on the issues, making them better informed and more reponsive legislators. It is arguable that too great a preoccupation with public reaction can inhibit or distort the legislative process, by turning leaders into followers. However, after repeated questioning of consultants, candidates, and party officials, it was difficult to find sufficient evidence to conclude that even a small number of candidates base their legislative votes or policy positions solely on public opinion polling or advice from pollsters.

Admittedly, consultancy, like most professions, has its ethical problems. Most importantly, there are no commonly accepted professional standards. From the survey, it is apparent that misrepresentations of abilities by political consultants, as well as unethical practices, do occur. On rare occasions a pollster may be accused of doctoring the numbers; media consultants and direct mail specialists have been accused of falsifying expense accounts. There are occasions, moreover, where consultants have consciously failed to act in the best interests of an informed electorate. One of the most famous "political strategy" directives in the annals of political history was written by pollster Patrick Caddell for Jimmy Carter, in the days leading up to the 1976 presidential election. In it he wrote, "Too many people have been beaten because they tried to substitue substance for style."[10] The 1988 presidential campaign of Governor Mike Dukakis was wrongly criticized for producing a video tape that shed a negative but legitimate light on the origins of opponent Senator Joe Biden's stump speeches. Failure to acknowledge responsibility for the video was a lapse of judgment that justly deserves disapproval. However, the attempt by key Dukakis political advisors to deflect responsibility for producing the video onto the rival campaign of Congressman Richard Gephardt was politics in its most unethical form, practiced by professionals with a lack of integrity.

But for the most part, the leading campaign consultants are reputable, hardworking people who care not only about winning elections but also about their impact on the democratic process. The pressure of the system has forced a few nonpartisan consultants to restrict themselves to one party, preventing them from working indiscriminately for candidates regardless of their party affiliation. Despite some accusations to the contrary, a sizeable number of consultants (particularly among younger consultants in established firms) specifically select as clients those who share their political ideology, and who, they believe, would truly make good senators, governors, or congressmen. Though the candidate's potential ability to raise money is generally among the criteria considered important by most consultants, his own personal wealth is not. Most consultants are not mercenary, and they hardly pose a threat to the democratic electoral process.

There are also numerous complaints that candidates, with the assistance of their professional advisors, have trivialized their election by using clever, negative advertising, making light of an opponent for such things as the opponent missing a vote or changing his mind on an issue. It would be difficult to defend the morality of the paid media campaign against Barry Goldwater in 1964, yet in every election cycle there are commercials (several of which were described in chapter 3) which, though universally considered offensive, are rooted in historical precedent. In America's first contested presidential election, Federalists branded Thomas Jefferson an anarchist, an atheist, and a coward; anti-Federalists lampooned Vice-President John Adams as a monarchist and an egoist. From the 1820s through the 1930s, campaigns were personal and vicious. Character attacks were the rule, not the exception, and distortions of a candidate's record were commonplace. Smear tactics in American politics not only predate the development of the political consulting profession and negative advertising, but were considerably more slanderous in the days before television.

In comparison, modern negative-on-negative advertising may attack one or two sentences in an opponent's commercial, but it also adds information to the general debate. Moreover, the ultimate effect of negative advertising is to focus attention on an elected office holder's voting record, and that in itself is important to the democratic process, a point often missed or ignored by the critics of current electioneering methods. To accuse an opponent of having raised taxes may be a disconcerting charge, but if it can be substantiated then it is a fair, if uncommendable, campaign tactic. To their credit, the candidates themselves are delivering more of the negative material, facing the camera head-on and telling the voters where they disagree with their opponents.

In an ideal world, campaigns would be structured so that they define the candidate's platform for the voters. As long as the information is truthful, then comparative advertising (a more enlightening form of negative advertising) fulfills this goal and should therefore remain a major element in campaigning. Once elected, senators and representatives will find they cannot vote irresponsibly and with disregard for the voters who put them in office. In this era of negative commercials, elected office holders will have to give more thought to how they vote – or face the consequences back home. As Michael Barone observed about the latest wave of negative ads: "They tell you more about candidates' positions on substantive issues than those ads you saw a few campaigns back showing a candidate in shirtsleeves strolling down the beach with his suitcoat slung over his shoulder."[11] Modern campaign technology exposes candidates to the electorate and renders office holders accountable to their constituents, both fundamental in the American political process.

Another anti-technology argument suggests that candidates can produce advertising with complete immunity. Columnist Tom Wicker maintains that consultants advise their candidate "to accuse the opponent of anything reprehensible that's remotely plausible; that failing, he should move on to charges that aren't even plausible."[12] If this were really the case, Congress would indeed have justification for passing legislation pertaining to reviewing, limiting, and, where applicable, barring paid political advertising. Fortunately, certain checks against false advertising are already in place. If a candidate's commercials are patently untrue, the news media can be expected to expose this. Another check is the opponent himself, who can challenge factual distortions or inaccuracies. Finally, there are the voters, the final arbiters, who have the ultimate power to judge, and punish, a candidate.

Media gurus have been accused of packaging clients so that the voter cannot distinguish between them. Said former Senator Herman Talmadge about today's advertising agencies, "They take some fellow, dress him up in their fashion, teach him to read from some idiot board for 20 seconds. You can't separate the men from the boys."[13] But if this were true, every successful candidate would look, speak, and act similarly. Such is not the case. One does not need to be handsome or even articulate to win. "Why is this man smiling?" asked a grinning Ed Zschau at a fundraising luncheon during his 1986 California Senate campaign, adding, "Because we know how we're going to win."[14] Zschau then went on to detail how millions of dollars were going to be spent on media advertising in his ultra-high technology campaign. Yet his opponent, Alan Cranston, a gaunt seventy-three year old veteran campaigner who could easily pass for eighty, was elected, even though he had been pitted against the much younger and more charismatic Zschau. Californians wanted a senator they could depend on, and for that reason they chose Cranston instead of Zschau.

South Dakota's Senator George McGovern, one of America's most articulate politicians, was defeated in 1980 by a candidate with a squeaky voice and a speech impediment, because his ideology more closely represented the voters of South Dakota than did McGovern's. When criticized for his difficulty in addressing large crowds, successful 1986 congressional hopeful Clyde Holloway explained, "I'm a farmer. I speak to plants. But I'm learning to talk."[15] Bruce Babbitt was one of the most popular governors in Arizona history, yet he had the television image of a stiff, awkward politician. When asked if this image would doom his presidential campaign, his response became one of the classic lines of the 1988 campaign: "If they can teach Mr. Ed [the TV horse] to talk, they can teach me."[16] In the 1980s, despite all the new techniques and gimmicks, it still takes more than an attractive image to win elections.

There has been the suggestion, following the 1986 elections, that there is too much paid media in politics today. In that year's South Dakota Senate race, both candidates were running as many as twenty radio ads a day, and had purchased all available television time weeks before the commercials were to air. Nevertheless, if the way to inform an often apathetic electorate is to run costly political advertisements during and around popular TV shows, it seems worth the price. The various modern campaign techniques have thus helped to reawaken the American people to the rough and tumble world of politics. How they act on this new awareness, time will tell.

Some observers would even ban television advertising altogether. "Truth, in politics, is a commodity packaged, twisted, stretched or ignored for convenience," concluded the *Washington Post* in an editorial following the 1986 elections.[17] Former senator and presidential candidate Eugene McCarthy concluded: "The most direct way of avoiding the socially corrupting effects of political advertising is by banning it altogether. . . . Striking these ads from the airwaves would go a long way toward . . . developing a better-informed electorate."[18] Such an alternative, however, would be far more damaging to the American electoral process. A public office holder seeks to justify his re-election on the basis of his performance and experience, whereas the opponent attacks him for that performance. The longer the voters dwell on this point, and the more evidence that is presented to them, the more likely they are to find something they do not like. Incumbents are usually better known than challengers and would stand to benefit if political advertising were regulated, limited, or even abolished. The ability to attack the incumbent, even if the attacks are somewhat slanted, is often the only way for the challenger to enter the campaign dialogue. Without having to answer to viable challengers, incumbents could ignore their opponents and run only vacuous fluff spots, devoid of issues and substance. Barring political advertising would further enhance an incumbent's already powerful position while decreasing his accountability in the political marketplace. Attacking an opponent is not unethical, and negative or comparative advertising can be a healthy addition to political discourse as long as it truthfully portrays what the opposition represents.

Recent candidates have complained, with justification, that the only way to get free media coverage for their campaign was to introduce a new TV ad. Said David Broder, veteran political columnist: "Too few papers monitored what was being said – or evaded – in the face-to-face campaigning. Too few pushed aggressively for news conferences and interviews in which the candidate would have to speak for himself – not hide behind his media managers."[19] It would be difficult to argue otherwise. Of the vast number of articles on the 1986 elections, a substantial proportion – perhaps half – focused on paid political advertising and other aspects of modern campaign technology, one-third dealt with money in politics, and only about 15 percent focused primarily on issues. The television networks, in the words of veteran political consultant Eddie Mahe, "cover the elections as though they were covering a horse race, disregarding what the horses are saying." While the news media criticize the dearth of in-depth issues in campaigns, they actually bear much of the responsibility for creating the very situation they have spent so much print and air time criticizing. Concluded former North Carolina Senator Jim Broyhill, "It's you news people who try to make a negative campaign. You just asked me a question to try to get me to hit on my opponent."[20]

But on the presidential level, the same candidates who craved free media in 1986 were burned by it in 1987. If 1986 was a warning to candidates about the senationalist and shallow concerns of the news media, few were prepared for, in the words of one observer, the "great witch hunt of 1987." The revelations among presidential hopefuls, of Gary Hart's infidelity, Joe Biden's exaggerated resumé, the raucous life style and premarital sex of Pat Robertson's youth, to say nothing of the accusations of cheating levelled against Jesse Jackson and the acknowledgements by Al Gore and Bruce Babbitt that they had smoked illegal substances in the past, all left voters dazed and candidates crying that enough was enough. Only 25 percent of the American public, according to a nationwide survey, felt the press acted properly in its coverage of the Gary Hart and Donna Rice affair, despite its serious implications.[21] Instead of fostering disourse on the important questions of the day, the press has become a self-appointed private detection agency, feverishly digging into the past of public officials in the hope of stumbling onto a good scandal or some example of "deviant" behavior. This notwithstanding, the press has also unearthed facts concealed by candidates who were less than honest or forthcoming; and public figures are in some ways being held to a more stringent standard now than at any time in the past. It is an undeniable role of the news media to challenge those candidates who are projecting an image contrary to who they really are. But the television advertising and the direct mail and the video tapes and the other modes of communication used by the 1988 presidential contenders have done more than the news media to tell voters who the candidates are and what they stand for.

The separation that once existed between a candidate's right to privacy and the public's right to know has been shattered. Yet those candidates who have the strength to demand that they be judged on their public record, not on their private life or on a mistake long past, should prosper in the new environment. As Bob Beckel, Walter Mondale's former presidential campaign manager, concluded in a *Washington Post* column, "If the candidates are confident that they have leveled with the public, they should then be confident enough to tell the press to 'get stuffed . . .' They can do this, to borrow a phrase, by Just Saying No."[22]

One of the great myths of the American political system is that the democratic ideal means candidates talking directly to the voters and appealing, face-to-face, for support. Envisioned as old-fashioned politics, it is a fantasy, and never really existed in twentieth-century America. There once was a time, about a century ago, when the candidate could literally walk his district and personally greet most of his constituents. Today, no candidate has enough time and energy to meet the roughly 600,000 people in his congressional district, or the millions of voters in his state. If the two Senate candidates in Florida could shake the hands of 120 people an hour for twenty-four hours a day, it would take three years to meet every individual who voted in the 1986 election. If they made ten speeches a day to audiences of 100 persons, it would take eight years to reach every voter.[23]

The introduction of television into the political landscape has enabled candidates, for the first time, to appear almost daily in the homes of their constituents. Although still far away in Washington, elected officials have become less obscure and more accountable figures to the average voter than in the days before television. Thanks to the media consultant, many American voters come to recognize the candidates' names and faces and learn something about the background of the people they are electing to statewide office. Thanks to pollsters, present-day voters have at hand far more information about the candidates than voters had in the 1950s or 1960s. Granted, the quality of information might be less than most would prefer, but today's voters still have the opportunity to acquire a sense of the personality and character of the candidate, and at least a superficial knowledge of his position on the issues.

At the same time, candidates also know more about the voters than they ever did before, derived both from secondary analysis of demographic and voter history, and directly, from their own polling data. If TV commercials tend to encourage superficiality in politics, the fact remains that TV is still the most efficient way and sometimes the only way for candidates to reach voters, especially in large states. The electorate's increasing dependence on television for news and information makes this expensive mode of communication an indispensable instrument for effective political speech. After all, the 30-second spot is still less superficial and more informative than the timeworn ritual of shaking hands and kissing babies. A forty-five-minute home video imparts more of a candidate's personality than an eight- to ten-minute campaign appearance.

In the final analysis, the responsibility for the campaign decisions remains with the candidate. "He's always in jeopardy of having the sex issue raised if he can't keep his pants on," warned Gary Hart advisor John McAvoy in 1987, several months before Hart, ignoring the advice, was caught with his pants down.[24] Consultants and advisors are hired, paid, and sometimes fired by the candidate, and the tactics employed during the campaign reflect on the candidate, not the paid professionals. Gary Hart's presidential pollster approved commercials for a 1984 primary without the candidate's knowledge and consent, and then was unable to have them taken off the air. The inability to have the spots killed became a major story, and Hart's opponent, on a nationally televised debate, asked voters whether a politician could run a nation when he could not even run his own campaign. They got the message.

Guided by his own intuition and integrity, the candidate can, and should, be the final determinant of campaign policy. Those candidates with a do-anything-to-win attitude have only themselves to blame when their campaign tactics backfire, and they lose. When former 1988 Democratic hopeful Joe Biden, responding to charges that he had plagiarized someone else's speech, said "I honestly did not know I was quoting somebody else," he was acknowledging to all who listened that he was a politician not in control.[25] Politicians cannot escape responsibility for cheapened or worthless campaign dialogue, and it is they, not the hired guns, who win and lose races. Concluded Indiana Congressman John Hiler, "On election day, there's only one name on the ballot, and that's mine – the candidate."

In summary, the current election laws have formulated the modern methods of campaigning, and, like it or not, the players must play by the rules. Neither candidates nor consultants nor party officials can rewrite or ignore them simply because they do not like them. Nor is the ultimate power with the politicians and their advisors. The political cemetery is full of candidates and consultants who tried, unsuccessfully, to dictate to the electorate. In a democracy, where the power of the vote is the power of the people, the voter is king.

The democratic political process in America depends on an interested and informed electorate. Campaigns of the 1980s have used modern technology effectively to provide more information than otherwise might have been available to the populace. Failure to utilize the latest advances in communication would increasingly detach the elected representative from the voter, and eventually the American political process could fail. It is of particular importance that candidates be given the opportunity to make their views known to the electorate, permitting a thoughtful evaluation of the candidates' personal qualities and their positions on vital public issues before the voter chooses among them on election day.

Once the bosses selected candidates in back rooms. Now we select them in public, in campaign by ordeal. Thomas Jefferson wrote: "I know no safe depository of the ultimate powers of society but the people themselves. It is our responsibility to inform their discretion by education." Clearly, an informed voter is a more effective voter. Jefferson expressed the goal. Modern campaign technology is providing the means to attain it.

# Appendix I

## Consultant questionnaire

The following is the complete survey originated by the author and presented during his personal interviews with America's leading political consultants. Numbers in the left-hand column give the order of presentation. Numbers in brackets designate the chapter and sequence in which particular survey questions appear in the text. Responses are all expressed in percentages.

1    [survey 1.1]    *What has been the single greatest change in electioneering in the past decade?*

| | |
|---|---:|
| Importance/impact/use of television | 43 |
| Federal election laws | 14 |
| Money in politics | 11 |
| Use/integration of modern technology and consultants | 9 |
| Role of the computer | 6 |
| Reduced role of the parties | 3 |
| Negative campaigning | 3 |
| Other responses | 11 |

2    [survey 1.3]    *What is the single most important factor in a political campaign today?*

| | |
|---|---:|
| Candidate | 66 |
| Money | 11 |
| Issues | 8 |
| Television | 6 |
| Strategy | 6 |
| Other | 3 |

3   [survey 7.1]   *Do technological innovations in electioneering generally start at the presidential level and filter down, or do they start at the statewide and congressional level and filter up?*

| | |
|---|---|
| Filter up from state and congressional level | 75 |
| Filter down from presidential level | 6 |
| Filter equally up and down (volunteered) | 19 |

4   [survey 1.2]   *Overall, which is more important in recent congressional and senatorial campaigns: issues, or the candidate's image and personality?*

| | Total | Pollsters | Media consultants | General consultants | Fundraisers |
|---|---|---|---|---|---|
| Image/ personality | 73 | 100 | 71 | 67 | 33 |
| Issues | 15 | 0 | 0 | 33 | 67 |
| Not separable/of equal importance (response volunteered) | 12 | 0 | 29 | 0 | 0 |

5   [survey 1.4]   *Are candidates better versed in the various aspects of the new campaign technologies than they were five years ago?*

| | |
|---|---|
| Yes | 75 |
| No | 25 |

6   [survey 2.4]   *How involved should the average candidate be in setting and executing the strategy and tactics of his campaign: very involved, somewhat involved, or little or no involvement?*

| | |
|---|---|
| Very involved | 39 |
| Somewhat involved | 46 |
| Little or no involvement | 15 |

7   *All things considered, who benefits more from the new technology, incumbents or challengers?*

| | |
|---|---|
| Incumbents | 58 |
| Challengers | 27 |
| Neutral (response volunteered) | 15 |

8  [survey 2.3]  *In general, which candidates are easier to work with, incumbents or challengers?*

|  | Total | Fundraisers | Pollsters | Media consultants | General consultants |
|---|---|---|---|---|---|
| Challengers | 65 | 100 | 86 | 56 | 55 |
| Incumbents | 22 | 0 | 14 | 33 | 17 |
| Equal | 13 | 0 | 0 | 11 | 28 |

9  [survey 2.2]  *Is your won-lost record very important to you and your firm?*

|  | Total | Media consultants | Pollsters | General consultants | Fundraisers |
|---|---|---|---|---|---|
| Yes | 59 | 78 | 62 | 50 | 0 |
| No | 41 | 22 | 38 | 50 | 100 |

10  [survey 2.1]  *The following factors are sometimes considered by consultants in their decision whether to take on a prospective client. Which factors are highly important, somewhat important, or of little importance in your decision?*

|  | Highly important | Somewhat important | Not important |
|---|---|---|---|
| Ideology | 50 | 29 | 21 |
| Electability | 41 | 24 | 35 |
| Candidate's personal wealth | 6 | 21 | 73 |

11  [survey 2.6]  *In general, are the great majority of political consultants worth the prices they charge?*

| Yes | 62 |
|---|---|
| No | 38 |

12  [survey 2.5]  *Do misrepresentation of abilities and unethical practices take place in the political consulting profession?*

| Yes | 88 |
|---|---|
| No | 12 |

13    *In which aspect of political consulting is misrepresentation or unethical behavior most likely to occur?*

|  |  |
|---|---|
| Media | 54 |
| General consultants | 31 |
| Direct mail | 15 |
| Polling | 0 |

14    [survey 4.1]  *How important are the national party organizations in the elections of their candidates: very important, somewhat important, or of little or no importance?*

|  | Total | Republican consultants | Democratic consultants |
|---|---|---|---|
| Very important | 41 | 65 | 7 |
| Somewhat important | 38 | 25 | 57 |
| Little or no importance | 21 | 10 | 36 |

15    [survey 4.2]  *Overall, is the importance of the national party organizations currently increasing or decreasing?*

|  | Total | Republican consultants | Democratic consultants |
|---|---|---|---|
| Increasing | 60 | 65 | 53 |
| Decreasing | 23 | 10 | 41 |
| Stable (response volunteered) | 16 | 25 | 6 |

16    [survey 8.1]  *In general, does the political action committee play a positive or negative role in American politics?*

|  | Total | Republican consultants | Democratic consultants |
|---|---|---|---|
| Positive | 44 | 65 | 14 |
| Negative | 47 | 30 | 72 |
| Neutral (response volunteered) | 9 | 5 | 14 |

17    *Do you expect the numbers and scope of independent expenditure campaigns to increase or decrease over the next few years?*

|  |  |
|---|---|
| Increase | 42 |
| Decrease | 29 |
| Remain roughly constant (response volunteered) | 29 |

18 *Overall, do you have a favorable or unfavorable impression of the current federal election laws?*

| | |
|---|---|
| Favorable | 19 |
| Unfavorable | 75 |
| No opinion (response volunteered) | 6 |

19 *What aspect, if any, of the federal election laws would you most like to see changed, or a new provision adopted? (Note: some consultants responded with more than one answer so responses total more than 100 percent.)*

| | |
|---|---|
| Raise/eliminate contribution limits | 43 |
| Abolish all election laws (except disclosures) | 28 |
| Restrict or eliminate PACs | 23 |
| Eliminate independent expenditures | 17 |
| Maintain laws as they are | 10 |
| Provide free TV air time | 10 |
| Adopt federal funding for House and Senate races | 6 |
| Limit campaign spending | 6 |

20 [survey 7.2] *Do you see the costs of political campaigns continuing to spiral upward in the upcoming election cycles?*

| | |
|---|---|
| Yes | 88 |
| No | 12 |

21 *Do you see the growth in political campaign technology as a positive or negative force in American democracy?*

| | |
|---|---|
| Positive | 73 |
| Negative | 6 |
| Neutral (response volunteered) | 21 |

# Appendix II

## Respondents to consultant survey and other interviewees

The following is a list of consultants interviewed for the survey, along with brief information on the number of clients they have represented (general election and presidential candidates only; since more than one pollster or media consultant is usually involved in presidential races, only the primary consultants are listed here). Unless otherwise stated, each is a senior partner in his consulting firm. The rankings of media consultants and pollsters for 1984 and 1986 are based on the number of Senate and gubernatorial clients represented by their firm. These figures are only occasionally available for general consultants and fundraisers.

### Media consultants

ROGER AILES   Nine statewide races in 1986 (rank 1); four statewide races in 1984 (rank 5 – tie); presidential candidates: Richard Nixon (1968), Ronald Reagan (1984), George Bush (1988); currently has more clients in the US Senate than any other Republican media consultant

ED BLAKELY   Associate in firm Smith and Harroff; three statewide races in 1986 (rank 9); Republican National Congressional Committee Communications Director in 1984

DAVID DOAK   Five statewide races in 1986 (rank 5); largest new media firm in 1986; presidential candidates: Richard Gephardt (1988); former associate of Robert Squier

JOHN DEARDOURFF   Seven statewide races in 1986 (rank 2 – tie); four statewide races in 1984 (rank 5 – tie); presidential candidates: George Romney (1968), Gerald Ford (1976), Howard Baker (1980)

ROBERT GOODMAN   Six statewide races in 1986 (rank 4); six statewide races in 1984 (rank 1 – tie); presidential candidates: George Bush (1980)

FRANK GREER   Five statewide races in 1986 (rank 5 – tie); presidential candidates: Walter Mondale (1984)

CHARLES GUGGENHEIM   One statewide race in 1986; presidential candidates: Robert Kennedy (1968), George McGovern (1972), Edward Kennedy (1980), Ernest Hollings (1984), recently retired from politics

DAVID SAWYER   Two statewide races in 1986; presidential candidates: Edward Kennedy (1980), John Glenn (1984), Gary Hart (1988)

ROBERT SQUIER   Seven statewide races in 1986 (rank 2 – tie); six statewide races in 1984 (rank 1 – tie); presidential candidates: Hubert Humphrey (1968), Edmund Muskie (1972), Jimmy Carter (1976); currently has more clients in the US Senate than any other Democratic media consultant

RAY STROTHER   Four statewide races in 1986 (rank 7 – tie); five statewide races in 1984 (rank 4); presidential candidates: Gary Hart (1984, 1988)

KEN SWOPE   Four statewide races in 1986 (rank 7 – tie); presidential candidates: George McGovern (1984)


## Pollsters

PAT CADDELL   Six statewide races in 1986 (rank 6 – tie); six statewide races in 1984 (rank 3 – tie); presidential candidates: George McGovern (1972), Jimmy Carter (1976, 1980), Gary Hart (1984), Joe Biden (1988); recently retired from politics

ARTHUR FINKELSTEIN   Six statewide races candidates in 1986 (rank 6 – tie); three statewide races in 1984 (rank 7); presidential candidates: Phil Crane (1980)

WILLIAM HAMILTON   Five statewide races in 1986 (rank 8); five statewide races in 1984 (rank 5); presidential candidates: Hubert Humphrey (1968), Edmund Muskie (1972), John Glenn (1984), Bruce Babbitt (1988)

R. HARRISON HICKMAN   Ten statewide races in 1986 (rank 4); largest new polling firm in 1986; presidential candidates: Paul Simon (1988); former associate of William Hamilton

PETER HART   Thirteen statewide races in 1986 (rank 2 – tie); ten statewide races in 1984 (rank 2); presidential candidates: Morris Udall (1976), Edward Kennedy (1980), Walter Mondale (1984); semi-retired from politics; currently has more clients in the US Senate than any other Democratic pollster

LANCE TARRANCE   Eight statewide races in 1986 (rank 5); six statewide races in 1984 (rank 3 – tie); presidential candidates: John Connally (1980), Jack Kemp (1988)

ROBERT TEETER     Seventeen statewide races in 1986 (rank 1); seventeen statewide races in 1984 (rank 1); presidential candidates: Richard Nixon (1972), Gerald Ford (1976), George Bush (1980, 1988); currently has more clients in the US Senate than any other Republican pollster

RICHARD WIRTHLIN     Thirteen statewide races in 1986 (rank 2 – tie); six statewide races in 1984 (rank 3 – tie); presidential candidates: Ronald Reagan (1980, 1984), Robert Dole (1988); White House pollster  1981–present

## Fundraisers

ROGER CRAVER     Presidential candidates: Morris Udall (1976), Edward Kennedy (1980), John Anderson (1980); most successful Democratic direct mail firm

BRUCE EBERLE     Presidential candidates: Ronald Reagan (1976); major conservative fundraiser

VICTOR KAMBER     Presidential candidates: Alan Cranston (1984); founder, PROPAC; leading fundraiser for organized labor

PETER KELLY     Democratic National Committee Treasurer (1979–81); Democratic National Committee Finance Chairman (1981–5); advisor to approximately twenty statewide races (1984–6)

ROBERT ODELL     Seven statewide races in 1986; presidential candidates: Gerald Ford (1976), Ronald Reagan (1984), George Bush (1980, 1988)

BRAD O'LEARY     Twelve statewide races in 1986; presidential candidates: Jack Kemp; president, American Association of Political Consultants

RICHARD VIGUERIE     Presidential candidates: George Wallace (1972), Phil Crane (1980), John Connally (1980), Jack Kemp (1988)

## General consultants/political advisors

LEE ATWATER     Two statewide races in 1986; presidential candidates: Ronald Reagan (1984), George Bush (1988)

CHARLIE BLACK     Three statewide races in 1986; presidential candidates: Ronald Reagan (1980, 1984), Jack Kemp (1988)

WALTER DEVRIES     One statewide race in 1986; presidential candidates: George Romney (1968); semi-retired from politics

DAVID KEENE     Presidential candidates: George Bush (1980), Robert Dole (1988)

EDDIE MAHE     Two statewide clients in 1986; presidential candidates: John Connally (1980), Ronald Reagan (1980, 1984)

JOSEPH NAPOLITAN     First major political consultant (1956); founder and past president, American Association of Political Consultants; presidential candidates: Hubert Humphrey (1968); semi-retired from American politics

LYN NOFZIGER   White House Political Director (1981–2); presidential candidates: Ronald Reagan (1976, 1980)

MATT REECE   Has worked in more than 200 races since 1960; presidential campaigns: Lyndon Johnson (1964), Robert Kennedy (1968), Hubert Humphrey (1968); past president, American Assocation of Political Consultants

BILL ROBERTS   One statewide client in 1986; founding partner of Spencer–Roberts in 1960 – left firm in 1974; presidential candidates: Nelson Rockefeller (1964)

ED ROLLINS   White House Political Director (1983–4); presidential candidates: Reagan-Bush campaign manager (1984), Jack Kemp campaign director (1988)

STUART SPENCER   Founded Spencer–Roberts firm in 1960; oldest Republican consulting firm in America; presidential candidates: Nelson Rockefeller (1964), Gerald Ford (1976), Ronald Reagan (1980, 1984)

## Additional interviews

The following were also interviewed for this book, but were not included in the consultant survey:

MARVIN CHERNOFF   Chernoff and Associates – retired from politics

ANDRE LETENDRE   Former congressional candidate, campaign manager and consultant

PAUL MANAFORT   Campaign Consultants, formerly Black, Manafort, Stone and Atwater

MIKE MURPHY   Murphey and Castellanos; media advisors to the Robert Dole for President campaign

CRAIG SHIRLEY   Keene, Shirley and Associates; former press secretary for the National Conservative Political Action Committee

GREG STEVENS   Campaign Consultants; media advisor to presidential candidate Jack Kemp; former campaign manager and chief of staff to New Jersey Governor Tom Kean

ROGER STONE   Campaign Consultants, formerly Black, Manafort, Stone and Atwater; consultant to presidential candidate Jack Kemp

## *Candidates*

JOHN ANDERSON   Former congressman and presidential candidate

HELEN BENTLEY   Maryland congresswoman

JAMES BUCKLEY   Former New York senator

ROBERT DORNAN   California congressman
COOPER EVANS   Former Iowa congressman
DEAN GALLO   New Jersey congressman
JOHN HILLER   Indiana congressman
GORDON HUMPHREY   New Hampshire senator
GEORGE MCGOVERN   Former senator and presidential candidate
STUART MCKINNEY   Former congressman (deceased)
JOHN ROWLAND   Connecticut congressman
ROBERT TORRICELLI   New Jersey congressman

## *Party Officials*

ED BROOKOVER   Former Field Director, Republican National Committee; currently National Republican Senatorial Committee Political Director
JEFF ELY   Former Political Director, Democratic National Committee
JOSEPH GAYLORD   Executive Director, National Republican Congressional Committee
THOMAS GRISCOM   Former Executive Director, National Republican Senatorial Committee; currently White House Communications Director
DAVID JOHNSON   Former Executive Director, Democratic Senatorial Campaign Committee
TOM KING   Former Political Director, Democratic Congressional Campaign Committee
WILLIAM LACY   Former Republican National Committee political director; former White House Deputy Political Director; currently strategy director for the Robert Dole for President campaign
BILL MCINTURFF   Director of Party Development, Republican National Committee

## *Other*

MICHAEL BARONE   *Washington Post* columnist and author of *The Almanac of American Politics*
DAVID BRODER   Nationally syndicated columnist
TERRY DOLAN   Founder and former director of the National Conservative Political Action Committee (deceased)
FRED WERTHEIMER   President of Common Cause

# Appendix III

## Interview with Raymond Strother (1984 media consultant to Gary Hart)

In the midst of producing commercials for several statewide candidates, Democratic media consultant Ray Strother was kind enough to give this author three extensive interviews totaling several hours. Strother discussed many topics, including the latest innovations in television advertising, the role of political consultants in modern campaigns, and even, in detail, his personal relationship with his clients.

The climax of our conversation was Strother's account of what he had done for Gary Hart, 1984 presidential candidate and, for a while, Democratic forerunner for the 1988 presidential race. It was Strother's television campaign that turned Hart, formerly an unknown senator from Colorado, into a media sensation. Experts cited Hart's commercials as the most innovative and effective television spots of all the 1984 national candidates. The respected *Campaigns and Elections* journal described them as "decidedly avant-garde, with a futuristic logo design and a dazzling technical device that opened the eyes of even the most jaded reporter."

Strother's story, which is given in his words and until now has never appeared in print, typifies the crucial aspects of modern campaign technology: mainly, the candidate–consultant relationship, the search for new campaign techniques, and the financial constraints in modern campaigns.

It was an affair of the heart for me. I wanted Gary Hart to win. I was still very angry about Vietnam – my brother had been killed there. Gary Hart came to see me in 1982 and said, "I like the things you're doing because they are honest. I don't think you would try to make a candidate something he is not." Hart did not want to be forced into theatrics or cosmetic changes. He was seeking a media consultant who would be more interested in *his* ideas and the substance behind them. When we first talked, he asked me to define my job, and I told him I was a communicator *for* the candidate, not a changer *of* the candidate. He said he'd like me to do his presidential race, and I agreed. He was my idea of who should be president. So I joined the race in the summer of 1983.

I knew immediately that people had to see Gary Hart – the man – and hear

245

Gary Hart – the man – to understand who he was and where he was coming from, and I knew I couldn't do it in 30-seconds. I needed a longer television piece. I talked to Hart and we agreed to a five-minute television program, which would take five days to shoot. The first day, I filmed Gary at Red Rock Park and at an anti-war meeting in a Denver Unitarian Church. When we finished, he had a while, so I asked him some questions, with a camera over my shoulder, and he'd answer. I told him to perform as though I was not there. We shot for a day, and that's all the time he had. It cost about $15,000 to shoot that day, but I still needed three or four more days. I contacted the campaign manager, and he told me that they would be lined up as soon as they got the money to pay for them.

There was never enough money to shoot more film. Then, in late 1983, the campaign manager called and asked if anything could be done with the film we already shot. I said, "No. I didn't shoot any cutaways. I didn't shoot anything extra." I told him all I have are interviews of Gary, and most of them are rather static. But the campaign manager said we had to do something because they needed television media. So I agreed to look at the film.

Hart was running on a campaign of change, a new generation of leadership, which to me suggested the age of the computer and of technology. I told my production manager to go to New York and to every major advertising house there and find out what's new in video technology, and bring me back some demo [demonstration] reels. He came back with a reel, something called a "Mirage," which came from England and was being used by the BBC. With this British device, you could reassemble a video picture millions of times, so that it looked like you were turning a page [now known as a page wipe].

I watched it again and again and again. You could do a lot with the picture. You could make it twirl or break up into "sand," gimmicky things that I really detested. But something intrigued me about this page turn. It said "change" to me. I had this film without cutaways. I had no way to get from a closeup to another closeup without a jump cut. So I took the Mirage and used the page turn to substitute for a jump cut, because they couldn't afford to shoot any more film. It solved the problem – the image of new technology and change – and it also allowed me to use film I already had.

Then I wanted something to suggest the new age Hart was running in, so I devised a grid on a piece of paper. We decided we had to use the grid because it was another subconscious suggestion about Hart, another form of communication. I also wanted to leave his name on the television screen for a long time because he was completely unknown in Iowa. So we used the grid and put Hart's name on it, and then I put a box on the grid, from which Hart could speak. It was placed above his name and within the grid.

That's how the spots came about. Hart had virtually no role in the creation of his TV commercials. He liked the commercials, though he did think that some of the early ones were slightly off target, that they weren't focused enough. But the truth was he himself wasn't focused enough. He was answering questions in four- or five-minute bursts, and he was never going to be satisfied since so much substance had to be taken out of his response. What he wanted was a four minute answer in 30 seconds.

Looking back, I wouldn't have done anything differently. It wasn't genius. It was simply solving a problem with technology. When we use technology, it is to solve a problem.

# Notes

## Introduction

1  *The Dallas Morning News*, 16 August 1987.
2  This author respectfully acknowledges that the number of successful female candidates increases with each election cycle. However, continual references to "his or hers" or "s/he" are cumbersome and, for ease in reading, will be avoided wherever possible.
3  Quotations that are not footnoted are from the author's personal interviews.

## 1  So you want to run for office? An overview of electoral politics in America

1  Hearings before the Senate Committee on Rules and Administration, *Proposed Amendments to the Federal Election Campaign Act of 1971* (Washington, DC, US Government Printing Office, 1986), p. 152.
2  Ibid., p. 25.
3  *Congressional Record*, 24 June 1985, p. H4757.
4  At the time of the Tillman Act, President Theodore Roosevelt told Congress in his annual message that "The need for collecting large campaign funds would vanish if Congress provided an appropriation for the proper and legitimate expenses of each of the great national parties, an appropriation ample enough to meet the necessity for thorough organization and machinery, which requires a large expenditure of money."
5  *Buckley* v. *Valeo* (424 US at 19).
6  Burton Sheppard, *Rethinking Congressional Reform* (Cambridge, Mass., Schenkman Books, 1985), p. 286.
7  Elizabeth Drew, *Politics and Money* (New York, Macmillan, 1983), p. 94.
8  Herbert Alexander and Brian Haggerty, *The Federal Election Campaign Act* (Los Angeles, Citizens' Research Fund, 1981), p. 84.
9  Congressional Quarterly, *Elections '86* (Washington, DC, Congressional Quarterly Press, 1986), p. 42.

10  *Wall Street Journal*, 10 October 1986.
11  *Washington Post*, 29 October 1986.
12  *Wall Street Journal*, 9 October 1986.
13  *Washington Post*, 12 August 1986 and 22 October 1986.
14  *Wall Street Journal*, 18 November 1987.
15  *Washington Post*, 22 July 1986.
16  Ibid.
17  *Advertising Age*, 2 November 1987, p. S-4.
18  *New York Times*, 27 October 1986.
19  *Washington Post*, 11 December 1987.
20  *Wall Street Journal*, 4 December 1987.
21  *Washington Post*, 17 October 1987.
22  *Washington Post*, 5 November 1986.
23  *Los Angeles Times*, 16 October 1986.
24  *New York Times Magazine*, 2 November 1986.
25  *Wall Street Journal*, 4 December 1987.
26  *USA Today*, 2 October 1986.
27  *Washington Post*, 2 November 1986.
28  *Washington Post*, 5 October 1986.
29  *Washington Times*, 22 October 1986, and *Washington Post*, 23 September 1986.
30  *Congressional Record*, 17 June 1985, p. S8267.
31  *New York Times*, 30 August 1986.
32  *Washington Post*, 13 October 1987.
33  *Washington Post*, 23 August 1986.
34  Ibid.
35  *Wall Street Journal*, 7 October 1986.
36  *Los Angeles Times*, 16 October 1986.
37  *New York Times*, 4 November 1986.
38  Hearings before the Senate Committee on Rules and Administration, *Campaign Finance Reform Proposals of 1983* (Washington, DC, US Government Printing Office, 1983), p. 50.
39  Hearings before the Senate Committee on Rules and Administration, *Proposed Amendments to the Federal Election Campaign Act of 1971*, p. 187.
40  *New York Times*, 26 August 1986.
41  *USA Today*, 3 September 1986.
42  Jack Germond and Jules Witcover, *Baltimore Sun*, 16 October 1986.
43  *Washington Post*, 10 November 1986.
44  *Los Angeles Times*, 6 December 1987.
45  *Washington Post*, 22 July 1986 and 10 November 1986.
46  *Washington Post*, 5 December 1987.
47  *USA Today*, 24 January 1987.
48  Hearings before the Senate Committee on Rules and Administration, *Proposed Amendments to the Federal Election Campaign Act*, pp. 32–33.
49  *Wall Street Journal*, 18 July 1986.
50  Federal Election Commission Press Release, 8 December 1985.
51  Federal Election Commission Report, 1984 North Carolina Senate.
52  Hearings before the Senate Committee on Rules and Administration,

*Proposed Amendments to the Federal Election Campaign Act*, p. 23.
53  *Washington Post*, 22 July 1986.
54  *Washington Post*, 10 November 1986.
55  *New York Times Magazine*, 2 November 1986.
56  *New York Times*, 14 November 1986.
57  *Washington Post*, 4 November 1986.
58  Hearings before the Task Force on Elections of the Committee on House Administration, *Campaign Finance Reform* (Washington, DC, US Government Printing Office, 1983), p. 2.
59  *Washington Post*, 22 July 1986.
60  *USA Today*, 22 July 1986.
61  Federal Election Commission Press Release, 18 October 1986.
62  Federal Election Commission Press Release, 10 May 1987.
63  *New York Times* 7 November 1986.
64  Hearings before the Senate Committee on Rules and Administration, *Campaign Finance Reform Proposals of 1983*, p. 152.
65  *Washington Post*, 14 September 1986.
66  *New York Times*, 13 September 1986.
67  *Los Angeles Times*, 15 October 1987.
68  *Washington Times*, 21 November 1986.
69  *Washington Times*, 23 October 1986.
70  *Washington Post*, 5 September 1986.
71  Ibid.
72  *Washington Times*, 23 October 1986.
73  *Washington Post*, 3 August 1986.
74  *New York Times*, 10 November 1986, and *Washington Post*, 23 November 1986.
75  *Wall Street Journal*, 24 September 1986.
76  Ibid.
77  Ibid.
78  *Washington Times*, 16 September 1986.
79  *Wall Street Journal*, 24 September 1986.
80  *Washington Post*, 22 October 1986.
81  Hearings before the Senate Committee on Rules and Administration, *Proposed Amendments to the Federal Election Campaign Act of 1971*, p. 7.
82  Quoted in *Wall Street Journal*, 7 November 1986.
83  Quoted in *Washington Post*, 20 November 1986.
84  Alexander and Haggerty, *The Federal Election Campaign Act*, p. 106.
85  Sheppard, *Rethinking Congressional Reform* p. 297.
86  Hearings before the Task Force on Elections of the Committee on House Administration, *Campaign Finance Reform*, p. 66.
87  Ibid.
88  Richard Joslyn, *Mass Media and Elections* (Reading, Mass., Addison-Wesley Publishing Co., 1984), p. 19.
89  *Washington Post* 7 October 1986.
90  *Washington Post*, 9 July 1986.
91  *New York Times*, 10 November 1986.
92  *Washington Post*, 9 July 1986.

93  *Washington Post*, July 9, 1986.
94  *Wall Street Journal*, 4 December 1987.
95  *USA Today*, 12 August 1986.

## 2 The wizards of American politics

1  Judith Trent and Robert Friedenberg, *Political Campaign Communication* (New York, Praeger Publishers, 1983), p. 7.
2  Compiled from *National Journal*, 11 October 1986, pp. 2432–41.
3  Ibid.
4  Stephen A. Salmore, *Candidates, Parties and Campaigns* (Washington, Congressional Quarterly Press, 1985), p. 89.
5  Compiled from *National Journal*, 11 October 1986, pp. 2432–41.
6  *New York Post*, 11 July 1986.
7  Hearings before the Senate Committee on Rules and Administration, *Campaign Finance Reform Proposals of 1983* (Washington, DC, US Government Printing Office, 1983), p. 75.
8  Quoted in *Congressional Quarterly*, 22 December 1984, p. 3152.
9  Salmore, *Candidates, Parties and Campaigns*, p. 195.
10  Dan Nimmo, *The Political Persuaders* (Englewood Cliffs, NJ, Prentice Hall, 1970), p. 13.
11  *Los Angeles Times*, 1 December 1987.
12  *Campaigns and Elections*, November/December 1986, p. 24.
13  Larry Sabato, *The Rise of Political Consultants* (New York, Basic Books, 1981), p. 24.
14  Ibid., p. 25.
15  Robert Agranoff, *The New Style in Election Campaigns* (Boston, Holbrook Press, 1976), p. 69.
16  Ibid., p. 59.
17  Hearings before the Senate Committee on Rules and Administration, *Campaign Finance Reform Proposals of 1983*, p. 111.
18  *National Journal*, 20 October 1986, p. 1981.
19  *Washington Post*, 18 November 1987.
20  Richard Joslyn, *Mass Media and Elections* (Reading, Mass., Addison-Wesley Publishing Co., 1984), p. 10.
21  Salmore, *Candidates, Parties and Campaigns*, p. 89.
22  Mario M. Cuomo, *Diaries of Mario M. Cuomo: The Campaign for Governor* (New York, Random House, 1984), p. 153.
23  Sabato, *The Rise of Political Consultants*, p. 33.
24  *Miami Herald*, 17 October 1986.
25  Stuart Rothenberg, *Ousting the Ins* (Washington, DC, Free Congress Research and Educational Foundation, 1985), p. 31.
26  *National Journal*, 2 August 1986, p. 1902.
27  *Campaigns and Elections*, July/August 1987, p. 41.
28  *Washington Post*, 18 November, 1987.
29  *National Journal*, 20 October 1984.
30  Vernon F. Anderson and Roger A. Van Winkle, *In the Arena* (New York, Harper and Row, 1976), p. 287.

31  Ibid.
32  *Washington Post*, 18 November 1987.
33  *Campaigns and Elections*, July/August 1987, p. 45.
34  Sidney Blumenthal, *The Permanent Campaign* (New York, Simon and Schuster, 1982), p. 187.
35  *Campaigns and Elections*, July/August 1987, p. 18.
36  *National Journal*, 20 October 1986.
37  *Washington Post*, 22 July 1986.
38  *National Journal*, 20 October 1984.
39  Joseph Napolitan, a political consultant with more than thirty years' experience, would look harshly on this remark. In an article he wrote for the July/August 1987 edition of the political journal *Campaigns and Elections*, Napolitan emphasized, "Do not have too much sympathy for a candidate. Not many candidates are drafted. Most of them are candidates because they want to be, because they want the glory and power. . . . They are there of their own volition."
40  *Campaigns and Elections*, July/August 1987, p. 18.
41  Schwartzman, *Political Campaign Craftsmanship* (New York, Van Nostrand Reinhold, 1984), p. 18.

## 3  The selling of the candidate

1  Larry Sabato, *The Rise of Political Consultants* (New York, Basic Books, 1981), p. 111.
2  Hearings before the Senate Committee on Rules and Administration, *Campaign Finance Reform Proposals of 1983* (Washington, DC, US Government Printing Office, 1983), p. 46.
3  See 1982 Neilson Rating Service Annual Report; 1980 US Census data.
4  Herbert Alexander and Brian Haggerty, *The Federal Election Campaign Act* (Los Angeles, Citizens' Research Fund, 1981), p. 97.
5  *Campaigns and Elections*, July/August 1986, p. 50.
6  *Wall Street Journal*, 24 October 1986.
7  *Washington Times*, 3 November 1986.
8  *Washington Post*, 10 November 1986.
9  *New York Times*, 27 November 1987.
10  *Washington Post*, 10 November 1986.
11  Ibid.
12  *New York Times Magazine*, 2 November 1986.
13  *Baltimore Sun*, 2 November 1986.
14  Barbara Hinkley, *Congressional Elections* (Washington, DC, Congressional Quarterly Press, 1981), p. 31.
15  *New York Times*, 24 October 1986.
16  Ray Hiebert, ed., *The Political Image Merchants: Strategies in the New Politics* (Washington, DC, Acropolis Books, 1971), p.99.
17  *New York Times*, 5 November 1986.
18  *Washington Post*, 4 August 1986.
19  *Washington Post*, 2 November 1986.
20  *USA Today*, 6 October 1986.

21  *USA Today*, 4 November 1986.
22  *Los Angeles Times*, 16 October 1986.
23  *Wall Street Journal*, 7 October 1986.
24  *Miami Herald*, 21 September 1986.
25  Ibid.
26  *Miami Herald*, 26 October 1986.
27  *Washington Times*, 3 November 1986.
28  *New York Times*, 22 October 1986.
29  *Washington Times*, 3 November 1986.
30  30 Stuart Rothenberg, *Ousting the Ins* (Washington, DC, Free Congress Research and Educational Foundation, 1985), pp. 21-22.
31  *New York Times*, 28 October 1986.
32  *Washington Post*, 5 OCtober 1986.
33  Ibid.
34  Ibid.
35  Ibid.
36  *New York Times*, 27 August 1986.
37  *New York Times*, 20 October 1986.
38  *Washington Post*, 5 October 1986.
39  *Christian Science Monitor*, 14 November 1986, and *Washington Post*, 30 October 1986.
40  *Christian Science Monitor*, 29 October 1986.
41  Stuart Rothenberg, *Winners and Losers: Campaigns, Candidates and Congressional Elections* (Washington, DC, Free Congress Research and Educational Foundation, 1983), p. 48.
42  *Washington Post*, 30 October 1986.
43  Gary Jacobson, *The Politics of Congressional Elections* (Boston, Mass., Little, Brown and Co., 1983), p. 68.
44  According to McConnell media consultant Roger Ailes, "When I first pitched McConnell the concept, he said, 'But they'll laugh at me.' I said, 'Mitch, you're forty-four points behind. They're already laughing at you. Who cares if you lose by forty-four or forty-eight points. I think this will work.' He had an incredible amount of guts to gamble on an unknown and untried concept, but that is the quality of a good candidate."
45  *Wall Street Journal*, 9 October 1986.
46  *New York Post*, 3 October 1986.
47  *New York Post*, 6 October 1986.
48  Ibid.
49  *Wall Street Journal*, 2 October 1986.
50  Thomas E. Mann and Norman J. Ornstein, *The American Elections of 1982* (Washington, DC, The American Enterprise Institute, 1983), p. 37.
51  *Washington Post*, 5 October 1986.
52  *Miami Herald*, 14 September 1986.
53  *Washington Post*, 27 October 1986.
54  Ibid.
55  *Washington Post*, 5 October 1986.
56  *Miami Herald*, 14 September 1986.
57  *Miami Herald*, 12 October 1986.
58  *Miami Herald*, 4 October 1986.

59 *National Journal*, 1 November 1986, p. 2621.
60 *Washington Post*, 27 October 1986.
61 Ibid.
62 *New York Times*, 5 November 1986.
63 *Washington Post*, 8 August 1986.
64 *Advertising Age*, 21 September 1987, p. 30.
65 *Washington Post*, 8 October 1986.
66 *Washington Post*, 18 October 1986.
67 *Washington Post*, 10 October 1986.
68 *Washington Post*, 29 February 1980.
69 Ibid.
70 Ibid.
71 *New York Times*, 22 October 1986.
72 *Wall Street Journal*, 3 November 1986.
73 *Washington Post*, 14 September 1986.
74 *Los Angeles Times*, 8 September 1986.
75 *Washington Post*, 7 August 1986.
76 *Washington Post*, 10 November 1986.
77 *Washington Post*, 25 October 1986.
78 *Washington Post*, 21 October 1986.
79 *Washington Post*, 25 October 1986.
80 *Washington Post*, 10 November 1986.
81 *Washington Post*, 31 October 1986.
82 *Washington Post*, 23 October 1986.
83 *Washington Times*, 31 October 1986.
84 Edward Costikyan, *How to Win Votes: The Politics of 1980* (New York, Harcourt Brace Jovanovich, 1980), p. 117.

## 4 The party's just begun

1 Austin Ranney, ed., *The American Elections of 1984* (North Carolina, Duke University Press, 1985), pp. 245–9. In the 1980 and 1982 elections, Republican Senate candidates won 81 percent of the elections decided by a margin of 4 percent or less.
2 Ray Hiebert, ed., *The Political Image Merchants: Strategies in the New Politics* (Washington, DC, Acropolis Books, 1971), p. 8.
3 Hiebert, *The Political Image Merchants*, pp. 22–3.
4 Larry Sabato, as quoted in Hearings before the Senate Committee on Rules and Administration, *Campaign Finance Reform Proposals of 1983* (Washington, DC, US Government Printing Office, 1983), p. 106.
5 *National Journal*, 1 November 1986, p. 2616.
6 Ibid., p. 2617.
7 Ibid.
8 *Washington Post*, 29 August 1986.
9 Robert Agranoff, *The New Style in Election Campaigns* (Boston, Mass., Holbrook Press, 1976), p. 19.
10 *Congressional Quarterly*, 2 July 1983, p. 1349.
11 Ranney, *The American Elections of 1984*, p. 249.

12  *Congressional Quarterly*, 12 December 1984, p. 3152.
13  *Washington Post*, 29 August 1986.
14  Ibid.
15  *Wall Street Journal*, 13 October 1986.
16  1986 Harriman Media Center handout.
17  Ranney, *The American Elections of 1984*, p. 248.
18  *Washington Post*, 30 September 1986.
19  *New York Times*, 7 November 1986, and *Washington Post*, 30 September 1986).
20  *Washington Post*, 30 September 1986.
21  Ornstein, quoted in Ranney, *The American Elections of 1984*, p. 249.
22  *Wall Street Journal*, 23 October 1986.
23  Frank Sorauf, *What Price PACs?* (New York, The Fund, 1984), p. 59.
24  *Congressional Quarterly*, 17 November 1984, p. 2979.
25  Burton Sheppard, *Rethinking Congressional Reform* (Cambridge, Mass., Schenkman Books, 1985), pp. 289–90.
26  *Congressional Quarterly*, 17 November 1984, p. 2979.
27  *Washington Post*, 2 October 1986.
28  Ibid.
29  Ibid.
30  *Campaigns and Elections*, March/April 1986, p. 10.
31  Gillian Peele, *Revival and Reaction* (Oxford, Oxford University Press, 1984), p. 65.

## 5  Politics through the mail

1  Herbert E. Alexander, *Financing Politics* (Washington, DC, Congressional Quarterly Press, 1984), p. 67.
2  Alexander, *Financing Politics*, p. 69. Most Democrat donors fall into the "liberal" category, particularly those on the McGovern donor list used by Carter in 1976.
3  Ibid.
4  Ibid., p. 70.
5  *National Journal*, 29 November 1986, p. 2884.
6  *Washington Post*, 16 September 1986.
7  Quoted in *Campaigns and Elections*, July/August 1986, p. 57.
8  Larry Sabato, *The Rise of Political Consultants* (New York, Basic Books, 1981), p. 236–7.
9  *New York Times*, 10 September 1986.
10  On the other hand, John Heinz, 1976 Republican Pennsylvania Senate candidate, had a very successful direct mail effort cut short by extensive press coverage of his great wealth and the huge sums of money he was spending on his own election. Contributors, after reading news accounts of the Heinz fortune, could not be convinced that their small donations would have any impact when the candidate, himself, was contributing about $2 million to his own race.
11  As quoted in *Washington Post*, 22 July 1986.
12  Sidney Blumenthal, *The Permanent Campaign* (New York, Simon and Schuster, 1982), p. 228.

13 *Public Opinion*, June/July 1979, p. 4.
14 *Campaign Insights*, 1 March 1976, p. 5.
15 Hearings before the Senate Committee on Rules and Administration, *Proposed Amendments to the Federal Election Campaign Act of 1971* (Washington, DC, Government Printing Office, 1986), p. 24.
16 Hearings before the Task Force on Elections of the Committee on House Administration, *Campaign Finance Reform* (Washington, DC, US Government Printing Office, 1983), p. 64.
17 Sabato, *The Rise of Political Consultants*, p. 57.
18 *New York Times*, 20 October 1986.
19 Sabato, *The Rise of Political Consultants*, p. 225.
20 Blumenthal, *The Permanent Campaign*, p. 233.
21 *Ibid.*, p. 218.
22 *Washington Post*, 30 October 1986.
23 *Washington Times*, 30 August 1986.
24 *Washington Post*, 8 August 1986.
25 *Washington Post*, 30 October 1986.
26 Blumenthal, *The Permanent Campaign*, p. 228.
27 Sabato, *The Rise of Political Consultants*, p. 241.
28 Ibid., p. 41.

## 6 The bad boys of politics: PACs and independent expenditures

1 *Congressional Record*, 11 August 1986.
2 Ibid.
3 *Congressional Record*, 11 August 1986, p. S11144, and Federal Election Commission Press Release, 1 December 1985.
4 Thomas E. Mann and Norman Ornstein, *The American Elections of 1982* (Washington, DC, The American Enterprise Institute, 1983), p. 88.
5 *Congressional Record*, 11 August 1986, p. S11167.
6 Ibid.
7 Ibid., p. S11148.
8 Ibid., p. S11163.
9 Ibid., pp. S11143 and S11171, and FEC Press Release, 10 May 1987.
10 *Congressional Record*, p. S11171.
11 Ibid., pp. S11151 and S11160.
12 Federal Election Commission press release, 10 May 1987.
13 Hearings before the Senate Committee on Rules and Administration, *Proposed Amendments to the Federal Election Campaign Act of 1971* (Washington, DC, US Government Printing Office, 1986), p. 20.
14 *Congressional Record*, 11 August 1986, p. S11143.
15 Larry Sabato, *PAC Power* (New York, Norton, 1985), pp. 110–11. Only two of the five senators, William Proxmire and David Boren, have not accepted any PAC contributions during their entire political careers.
16 *Congressional Record*, 11 August 1986, p. 11150.
17 Sabato, *PAC Power*, p. 112.
18 Michael J. Malbin, ed., *Money and Politics in the United States*

(Chatham, NJ, Chatham House, 1984), p. 132.
19 *Washington Post*, 2 November 1986.
20 *USA Today*, 7 October 1986.
21 Hearings before the Senate Committee on Rules and Administration, *Proposed Amendments to the Federal Election Campaign Act of 1971*, p. 115.
22 *Washington Post*, 2 December 1985.
23 *Congressional Record*, 11 August 1986, p. S11162.
24 *Washington Post*, 21 August 1983.
25 *Congressional Quarterly*, 12 March 1983, p. 505.
26 *National Journal*, 11 October 1986, pp. 2440–1.
27 *Congressional Record*, 11 August 1986, p. S11149.
28 *Washington Post*, 2 November 1986.
29 Ibid.
30 Federal Election Commission press release, 10 May 1987.
31 Mann and Ornstein, *The American Elections of 1982*, p. 91.
32 *Washington Post*, 26 July 1986.
33 Sabato, *PAC Power*, p. 75.
34 Ibid.
35 Mann and Ornstein, *The American Elections of 1982*, p. 91.
36 *USA Today*, 7 October 1986.
37 *Congressional Record*, 11 August 1986, p. S11158.
38 *Washington Post*, 22 July 1986.
39 Malbin, *Money and Politics in the United States*, p. 132.
40 Ibid., pp. 263, 306–7.
41 Ibid., p. 266.
42 *New York Times*, 18 October 1987.
43 *Washington Post*, 22 July 1986.
44 Federal Election Commission press releases, 3 October 1982, 6 January 1983, and 29 April 1983.
45 Clark Wallace, President of the National Association of Realtors, quoted in Hearings before the Senate Committee on Rules and Administration, *Proposed Amendments to the Federal Election Campaign Act of 1971*, p. 318.
46 Ibid.
47 Larry Sabato, in Mann and Ornstein, *The American Elections of 1982*, p. 97.
48 *Congressional Quarterly*, 17 May 1980, p. 1333.
49 Sabato, *PAC Power*, p. 112.
50 *Congressional Record*, 11 August 1986, p. S11162.
51 *Washington Post*, 22 July 1986.
52 *New York Times*, 2 November 1986.
53 Malbin, *Money and Politics in the United States*, p. 160.
54 2 USC 431, p. 45.
55 Frank Sorauf, *What Price PACS?* (New York, The Fund, 1984), p. 54.
56 *Washington Post*, 10 August 1980.
57 *Washington Post*, 5 November 1982.
58 Ibid.
59 *National Journal*, 6 December 1986.

60 *Wall Street Journal*, 4 December 1986.
61 *Miami Herald*, 26 October 1986.
62 *Washington Post*, 2 November 1986, and *National Journal*, 6 December 1986.
63 *Miami Herald*, 26 October 1986.
64 Hearings before the Senate Committee on Rules and Administration, *Proposed Amendments to the Federal Election Campaign Act of 1971*, p. 146, and interview with Terry Dolan, April 1986.
65 Congressional Quarterly, *Dollar Politics* (Washington, DC, Congressional Quarterly Press, 1982), p. 87.
66 *National Journal*, 6 December 1986.
67 Congressional Quarterly, *Dollar Politics*, p. 86.
68 Ibid., p. 87.
69 Stephen A. Salmore, *Candidates, Parties and Campaigns* (Washington, DC, Congressional Quarterly Press, 1985).
70 Hearings before the Senate Committee on Rules and Administration, *Proposed Amendments to the Federal Election Campaign Act of 1971*, p. 68.
71 Ibid.
72 Federal Election Commission report for Illinois, 1984.
73 Hearings before the Senate Committee on Rules and Administration, *Campaign Finance Reform Proposals of 1983*, p. 57.
74 *Washington Times*, 23 September 1986.
75 *National Journal*, 2 August 1986.
76 Mann and Ornstein, *The American Elections of 1982*, p. 101.
77 Hearings before the Senate Committee on Rules and Administration, *Campaign Finance Reform Proposals of 1983*, p. 59.
78 *National Journal*, 6 December 1986.
79 *Washington Times*, 11 July 1986.

## 7 Modern campaign technology in the 1990s

1 *Fortune*, 21 December 1987, p. 131.
2 A 1987 Brady Group company handout.
3 *Washington Post*, 20 January 1986.
4 Gary Mauser, *Political Marketing* (New York, Praeger, 1983), p. 9.
5 Michael Nelson, ed., *The Elections of 1984* (Washington, DC, Congressional Quarterly Publications, 1985), p. 266.
6 *Campaigns and Elections*, November/December 1986, p. 9.
7 *Congressional Quarterly*, 22 December 1986, p. 3153.
8 Andrew Buchsbaum, *Independent Expenditures in Congressional Campaigns* (New York, Democracy Project, 1982), p. 67, and interview with Raymond Strother, August 1986.
9 *Washington Post*, 14 March 1982.
10 Buchsbaum, *Independent Expenditures in Congressional Campaigns*, p. 70.
11 *Los Angeles Times*, 8 December 1987.
12 *New York Times*, 17 October 1987.

13  *Campaigns and Elections*, September/October 1986, p. 64.
14  Larry Sabato, *The Rise of Political Consultants* (New York, Basic Books, 1981), p. 256.
15  *Campaigns and Elections*, January/February 1987, p. 12.
16  Ibid.
17  *Congressional Quarterly*, 22 December 1984.


### 8  Candidates, consultants, and the American democratic process

1  *Washington Times*, 5 November 1986.
2  Hearings before the Senate Committee on Rules and Administration, *Proposed Amendments to the Federal Election Campaign Act of 1971* (Washington, DC, US Government Printing Office, 1986), p. 147.
3  Larry Sabato, *PAC Power* (New York, Norton, 1985), p. 97.
4  Ibid., p. 110.
5  Hearings before the Senate Committee on Rules and Administration, *Proposed Amendments to the Federal Election Campaign Act of 1971*, p. 3.
6  *New York Times*, 14 November 1986.
7  *New York Times*, 7 November 1986.
8  *Congressional Quarterly*, 22 December 1984, p. 3140.
9  *Campaigns and Elections*, November/December 1986, p. 3.
10  Bruce Altschuler, *Keeping a Finger on the Public Pulse* (London, Greenwood Press, 1982), p. 3.
11  *Washington Post*, 2 November 1986.
12  *New York Times*, 14 November 1986.
13  *New York Times*, 6 October 1986.
14  *Washington Post*, 24 September 1986.
15  *USA Today*, 27 October 1986.
16  *New York Times*, 17 October 1987.
17  *Washington Post*, 10 November 1986.
18  *Campaigns and Elections*, July/August 1986, p. 12.
19  *Washington Post*, 2 November 1986.
20  *Baltimore Sun*, 15 October 1986.
21  *USA Today*, 6 November 1987.
22  *Washington Post*, 20 November 1987.
23  *Christian Science Monitor*, 14 October 1986.
24  *Dallas Morning News*, 10 May 1987.
25  *Dallas Morning News*, 18 September 1987.

# Further reading

Abramson, Paul, R., Aldrich, John H., and Rohde, David N. *Change and Continuity in the 1984 Elections*. Washington, DC, Congressional Quarterly Press, 1986.

Agranoff, Robert. *The New Style in Election Campaigns*. Boston, Mass.: Holbrook Press, 1976.

Alexander, Herbert E. *Financing Politics*. Washington: Congressional Quarterly Press, 1984.

——. *Financing the 1980 Election*. Mass.: Lexington Books 1983.

——. *PACs and Parties*. Los Angeles: Citizens' Research Foundation, 1984.

——, and Haggerty, Brian A. *The Federal Election Campaign Act*. Los Angeles: Citizens' Research Fund, 1981.

Altschuler, Bruce. *Keeping a Finger on the Public Pulse*. London: Greenwood Press, 1982.

Anderson, Vernon F., and Van Winkle, Roger A. *In the Arena*. New York: Harper and Row, 1976.

Barone, Michael, and Ujifusa, Grant. *The Almanac of American Politics: 1986*. Washington: National Journal, 1985.

Blumenthal, Sidney. *The Permanent Campaign*. New York: Simon and Schuster, 1982.

Broder, David. *The Party's Over: The Failure of Politics in America*. New York: Harper and Row, 1972.

Buchsbaum, Andrew. *Independent Expenditures in Congressional Campaigns*. New York: Democracy Project, 1982.

Campbell, Angus, Converse, Philip E., Miller, Warren E., and Stokes, Donald E. *Elections and the Political Order*. New York: John Wiley and Sons, Inc., 1966.

——. *The American Voter*. New York: John Wiley and Sons, Inc., 1960.

Chagall, David. *The New Kingmakers*. New York: Harcourt Brace Jovanovich, 1982.

Chester, Edward W. *Radio, Television and American Politics*. New York: Sheed and Ward, 1969.

Congressional Quarterly. *Dollar Politics*. Washington, DC, Congressional Quarterly Press, 1982.

———. *Elections '86*. Washington, DC: Congressional Quarterly Press, 1986.

———. *The Elections of 1984*. Washington, DC: Congressional Quarterly Press, 1985.

Costikyan, Edward N. *How to Win Votes: The Politics of 1980*. New York: Harcourt Brace Jovanovich, 1980.

Cuomo, Mario M. *Diaries of Mario M. Cuomo: The Campaign for Governor*. New York: Random House, 1984.

DeVries, Walter, and Tarrance, Lance, Jr. *The Ticket-Splitter: A New Force in American Politics*. Grand Rapids, Mich.: William B. Eardmans Publishing Co., 1972.

Diamond, Edwin, and Bates, Stephen. *The Spot: The Rise of Political Advertising on Television*. Cambridge, Mass.: MIT Press, 1984.

Drew, Elizabeth. *Politics and Money*. New York: Macmillan, 1983.

Dyk, Timothy. *Campaign '84*. New York: Practicing Law Institute, 1983.

Epstein, Edwin M. *The Corporation in American Politics*. Englewood Cliffs, NJ: Prentice-Hall Inc., 1969.

Fenno, Richard. *Home Styles: House Members in their Districts*. Boston: Little, Brown, 1978.

Goldenberg, Edie N., and Traugott, Michael, W. *Campaigning for Congress*. Washington, DC: Congressional Quarterly Press, 1984.

Hiebert, Ray, ed. *The Political Image Merchants: Strategies in the New Politics*. Washington, DC: Acropolis Books, 1971.

Hinckley, Barbara. *Congressional Elections*. Washington, DC: Congressional Quarterly Press, 1981.

Jacobson, Gary C. *The Politics of Congressional Elections*. Boston, Mass.: Little, Brown and Co., 1983.

———, and Kernell, Samuel. *Money in Congressional Elections*. New Haven, Conn.: Yale University Press, 1980.

———. *Strategy and Choice in Congressional Elections*. New Haven, Conn.: Yale University Press, 1981.

Joslyn, Richard. *Mass Media and Elections*. Reading, Mass.: Addison-Wesley Publishing Co., 1984.

Lipset, Seymour Martin, ed. *Emerging Coalitions in American Politics*. San Francisco: Institute for Contemporary Studies, 1978.

McGinniss, Joe. *The Selling of the President, 1968*. New York: Trident Press, 1969.

MacNeil, Robert. *The People Machine: The Influence of Television on American Politics*. New York: Harper and Row, 1968.

Malbin, Michael J., ed. *Money and Politics in the United States*. Chatham, NJ: Chatham House, 1984.

———, ed. *Parties, Interest Groups and Campaign Finance Laws*. Washington, DC: American Enterprise Institute, 1980.

Mann, Thomas E. *Unsafe at Any Margin*. Washington, DC: American Enterprise Institute, 1978.

———, and Ornstein, Norman J. *The American Elections of 1982*. Washington, DC: American Enterprise Institute, 1983.

Mauser, Gary. *Political Marketing*. New York: Praeger, 1983.

Napolitan, Joseph. *The Election Game and How to Win It*. Garden City, NY: Doubleday, 1972.

Nelson, Michael, ed. *The Elections of 1984*. Washington, DC: Congressional Quarterly Publications, 1985.

Nie, Norman H., Verba, Sidney, and Petrocik, John R. *The Changing American Voter*. Cambridge, Mass.: Harvard University Press, 1976.

Niemi, Richard G., and Weisberg, Herbert F. *Controversies in American Voting Behavior*. San Francisco: W.H. Freeman and Co., 1976.

Nimmo, Dan. *The Political Persuaders*. Englewood Cliffs, NJ: Prentice-Hall, 1970.

Patterson, Thomas E., and McClure, Robert D. *The Unseeing Eye: The Myth of Television Power in National Politics*. New York: G.P. Putnam's Sons, 1976.

Peele, Gillian. *Revival and Reaction*. Oxford: Oxford University Press, 1984.

Polsby, Nelson W. *Consequences of Party Reform*. Oxford: Oxford University Press, 1983.

Pomper, Gerald. *Elections in America*. New York: Longman, 1980.

——. *Voters' Choice*. New York: Harper and Row, 1975.

Ranney, Austin. *Channels of Power: The Impact of Television on American Politics*. New York: Basic Books, 1983.

——, ed. *The American Elections of 1984*. North Carolina: Duke University Press, 1985.

Rosenbloom, David Lee. *The Election Men: Professional Campaign Managers and American Democracy*. New York: Quadrangle Books, 1973.

Rothenberg, Stuart. *Dusting the Ins*. Washington, DC: Free Congress Research and Educational Foundation, 1985.

——. *Winners and Losers: Campaigns, Candidates and Congressional Elections*. Washington, DC: Free Congress Research and Educational Foundation, 1983.

Sabato, Larry. *PAC Power*. New York: Norton, 1985.

——. *The Rise of Political Consultants*. New York: Basic Books, 1981.

Salmore, Stephen A. *Candidates, Parties and Campaigns*. Washington, DC: Congressional Quarterly Press, 1985.

Schwartzman, Edward. *Political Campaign Craftsmanship*. New York: Van Nostrand Reinhold, 1984.

Sheppard, Burton D. *Rethinking Congressional Reform*. Cambridge, Mass.: Schenkman Books, 1985.

Sorauf, Frank J. *What Price PACs?* New York: The Fund, 1984.

Trent, Judith S., and Friedenberg, Robert V. *Political Campaign Communication*. New York: Praeger, 1983.

Viguerie, Richard A. *The New Right: We're Ready to Lead*. Falls Church, VA: Viguerie Co., 1981.

White, Theodore H. *America in Search of Itself: The Making of the President: 1956–1980*. New York: Harper and Row, 1982.

Wolfinger, Raymond E., and Rosenstone, Steven J. *Who Votes?* New Haven, Conn.: Yale University Press, 1980.

*Congressional Testimony*

Hearings before the Senate Committee on Rules and Administration, *Campaign Finance Reform Proposals of 1983* (26, 27 January 1983; 17 May 1983; 29 September 1983).

Hearings before the Senate Committee on Rules and Administration, *Proposed Amendments to the Federal Election Campaign Act of 1971* (5 November 1985; 22 January 1986; 27 March 1986).

Hearings before the Task Force on Elections of the Committee on House Administration, *Campaign Finance Reform* (9, 16, 21, 23 June 1983; 8 July 1983; 22, 23 August 1983; 12 October 1983).

Hearings before the Task Force on Elections of the Committee on House Administration, *Contribution Limitations and Independent Expenditures* (10 June 1982; 28 July 1982).

*The Congressional Record*: 1983–7.

# Index